GLOBALIZATION and ITS EFFECTS ON URBAN MINISTRY in the 21st CENTURY

GLOBALIZATION and ITS EFFECTS ON URBAN MINISTRY in the 21st CENTURY

SUSAN S. BAKER, EDITOR

WILLIAM CAREY
LIBRARY

Globalization and Its Effects on Urban Ministry in the 21ˢᵗ Century
Copyright © 2009 by Susan S. Baker

Unless otherwise noted, all scripture is taken from the HOLY BIBLE, NEW INTER-
NATIONAL VERSION®. Copyright © 1973, 1978, 1984 International Bible Society.
Used by permission of Zondervan. All rights reserved. The "NIV" and "New Internation-
al Version" trademarks are registered in the United States Patent and Trademark Office
by International Bible Society. Use of either trademark requires the permission of
International Bible Society.

Published by William Carey Library
1605 E. Elizabeth Street
Pasadena, CA 91104
www.missionbooks.org

Naomi Bradley, editorial manager
Johanna Deming, assistant editor
Hugh Pindur, graphic designer

William Carey Library is a ministry of the
U.S. Center for World Mission
www.uscwm.org

20091STCHG1000

Library of Congress Cataloging-in-Publication Data

Globalization and its effects on urban ministry in the 21st century : a
festschrift in honor of the life and ministry of Dr. Manuel Ortiz / Susan S.
Baker, editor.
    p. cm.
  Includes bibliographical references (p.   ).
  ISBN 978-0-87808-006-9
  1. City missions. 2. Globalization--Religious aspects--Christianity. I.
Ortiz, Manuel, 1938- II. Baker, Susan S., 1945-
  BV2653.G54 2009
  253.09173'2--dc22
                        2008049811

DEDICATED TO:

Manuel Ortiz

For his life of service in God's urban kingdom

Contents

Preface

This volume has been compiled with two intentions. First, it is meant to be a fest-schrift in honor of the life of Manuel (Manny) Ortiz both in grassroots inner city ministry and as an academician, primarily at Westminster Theological Seminary where he has taught in the Urban Mission program for the past twenty-one years. The second intention of this volume is that it is meant to be a stand-alone textbook developed around issues that are at the forefront of mission dialogue as we enter the 21st century. Some of these issues are not new, but they do take on a different face as we recognize the effects of globalization in this world.

The book is organized around the four overarching themes of globalization, reconciliation, church planting, and leadership development. Our authors come from around the world—South Africa, Nigeria, Serbia, England, Northern Ireland, Ecuador, and the U.S. The U.S. authors include those who are Asian, Puerto Rican, and Anglo, all committed to the mission of Christ in our urban settings. This scope of authorship was always a priority with Manny as he searched out references from non-Western authors.

Many people were involved in the compilation of this work. My special thanks goes to Tim Witmer who was an encouragement from the beginning and helped me think through the organization of material and possible authors. I also want to thank the other members of the Practical Theology department at Westminster as they kept the festschrift discussion alive. Sandy Finlayson, Westminster's librarian, assisted in the process of locating a publisher, and Carl Trueman, Westminster's academic dean, also gave his support.

I want to thank the editorial board of William Carey Library for agreeing to publish this book and working with me throughout the proposal and review processes. A special thanks is due Naomi Bradley, Johanna Deming and Hugh Pinder for their work producing the book for our publisher.

Acknowledgements would never be complete without thanking all these wonderful authors for their hard work and commitment to this project. In this regard I want to especially thank the *Westminster Theological Journal* for giving us permission to reprint an essay from the late Harvie Conn.

Finally, we want to thank the Lord for instilling in all of us his heart for the poor, the marginalized, the hurting ones found in cities around the world. We also thank him for his graciousness in allowing us to complete this volume.

The Convergence of Colleagues: Westminster's Urban Program

SUSAN S. BAKER, ROGER S. GREENWAY, AND WILLIAM C. KRISPIN

As the preface stated, one of our purposes for this volume was to honor the life and ministry of Manuel Ortiz, Manny to all who know him, especially as he trained so many at Westminster Theological Seminary by bringing the urban grassroots into the classroom. Manny holds a special place in the lives of many around the world. This essay is meant to show how, in God's providence, a number of people's lives moved from diverse backgrounds to become intertwined with Manny's, encouraging him and mentoring him as he then encouraged and mentored others in following Christ in urban mission. We will be looking at brief histories of some of the men and women who were responsible for developing Westminster's urban program and how, over many years, Manny's life kept bumping into theirs, sometimes for short intervals and other times for long-term relationships. We will also look at how others not connected with Westminster have spoken into his life and challenged him to become the man of God that he has become. This essay will be the only place where we talk about Manny directly as the rest of this volume has been organized to fulfill our second purpose, that of developing a stand-alone text.

We will start with short individual histories leading up to 1972 when God started bringing all of us together. From that point we will build divergent paths that continue to cross through the present. We will conclude with a tribute to Manny.

MANNY'S EARLY YEARS

Manny was born in New York City to Manuel and Luisa Ortiz, first generation Puerto Rican migrants from La Isla. The oldest of three children, he grew up in "el barrio" where he learned first hand about prejudice. In his own words Manny says,

> [It] started with my first visit to the farms of New Jersey, where I saw my relatives working as cheap labor and living in shacks under horrible conditions, and continued to the streets of Spanish Harlem, where we learned that because we were Puerto Ricans we could not walk outside of our neighborhood for fear of violent attacks.[1]

He often relates how he had to run to school through an Italian section. If he had slowed down, he could have been beaten. He writes further,

> Though I lived in a mixed neighborhood comprised of Hispanics, African-Americans and Italians, other areas were culturally defined. I was chased or robbed at times by Italians because I was Puerto Rican. I was a stranger in the African-American community because I was Puerto Rican. I had to make survival my top agenda every day.[2]

Although these experiences were painful, they were also Manny's first experiences of dealing with multi-ethnicity. In time he had friends who were Italian, Irish, and African American, and many of these friendships remain today.

Manny's parents were Roman Catholic, and part of his schooling was in parochial schools. Manny finished high school and joined the Marines at age 17. After his stint in the Marines, he came home and eventually owned an after-hours club. In 1962 he married Blanca Nieves Otero. Meanwhile, Manny's father had accepted the Lord and had been fervently praying for the rest of his family. After seven years, Manny's mother also accepted the Lord and joined her husband in prayer for the children. Finally, when Manny was 30, the Lord saved him through the ministry of a German Baptist church in Long Island, and his life was dramatically changed. Blanca immediately noticed the change, and although she resisted, the Lord claimed her just two weeks later.

Manny's pastor recognized the gifts God had given Manny and urged him to go to a Bible school. One year later, in 1968, Manny moved his family to the Bartram Village Apartments, a housing project in southwest Philadelphia, and he attended the Philadelphia College of Bible (PCB). At a time when "mature" men and women were not yet going back for undergraduate degrees, Manny was not only older than

---

1 Manuel Ortiz, *The Hispanic Challenge: Opportunities Confronting the Church* (Downers Grove, IL: InterVarsity Press, 1993), 13.
2 Ibid., 61.

most of his classmates but he also found himself behind many of them. This was not only a humbling, even humiliating, experience, but it was made worse as he was one of the few non-Anglos; he felt it reflected on who he was as a Puerto Rican. He had to work extremely hard at his studies all the while supporting a family. This time also helped him grasp the nature of institutional sin as he realized the New York City's public schools inadequately equipped him to continue his education. He developed a fervor for providing Christian alternative education models in inner cities as well as encouraging Christians to participate in the public schools in those areas so there would be a voice for justice in the educational institutions.

Although Manny and Blanca felt more at home in a Hispanic church, Manny believed people should worship in their own community. The projects' population was almost totally African American, so Manny and his family joined the Christian Union Baptist Church, an African American church in southwest Philadelphia. Manny and Blanca led the youth group in that church and had a summer ministry at the New Jersey shore. In time Manny became ordained through that church. God used these experiences to instill in his heart the concepts of incarnational living as well as the importance of parish ministry. In 1972 Manny graduated from PCB with a degree in theology.

HARVIE CONN'S EARLY YEARS

Harvie Conn was a unique urbanologist and missiologist. Although he passed away in 1999, any volume depicting the influences on Manny's life would be incomplete without including Harvie. The following information comes from a website on "Harvie Conn: The Man and His Writings."

> Dr. Conn was born in Regina, SK, Canada in 1933, and became an American citizen in 1957. He received an AB from Calvin College in 1953, a BD in 1957, and a Th.M. in 1958 both from Westminster Theological Seminary. He was awarded a Litt.D. from Geneva College in 1976.

> In 1957, Harvie began a church planting ministry in New Jersey. Later he went to Korea as an itinerant preacher in churches. He also taught New Testament at the General Assembly Theological Seminary in Seoul for

ten years, as well as carrying on a ministry of evangelism there among prostitutes and pimps.[3]

As Ortiz, Barker, and Logan articulate, the "one thing that was extremely important to [Harvie] was God's concern for the poor. He taught, preached, and lived in such a manner that it seemed to be a high calling for him."[4] He loved the city and his heart ached for the victims of injustice, marginalization, and discrimination that filled our inner cities. He spoke, wrote, and taught about issues of urbanization, globalization, contextualization, and reconciliation with a view to proclaiming justice and justification. As the blog above reported, Harvie spent ten years in Korea. "He worked with prostitutes in the red-light district because he knew that women were being oppressed, and they were usually the ones who were poor and powerless."[5] In 1972 he began teaching apologetics and missions at Westminster Theological Seminary.

BILL KRISPIN'S EARLY YEARS

Bill grew up in a Christian home on the near north side of Chicago. He came to Westminster Theological Seminary in 1965 with the intent of returning to Chicago for ministry. During his second year of seminary, he served as an intern at Tenth Presbyterian Church in Center City Philadelphia. Dr. Di Gangi, then pastor of the church, knowing Bill's interest in urban ministry, gave him the assignment to work with a youth group at the Evangel Presbyterian Church in South Philadelphia. This congregation had been without a pastor for many years and was down to a handful of elderly believers who no longer lived in the changing community where the church building was located. The congregation was in its final years of life. At the same time, a vibrant youth ministry of over 100 young people was carried on by Mrs. Hannah McFetridge, a member of Evangel in her 70's. Bill counts himself blessed to be an apprentice

---

3 "'Conn'-versation: Reviving and Applying the Legacy of Harvie Conn to Today's Changing World," http://connversation.worldpress.com/harvie-conn-the-man/ accessed 4/23/08.

4 Manuel Ortiz with William S. Barker and Samuel T. Logan, Jr., "Introduction," in Manuel Ortiz and Susan S. Baker, eds., *The Urban Face of Mission: Ministering the Gospel in a Diverse and Changing World* (Phillipsburg, NJ: Presbyterian & Reformed Publishers, 2002), 1.

5 Ibid.

under her tutelage which also gave him the opportunity to connect to South Philadelphia.

There wasn't much talk of urban missions among Westminster students in those days. Single students ate in a student-run dining club. At most tables the conversation focused on the hot theological topic of the day. The only table where real missional conversation was to be found was the table of mostly Chinese international students. There, Wilson Chow, Che Bin Tan, and Sam Kau along with others would discuss the mission concerns of Jonathan Chao, a recent graduate of the seminary. Jonathan talked with anyone who would listen. He had a vision for a Chinese seminary—by Chinese and for Chinese—in Hong Kong. That vision was to become a reality with the beginning of the China Graduate School of Theology in 1973.

Jonathan Chao also cut hair in the basement of Machen Hall at Westminster to earn some money. He talked to the "captive" in his chair about only one thing—China and theological education for training leadership for the Chinese harvest that was sure to come. At the time, Bill was sure God wasn't calling him to China, and He certainly wasn't calling him to be involved in theological education. Bill was an urban guy who wanted to see Christ proclaimed on the streets of the city. But Jonathan still would give the challenge. He would tell Bill not to forget to train up future leaders. He would say that we have to care about the continuation of ministry to the generations that would follow after us. Otherwise, our ministries would die with us. At the time Bill didn't realize that God would use those conversations to move him into urban theological education. He still marvels at that and has learned not to say, "never will I..."

Another person who influenced Bill was Dr. Jack Miller who affirmed his interest in urban ministry and encouraged him to stay in Philadelphia to do urban church planting. Miller's challenge to the Orthodox Presbyterian Church resulted in a call to Bill to plant a church in South Philadelphia along with his wife Mary.

In 1969 while ministering at Emmanuel Chapel (OPC), a Baptist minister invited Bill to Thursday morning prayer with city pastors. That group of pastors became his mentoring lifeline. They began to pray with and for Bill. Their encouragement was life-giving to Bill.

Also in 1969, Philadelphia's school system was headed for a long teachers' strike. Gang warfare was at its peak during those years. And the group of pastors had a burden that children were not able to go to school, would be on the streets, and would be vulnerable. They prayed throughout the month of August and then became determined to start a school—three weeks later! Bill was the skeptic but, miraculously, three weeks later to the day, the school opened in a rent-free facility with four teachers, fifty-three students, and all the supplies they needed.

Two years later, from that same group of pastors, a second educational opportunity arose. Most of the pastors did not have seminary training but had attended non-formal evening Bible institutes which gave them an overview of biblical content and basic doctrine but little theological reflection or practical ministry training. Bill was the only seminary graduate, so they challenged him to speak with Westminster about partnering with them, despite numerous barriers. Again Bill was skeptical, this time that a Reformed seminary would partner with Pentecostal and Baptist urban African American pastors who could only take classes on evenings and weekends, but he took the idea to the seminary in 1971. The Lord did another miracle, and after just one meeting Westminster's urban program was spawned and the Westminster Saturday Seminar began.

ROGER GREENWAY'S EARLY YEARS

Roger Greenway graduated from Calvin College and then went on to Calvin Theological Seminary. While still a student at the college he met Harvie Conn and they became lifelong friends. Roger served twenty years with Christian Reformed World Missions, first in Sri Lanka and later in Latin America where his passion for contextual theological education was born.

Roger had lived in Mexico City during a time when it was rapidly becoming the world's largest metropolitan area, with more people clustered in that one city than all the people in New York and Los Angeles together. He had seen the miles and miles of slums that encircled Mexico City, had helped to plant churches in some of them, and had found the residents amazingly open to hearing the gospel. In addition, he had experienced the frustration of teaching in a seminary belonging to a denomination that was extremely reluctant to take cities seriously. Its vision for mission was someplace "over the river and up the hill," not on the 20th floor of an apartment house or two subway rides away. To put it simply, he taught in a "rural" seminary located in a megacity.

When Roger joined the faculty at the *Seminario Juan Calvino* in 1963, Mexico City was in a race with Tokyo and Sao Paulo for the title of the world's largest city. However, rather than recognizing and seizing the opportunity to present the gospel to the tens of thousands pouring into the city and multiplying churches among them, the seminary drew its students from rural villages, places that were gradually being depopulated due to migration to the city. The focus of the seminary remained on training rural pastors.

Eventually Roger teamed up with a Presbyterian pastor who earlier had been a Catholic priest. Pastor Efren Haro Robles understood Mexican people inside and out, and the two of them shared the vision of a training institute totally committed to urban church development. They studied Mexico City from one end to the other and identified the more responsive areas of population. They then rented two houses in the heart of the city, enlisted a group of like-minded Mexican students and part-time teachers, and began the urban institute that they had envisioned. Instructors and students spent hours together each week evangelizing house to house and forming new groups in the congested neighborhoods and apartment buildings of the city. Students were told up front that no one would receive a certificate without having been a vital part of a successful church-planting team. At the end of the first four years, fifty men and women had received certificates and more than fifty house churches had been started, about half of which later developed into established churches.

Over time the Mexico City urban institute strayed from the vision that gave it birth and was swallowed up by a traditional theological school. Roger learned from its demise that visions can be lost when they are not regularly monitored, when in-course corrections are neglected, and new leaders are not carefully chosen.

SUE BAKER'S EARLY YEARS

Sue grew up as part of the American dream. Her maternal grandfather was a German immigrant at the turn of the century, entering the U.S. as a young toddler in 1900. Her father read every Horatio Alger book he could find and went from a poor rural life in a small town in New Jersey to providing a comfortable middle-class suburban lifestyle for Sue and the rest of her family in Bucks County, Pennsylvania. Just before high school she and her family moved to Boca Raton, Florida. While in high school Sue met a girl from Chicago and remarked, "I will *never* live in a big city like Chicago!"

Sue then went to Wheaton College and became involved in a voluntary ministry program from the college that landed her in the projects of Chicago's south side. While there, Sue and her now husband Randy came under the tutelage of Rev. Richard Gleason, who had established a church and was working with youth from the projects for many years. Rev. Gleason taught them the necessity of incarnational ministry, of caring for justice and for the poor, of making long-term commitments to a community, and much more that they would take with them throughout a lifetime of urban ministry.

After Sue's graduation, she and Randy married and moved into Chicago. Through God's providence they became involved in ministry in the Puerto Rican barrio. They purchased a home and converted the basement and backyard into a youth center with a swing set for the younger children and a basketball court for the older ones. A couple years later they purchased twenty acres on a small lake in Michigan and, with only the help of the youth center older boys and girls, they built two cabins and a separate washroom and began having summer camp programs. They also were appalled at the lack of concern in the educational system for their young people's growth. Their own oldest child was reaching school age, and they were in a quandary about what to do with her education. They knew God wanted them to stay in their community, so they prayerfully began looking for educational options. This brought them into the period of convergence.

THE BEGINNING OF CONVERGENCE

The years 1972 and 1973 were important ones for bringing all these individuals together. During the summer of 1972 Manny was driving a school bus taking children from Bill Krispin's neighborhood for a day camp experience. One day he stopped at Bill's doorstep and introduced himself. Bill learned that he was from New York and was then living with his wife and children in the projects. Manny learned that Bill was from Chicago and was a graduate of Westminster Seminary. Manny was still a young Christian and had just finished at PCB, and he was longing to hear more about Van Til and his apologetics. He would go to Bill's house early each morning for coffee and dialogue on Bill's front steps.

From these meetings, besides the knowledge that Manny received, three important events took place. First, Manny accepted a teaching job for one year at one of the elementary schools begun through the initiative of the group of pastors with whom Bill regularly met. This further nurtured his commitment to alternative Christian education. Second, he was asked to teach a class at the Westminster Saturday Seminars where he met Harvie Conn for the first time. Finally, when a position opened up in the church in Chicago attended by some of Bill's family members,

Bill recommended Manny for the position, and Manny accepted, packing up and leaving for Chicago the summer of 1973.

Meanwhile, Harvie Conn, who had just recently arrived at Westminster to begin teaching, started to realize that the Saturday seminars needed to be more formalized, so over the next three years he developed a three-year curriculum of evening, non-formal courses, and the program's name was changed to the Westminster Ministerial Institute.

Taking a turn in the road to follow Manny to Chicago, we find that the church to which he had been called had a number of buildings, and he immediately asked permission to start a Christian school in one of them. He contacted the school in Philadelphia where he had previously taught and they gave him much advice. They also gave him the names of a couple who were involved in youth ministry, Randy and Sue Baker, with the idea that they, too, might embrace the idea of a Christian school. Salem Christian School was begun just a little over a month later.

That was thirty-five years ago, and the Bakers and the Ortizes have remained firm friends and co-laborers ever since.

Still a very young Christian, Manny had the wisdom of seeking other pastors to come alongside him to provide mutual support. Many of his attempts proved short-lived as the other pastors backed out, but one African American pastor, the late Rev. Clarence Hilliard, became both a friend and a mentor. Together Clarence and Manny strove for reconciliation, not just between blacks and whites or Hispanics and Anglos but also between blacks and "browns." They put together a symposium of black and Hispanic leaders across the country to speak on these issues. This event was one of the highlights of Manny's stay in Chicago. One of the plenary speakers at that symposium was Dr. Orlando Costas, a Puerto Rican evangelical theologian who tragically passed away while still in his 40's. Orlando both personally and through his writings became another influential force in Manny's life, and they developed a deep friendship.

After four years in Chicago, in 1977, Manny left the church that had called him there and embarked on a life of church planting. A core group of four families, including the Bakers and Ortizes, began Spirit and Truth Fellowship as a church plant in Chicago with a strategy to reproduce itself in a very unique missional cell group format. Over seven years the team saw the reproduction process which culminated in three new churches developed from cell groups with leadership trained and mentored by Manny, and later one more church. At the same time, the team began a second school, Humboldt Community Christian School, and other ministries. The plan was to train indigenous leaders to take over all the ministries, and by 1987 the team families had worked their way out of jobs. Part of the training for these new leaders took place through a collaborative effort with Calvin Theological Seminary. Begun from the grassroots and then joined by Calvin, The Apprenticeship School for Urban Ministry (TASUM) started with Manny as the executive director and Sue as the administrator. Both Harvie and Roger made the trip from Philadelphia to teach at TASUM. At the same time Manny was developing his teaching skills by teaching courses at several institutions in the Chicago area and even traveling to Westminster to teach a course. In terms of his own education, Manny completed a Master of Arts in Missiology degree from Wheaton Graduate School and had begun a Doctor of Ministry in Urban Mission degree at Westminster with Harvie Conn as his adviser.

Back in Philadelphia, Roger joined Harvie at Westminster in 1982 and became a part of Westminster's urban program until 1986 when the Synod of the CRC appointed him to become the Executive Director of Christian Reformed World Ministries. He held that post until 1990 when he moved over to Calvin Theological Seminary to teach Missiology. His departure from Westminster opened the door to invite Manny to fill the vacancy in their urban program, so in the summer of 1987 Manny once again packed up his family for a move across country to return to Philadelphia, this time with Randy and Sue Baker and their family.

THE RETURN TO PHILADELPHIA

Never did Manny think that he, a Puerto Rican from Spanish Harlem who had virtually never lived outside a major city, would be called to a predominantly white suburban seminary. At a time when most people thought of crossing cultures as something done by white Westerners called to be missionaries, Manny found himself pressed to cross cultures in the opposite direction. Soon after he came to Westminster, Manny completed his D.Min. in Urban Mission.

It was difficult for Manny to make the transition to WTS, but he also struggled with his heart for planting churches and being involved in grassroots ministry. He attempted to make the two worlds meet by mentoring students to pastor a new church plant being formulated by Manny, his wife, and the Bakers. However, in 1995, the Lord made it clear that Manny was to pastor this church plant, also named Spirit and Truth Fellowship (STF), and train church planters through STF. As of this writing STF has spawned four more churches with a fifth in process. It also has begun an elementary school, Hunting Park Christian Academy, and a community outreach center, Ayuda Community Center.

Harvie Conn's passing in 1999 left an opening in the urban program. Sue Baker left her post at The Center for Urban Theological Studies to come on staff at Westminster as a part-time administrator and part-time faculty member, to assist Manny in the further development of the program. As of this writing, Manny and Sue are transitioning into retirement from the seminary. Their hearts have been captured by the needs of the fledgling church plants, and they will be formulating and directing the Church Planting Center as a new venture supported by STF to provide non-formal, informal, and formal education for church planters and potential church planters along with research assistance.

THE CENTER FOR URBAN THEOLOGICAL STUDIES

By 1975 it had become evident that something much more than the Westminster Ministerial Institute was needed, and the Center for Urban Theological Studies (CUTS) was born in 1978 as an inner-city, multi-racial base for an urban program. The amazing thing about CUTS' beginnings is that three uniquely different institutions joined into a partnership to bring this dream to fruition. The first partner was an inner city training center (CUTS) composed largely of non-Reformed church leaders from African American communities. The second was Geneva College, a largely white Christian college located in western Pennsylvania. Many city church leaders wanted, but could not get, accredited college-level training from a Christian standpoint and in a format that fit their needs, educational backgrounds and work schedules. Furthermore, the training had to be offered in a location that was easily accessible to inner city residents. Geneva was willing to enter into a creative new partnership for the purpose of offering accredited college-level Christian education in inner city Philadelphia. The third partner was Westminster Theological Seminary whose Ministerial Institute precipitated this partnership.

All parties to this partnership had to consider the risks involved, and Bill recounts how a constitution was hammered out to address such issues as racism and a call to racial reconciliation. The biggest barriers on this issue were the corporate as well as individual dimensions of racism and acknowledgement that the racial divide of the church was a white generated schism. A second issue was an understanding of the oral confessional tradition of the African American churches and the written tradition of the white churches. Particularly important was the acknowledgement that the oral tradition of the African American church was a viable, vital affirmation of biblical Christianity in the context of a suffering church. Also of note was the strong affirmation given to the catholicity of the church, even with all its alienation and fragmentation. It is out of unity in Christ that we were compelled to labor together for the growth and development of all parts of the body. A final issue was that of figuring out how such theologically diverse entities could work together in a teaching ministry. What resulted was an understanding of "Learning Together with an Open Bible."

CUTS has had an impact. Large numbers of the over 1,500 CUTS/Geneva College grads have gone on to area institutions to earn master and doctoral degrees. The alumni of CUTS are serving today in over 500 churches in the Philadelphia area. They have also been dispersed nationwide to serve in over twenty-five cities and some minister in cities overseas. A number of students from Westminister's main campus took graduate courses at CUTS and some of its professors offered their teaching services. This helped to keep the inner city and its churches before the eyes of the seminary community. Without question the CUTS connection opened the eyes of some seminarians to the rich spiritual assets as well as the needs found in African American and ethnic churches. A number of young men and women who combined studies on the main campus with classes at CUTS went on to dedicate their lives to urban ministries.

Although the partnership between Westminster and CUTS led to the establishment of the M.A. in Missiology degree which, beginning in 1980, was facilitated and coordinated at the CUTS location, it became evident that there was a built-in fatal flaw. It was a terminal degree within the Westminster system. This meant that the courses taken could not be applied to another degree program within Westminster, largely because of the biblical language-based prerequisite degree requirement of other degrees offered by the seminary. This had the effect that the pool of interested students was small in comparison to the larger church constituency in Philadelphia.

CUTS was also influential in the lives of all the individuals about whom we have been speaking. Harvie and Bill developed the M.A. in Missiology degree to be taught there. Bill was the Executive Director for over twenty years. Roger taught there for four years and counts it as one of the highlights of his ministry. After returning to Philadelphia, Manny taught there in Westminster's program. Sue taught in the Geneva undergraduate program for six years and wrote much of the curriculum for one of the bachelor programs.

WESTMINSTER'S URBAN PROGRAM

The final arena which brought Roger, Harvie, Bill, Sue, and Manny together was Westminster's urban program. This intertwined journey would not be complete without understanding who Westminster is.

A vision that is repeatedly articulated and warmly embraced becomes a compelling force that moves people and institutions to new and greater heights. Eight decades ago it was a great vision that led to the birth of Westminster Theological Seminary, and the school's uncompromising loyalty to the sacred Scriptures and the Presbyterian and Reformed confessions still witnesses to the clarity and strength of that vision.

Visions are born at special times and in response to particular circumstances. They can grow stronger from one generation to another, or they can wither and die. Visions that have potential for advancing Christ's kingdom encounter resistance from many quarters. It takes a lot to keep a God-honoring, gospel-advancing vision alive. For that reason, Christian people and institutions need to reflect occasionally on the visions they cherish, and evaluate how well they are doing.

The vision for an urban mission program at Westminster, as Harvie described it to Roger, was to build on the foundation of the seminary's strong biblical and Reformed heritage and to offer degree programs of urbanized theological education that would enable a new generation of pastors, teachers and missionaries to give strong leadership in a rapidly urbanizing world.

Roger knew this vision was needed from the global standpoint, for, as we have seen, he had served as a missionary, as a pastor, and as a seminary instructor in major cities overseas. Based on his study and experiences he was passionate about reshaping theological education in ways that prepared leaders for urban ministries in North America and worldwide.

In the early 1980s Westminster became the first evangelical seminary to offer academic programs focused on urban mission studies from entry-level master's work through doctoral studies. It now offers a certificate program as well.

At a time when D.Min. degrees were becoming popular, Westminster broke new ground among seminaries by offering a D.Min. in Urban Mission. From the beginning, under the leadership of Harvie Conn, this program attracted a number of people serving as pastors or missionaries overseas. It is this aspect of the Westminster urban program that most excited Roger and continues to excite Manny and Sue.

Westminster's D.Min. in Urban Mission continues to make an impact. The size of its impact can be only partly measured because the results are in widely scattered cities from Australia to Brazil, Chile, Peru, Mexico, South Korea, countries of Eastern and Western Europe, African nations, and North America. It is important to note that this program has inspired urban leaders in a variety of locations to develop programs that fit their cities and the needs of their churches and schools.

Soon after moving to Philadelphia, Roger started the *Urban Mission* journal under the auspices of Westminster. At that time, the bias against things urban was so strong that a friendly editor of a leading evangelical magazine advised him not to use the word "urban" in the title. The purpose of the journal coincided with the vision that Harvie and Roger shared from the start, to turn the attention of schools, churches and mission organizations toward the world's growing cities, and to do it in keeping with the depth and breadth of Westminster's Reformed theology.

Most North American Christians still thought that reaching a city for Christ meant "Billy Graham" size crusades and Skid Row rescue missions. Overseas missions was thought of in terms of teeming jungles, villages with grass huts and missionaries wearing pith helmets. Mission agencies kept pouring their financial and people resources into remote locations while ignoring the millions of city dwellers who needed to know Christ and become engrafted into his Church.

The problem was not exclusively North American. Christians around the world needed to be informed and awakened to the enormous demographic changes that were occurring on nearly all continents. Harvie and Roger concluded that one of the best ways to address this issue was to publish a journal entirely devoted to informing readers of the facts regarding urbanization, of the needs and challenges of urban ministry, and of models of effective urban programs from every part of the world. At the same time, the journal would advertise, and hopefully build up, the urban program offered at Westminster.

After six years Harvie took over as editor of the journal until shortly before his death in 1999. Its demise was a great loss. People still speak of articles they read years ago in *Urban Mission* and how they were enlightened and motivated by what they read. With more than half the world's unsaved, unchurched and suffering people residing in cities, Christian mission still needs a journal like *Urban Mission*, an advocacy journal that is evangelical and addresses urban issues with the breadth of perspective that emerges from good Reformed theology.

Reformed theology, taught and applied, is the hope of the city. Please remember that, Westminster, and don't lose the vision. Remember the city. God has used you to be salt and light, a planting of the Lord for the display of his splendor (Isaiah 61:1-4).

A TRIBUTE TO MANNY

Bill Krispin sums up the sentiment of all the authors of this essay, as well as the rest of the authors represented in this volume when he states that Manny has been the quintessential urban pastor/scholar. Serving as the pastor at Spirit and Truth Fellowship, Philadelphia, while at the same time serving as a professor at Westminster Theological Seminary, has been no small accomplishment. His scholarly work through teaching and writing has profoundly influenced many, and his mentorship and encouragement have touched scores of urban practitioners. His love of people has been a blessing to many in the trenches. His passion for the last, the least, and the lost has been contagious. Few have been able to juggle well the demands of such responsibilities.

Roger Greenway adds that Manny not only projected the urban vision on a widening screen, he enhanced basic elements of the vision itself. Manny has been a skilled practitioner of urban ministry, but he has also been a scholar. He represents the kind of scholar whom Edmund P. Clowney, Westminster's first president, described as a man who could move easily from his "study to the streets."

Sue Baker counts it a privilege to have been a part of the ministry team with Manny both in Chicago and Philadelphia planting churches and beginning schools. Now, for the last ten years she has also team taught with Manny at Westminster. Knowing Manny in both arenas of his life has allowed Sue to say confidently that he is a man who "walks the talk." He is also, above all else, a pastor. He cannot help himself—it's who God created him to be. This has been one of his most valuable gifts to Westminster as he has pastored literally hundreds of students. It is not unusual to overhear a conversation on campus between two students in which one student asks the other where he's been and the second student replies, "I've just been talking with Pastor Manny."

We all want to say, "Thank you, Manny."

Introduction:
Globalization, Urbanization and Mission

SUSAN S. BAKER

Globalization is a word describing a plethora of phenomena that tend to make the world seem smaller as interconnections form a web around it. As a word, globalization has become one of literature's latest buzz words and could quite possibly be the most overly used word around. This book is yet another volume organized under the umbrella of globalization. The particular tack we will be taking is to view the intersection of globalization and urbanization as God's provision for expanded mission.

No, this isn't the first book to view globalization through the eyes of mission. We don't want to repeat or replace what has already been done, but we do aim to add to that literature with some unique essays focusing on the four general areas of globalization, reconciliation, church planting, and leadership development. Within each of these areas we provide views from both the U.S. and other countries and have included a number of case studies to illustrate the themes. But before introducing each of these themes and the individual contributions further depicting these themes, we will take a more general look at globalization, its intersection with urbanization, and how both these phenomena join together to influence missions.

GLOBALIZATION AND URBANIZATION

Urbanization began in earnest with the start of the industrial revolution, in the late 18th and early 19th centuries. In many ways missions and the church as a whole did not take advantage of the phenomenon of urbanization. Churches shunned cities as being dirty, crime-ridden, and certainly not a place to raise a family (even though they extolled the virtues of those who chose to go overseas and live in exotic areas that were much more dangerous). This has not changed much. Major cities in the U.S. have long dealt with "white flight," and now they are also dealing with black flight and brown flight, leaving the cities to the most destitute and desperate with nothing more than a spiritual vacuum where the church should be. Should we really be all that surprised at the growth of Islam in many of our cities? Now we not only have continued, but relatively slow, urbanization in the West, we also have burgeoning urbanization in the Two-Thirds World, and all this urbanization is inextricably intertwined with globalization.

> Most of the global population growth in the coming decades will be urban. Today, around 45 percent of the world's people live in urban areas, but that proportion should rise to 60 percent by 2025 and to over 66 percent by 2050. The result will be a steadily growing number of huge metropolitan complexes that could by 2050 or so be counting their populations in the tens of millions.[1]

Schreiter expresses it this way, "Half of the global population now lives in cities. These cities are increasingly internationalized, creating complex multicultural mosaics.... These emerging city-states house the commercial nodes of today's global network of about forty thousand transnational corporations acknowledged by the United Nations."[2]

But we're getting ahead of ourselves. The one word used by almost all writers to describe or define globalization is interconnectedness. "The symbol for this connectedness which emerged in the 1990s, is the Internet and the World Wide Web.... But interconnectedness has a downside.... This is *exclusion*, a theme that has been reflected upon by those who not only do not benefit from globalization, but are disadvantaged and oppressed by it."[3] Viv Grigg explains that there are "a few powerful cities in the West and North, linked by global technologies, dominated by a few multinational corporations and banks."[4] This power network of businesses is at the heart of exclusion.

Another characteristic of globalization is compression. "The social counterpart of the microchip [which has been manufactured to hold more and more data] is the

---

1 Philip Jenkins, *The Next Christendom: The Coming of Global Christianity* (Oxford: Oxford University Press, 2002), 93.
2 William R. O'Brien, "Mission in the Valley of Postmodernity," in Howard A. Snyder, ed., *Global Good News: Mission in a New Context* (Nashville: Abingdon Press, 2001), 18-19.
3 Robert J. Schreiter, "Globalization and Reconciliation," in Robert J. Schreiter, ed., *Mission in the Third Millenium* (Maryknoll, NY: Orbis Press, 2001), 125, emphasis in original.
4 Viv Grigg, *Cry of the Urban Poor* (Monrovia, CA: MARC, 1992), 88.

global city. There are now more than four hundred cities in the world that have a population of more than a million inhabitants.... Here human beings are compressed into spaces that cannot sustain them at any level of humanness."[5]

Finally, along with interconnectedness and compression we find deterritorialization. "This is most evident in the flow of communication and the distribution of wealth in the world today.... The wealthy cities in poor countries may identify more with one another than with the disadvantaged denizens of their own country."[6]

Now that we have explored the connection between globalization and urbanization, what does that have to say to how we do mission? "Rich pickings await any religious groups who can meet these needs of these new urbanites, anyone who can at once feed the body and nourish the soul. Will the harvest fall to Christians or Muslims? And if to Christians, will the winners be Catholics or Pentecostals?"[7]

MISSIONS

What does God have to say about globalization? Is it a fluke, or does it have purpose in his overarching plan for humanity?

> The movement and presence of people around the globe are not simply products of market forces. Globalization is not simply the product of a human desire for betterment, a working out of aggression, or a flight from danger. Rather, God himself orchestrates the globalizing phenomenon of human migration. The fundamental fact of population migration, the presence of people of many cultures living together the world over, is not a theological "problem." It is a phenomenon we are called to embrace and even to engage.[8]

Escobar writes, "A crucial question to ask is how Christian mission is going to take place in this new world. Should Christian mission simply ride the crest of the globalization wave?"[9] Marcelo Vargas poses another question, "How does Christian

---

5 Schreiter, "Globalization and Reconciliation," 126.
6 Ibid., 126-7.
7 Jenkins, *The Next Christendom*, 94.
8 Michael Pocock, Gailyn Van Rheenen, and Douglas McConnell, *The Changing Face of World Missions: Engaging Contemporary Issues and Trends* (Grand Rapids, MI: Wm. B. Eerdmans Publishing Co., 2003), 30.
9 Samuel Escobar, *The New Global Mission: The Gospel from Everywhere to Everyone* (Downers Grove, IL: InterVarsity Press, 2003), 56.

mission question globalization?"[10] We don't pretend we can answer these questions in such a short space, but we would be remiss if we did not at least present them to you.

The whole issue of Western secularization has caused us to rethink mission. "The U.S.A. is a vast secular mission field with many cultures and subcultures. Are we imaginative enough and compassionate enough to sponsor and unleash many forms of indigenous Christianity in this land?"[11] Murray believes the only way for the West to turn around and embrace the truths of the gospel is to accept that it is no longer the center of Christianity and that it must move to the margins.

> Becoming again a marginal mission movement means rejecting many attitudes and assumptions inherited from Christendom. The invitation is to return to our roots and recapture the subversive pre-Christendom dynamism that turned the world upside down from the margins. Repositioning our churches—theologically, attitudinally and strategically—on the margins is essential.[12]

On the other side we have the marginalized, poor, and oppressed. It is important that they, too, are a part of the mission, and in fact they are, as Southern missionaries are flooding the world. "There is an element of mystery when the dynamism does not come from people in positions of power or privilege, or from the expansive dynamism of a superior civilization, but from below—from the little ones, those who have few material, financial or technical resources but who are open to the prompting of the Spirit."[13] It is also important that Christians respond to the needs of the marginalized.

> In many places in the twenty-first century, Christian compassion will be the only hope of survival for victims of the global economic process. The challenge for missionaries will be how to avoid the pitfalls of missionary paternalism and of the failed secular welfare system. Only the redemp-

---

10 Marcelo Vargas, "Can the global replace the local? Globalization and contextualization," in Richard Tiplady, ed., *One World or Many? The Impact of Globalisation on Mission* (Pasadena, CA: Wm. Carey Library, 2003), 208.

11 George G. Hunter, III, "The Case for Culturally Relevant Congregations," in Howard A. Snyder, ed., *Global Good News: Mission in a New Context* (Nashville: Abingdon Press, 2001), 105.

12 Stuart Murray, *Church After Christendom* (Waynesboro, GA: Paternoster Press, 2004), 155.

13 Escobar, *The New Global Mission*, 19.

tive power of the gospel transforms people in such a way that it enables them to overcome the dire consequences of poverty.[14]

"Jesus' reign is global. Eternal glory and power are ascribed to him. We are his people with a mission. We are his priests and servants, locally... and globally."[15] How is this happening? Escobar helps us here.

> The biblical perspective on mission has a global vision and a global component that comes from faith in God the Creator and his intention to bless all of humankind through the instruments he chooses. At the same time, God is forming a new global people from races, cultures and languages spread over the whole earth, a people who cannot do less than have a global vision but who live their vision in the local situation where God has placed them. The contemporary globalization process has to be evaluated from that biblical perspective.[16]

We have attempted to bring globalization and urbanization together so that the Christian church could respond missionally—globally and locally. At this point we will turn our attention to the rest of this book and see how the various essays fit in with the processes we have established.

ORGANIZATION OF THE BOOK

As mentioned earlier, this book is organized around four major themes. These particular themes were chosen as they epitomize the contributions by Manuel Ortiz to missions, both at the grassroots level and in academia.

Globalization

As with urbanization, globalization has taken many Christians (churches, denominations, mission agencies, theological schools) by surprise, but Goudzwaard tells us this should not have happened.

---

14 Ibid., 65-6.

15 Lois McKinney Douglas, "Globalizing Theology and Theological Education," in Craig Ott and Harold A. Netland, eds., *Globalizing Theology: Belief and Practice in an Era of World Christianity* (Grand Rapids, MI: Baker Academic, 2006), 280.

16 Escobar, *The New Global Mission*, 63.

Globalization should not surprise Christians, who confess that God created one world and sent forth the first man and woman to populate and steward the entire earth. Nor are Christians shocked by the fact that much of the populating, and "stewarding" has amounted to destruction, oppression, and unspeakable poverty. From Adam and Eve's first disobedience has sprung a history of multigenerational disobedience to the Creator, who entrusted us with so much.[17]

Not only should we not be surprised at globalization from an understanding of God's purpose in Creation, we can also see evidences of this phenomenon throughout the ages.

The reality is that globalization has developed over centuries as people have engaged in trade, conquest, and religious expansion. Globalization has progressed in fits and starts. The rapid expansion of peoples and ideas, followed by stagnation or reaction has been going on throughout human history. The more modern version of globalization has been linked to the appearance of capitalism and especially to the recent mobility of capital.[18]

How does globalization actually affect us? Robert Schreiter suggests, "Globalization has already so woven itself into the fabric of the world that it is not likely—as an economic, political, and sociocultural phenomenon—to disappear quickly."[19] Pocock et al. add, "Like it or not, many new technologies have the potential to change everything from the way we work to our worldview."[20] Araujo echoes this by pointing out, "The danger of globalization for Christians today is in its power to shape not only how we live, but also how we think and how we place ultimate value on things."[21]

---

17 James W. Skillen, "Foreword," in Bob Goudzwaard, *Globalization and the Kingdom of God* (Grand Rapids: Baker Books, 2001), 8.

18 Pocock et al., *The Changing Face,* 23-4.

19 Schreiter, "Globalization and Reconciliation," 131-2.

20 Pocock et al., *The Changing Face,* 157.

21 Alex Araujo, "Globalization and the church," in Richard Tiplady, ed., *One World or Many? The Impact of Globalisation on Mission* (Pasadena, CA: Wm. Carey Library, 2003), 233.

In chapter one, Susan Baker looks at the areas of globalization we have just highlighted—technology, economics, politics, culture, population movement, and religious movement. This chapter is meant to be an overview of how each of these elements have positive and negative characteristics, how they can be used by the Lord or by the powers of this world.

Contextualization has been a mission topic first given prominence in 1972 when it became a discussion in theological education.

> It is hardly controversial today to claim that the communication and local expression of the (unchanging) gospel of Jesus Christ must be adapted to changing cultural dynamics. Contextualization is thus now an accepted part of the missiological and theological agenda, even if lingering questions remain about what it means and how we should go about it. [22]

Although this may be true, "The new global dimension of Christianity has brought a new sensitivity to the fact that the text of Scripture can be understood adequately only within its own context, and that the understanding and application of its eternal message demands awareness of our own cultural context."[23]

The late Harvie Conn wrote and taught a great deal about contextualization. Chapter two is a reprint of one of his articles about this significant topic. He recognizes the usual hesitancy associated with contextualization, that of syncretism, but then goes on to point out the failure of the Reformed and evangelical community to consider historical context in their theology.

We now turn our attention to two different parts of the world and how globalization is affecting them. Arias explains why globalization causes so much concern for those in the South.

> "Global" is *in* these days.... Such "global" language has raised some misgivings, especially in the Two-Thirds World. Its origin in the so-called First World—and the adoption of the vision and language of the free market and of the prophets of the transnational corporations who live, move, and have their being in the matrix of "international and

---

22 Harold A. Netland, "Introduction: Globalization and Theology Today," in Craig Ott and Harold A. Netland, eds., *Globalizing Theology: Belief and Practice in an Era of World Christianity* (Grand Rapids, MI: Baker Academic, 2006), 16.

23 Escobar, *The New Global Mission*, 21.

global trends"—produces uneasiness. Some Christian leaders suspect that "global" plans and schemes are merely another version of old Western ethnocentrism in theology and missions. We have already had five hundred years of Western globalization of mission, beginning with Columbus.[24]

This is the theme of chapter three, written by Naas Ferreira, a South African. He views globalization as the fourth wave of outside manipulation and interference in Africa's past, present and future.

Finally, Michael Eastman, in chapter four, speaks from the other spectrum—that of post-Christian London. However, he does not see the demise of Christianity in London but rather a renewal—a renewal that is coming from the South, from African and Afro-Caribbean churches that are being planted in response to these populations as they filter into London.

We will close this section with words from Pocock et al.

> If we do not understand the phenomenon of globalization, we will miss golden opportunities for service, and we will fail to understand the antagonism that swirls around us.... God has a purpose in globalization, and while we may not have clarity on that purpose, he will not permit it to be thwarted.[25]

Reconciliation

Globalization is not only about interconnectivity but also about an increased knowledge of that interconnectedness. We find ourselves rubbing shoulders with those who are different from us. Denominations, agencies/organizations, churches, and individuals are all struggling with how to respond to what is going on around them. Unfortunately, an integral part of our sin nature seems to be an innate shying away from if not downright antagonism toward that which is different. As Christians we must all repent of this on both the individual and institutional levels.

First, let us look at what we mean by reconciliation. Robert Schreiter writes, "Reconciliation is about making peace, seeking justice, healing memories, rebuilding societies."[26] He goes on to explain it a bit more.

---

24 Mortimer Arias, "Global and Local: A Critical View of Mission Models," in Howard A. Snyder, ed., *Global Good News: Mission in a New Context* (Nashville: Abingdon Press, 2001), 55, emphasis in original.

25 Pocock et al., *The Changing Face,* 29.

26 Schreiter, "Globalization and Reconciliation," 139.

> The cry for reconciliation grows out of an acute sense of the brokenness experienced on such a broad scale in the world today. It arises as people try to rebuild their lives in the ruins of ideological projects, civil conflict, the consequences of human malice and greed. It breaches the darkness of memory recovered from a painful past and the loss which that memory evokes.... Christian understanding of reconciliation begins with the work of God in our lives, a work that has been made manifest to us in the life, death, and resurrection of Jesus Christ.[27]

Manuel Ortiz begins this section in chapter five by addressing reconciliation on an institutional level. He bemoans our continued discussions at conferences and denominational meetings when all that needs to be said has already been said. It is time for action—a reconstruction of the past, present, and future of our institutions.

In talking about race relations in the U.S., we are tempted to think in terms of black and white, or possibly Hispanic and Anglo. But racial discrimination was overtly practiced against both Chinese and Japanese in the U.S. In chapter six, Jeffrey Jue describes the history of institutional discrimination against Chinese in the U.S., including, and maybe especially, within the Christian church and how the church ought to be reaching out its hand in reconciliation to the Chinese church.

Before looking at two examples of physically violent expressions of prejudice in parts of the world, let us look at the violence perpetuated more subtly through the unequal distribution of resources throughout the world, even among our Christian brothers and sisters. Watson explains that "52 percent of the world's Christians live in affluence, 14 percent in moderate poverty, and 13 percent, or 95 million, in abject poverty."[28] This should not be. Mark Gornik, in chapter seven, brings us his reflections on Isaiah 32:17, which indicates that there can be no peace if there is no justice.

Finally, when we speak of reconciliation, the image of violent conflicts is often evoked. Kirk reminds us,

> There should be no need to justify the Christian's role in overcoming violence and building peace as an indispensable aspect of his or her calling

---

27 Ibid., 140.

28 David Lowes Watson, "The Mystery of Evangelism: Mission in an Age of Cosmic Discovery," in Howard A. Snyder, ed., *Global Good News: Mission in a New Context* (Nashville: Abingdon Press, 2001), 31.

to mission... peace through the genuine reconciliation of hostile parties is a fundamental aspect of the good news of Jesus and the kingdom.[29]

To understand the devastation of violence and yet the beauty of reconciliation, we cannot afford to omit the writing of Miroslav Volf. He recognizes, first of all, that there are overt and also subtle manifestations of violence. "Cultural conflicts are by no means simply a feature of societies that have not yet tasted the 'blessings' of modernization.... More subtle but nonetheless real wars between rivaling cultural groups are threatening to tear the fabric of social life in many Western countries."[30] A native Croatian, he witnessed his homeland torn apart through what has been known as "ethnic cleansing." He implores the church and theological institutions, "*to place identity and otherness at the center of theological reflection* on social issues."[31]

From the same region as Volf, Ondrej Franka (a Slovak living in Serbia and ministering to Bosnian refugees), writes in chapter eight about the church in Serbia and how it can make a difference in that devastated region. With the displacement of so many refugees, Franka is faced with the question of what is the Lord's purpose in this? Part of the answer he has found is that through the ministry to Bosnian refugees, Bosnian Christians are returning to Bosnia as evangelists and church planters, spreading the gospel to those who would never have been receptive to outsiders.

Volf continues with words that can ring true regardless of the "reason" for violence. "As God does not abandon the godless to their evil but gives the divine self for them in order to receive them into divine communion through atonement, so also should we—whoever our enemies and whoever we may be."[32] William Shaw, in chapter nine, describes what has happened to his homeland, Northern Ireland, in what many think of as religiously-based violence but which he explains is actually more nationalistic violence. He brings us a case study of a Protestant community organization attempting to build a bridge in an especially destroyed Roman Catholic section of Belfast.

"The gospel is *global* good news. Thinking globally, God acted locally. The gospel is good news about personal, social, ecological and cosmic healing and reconcili-

---

29 J. Andrew Kirk, *What is Mission? Theological Explorations* (Minneapolis: Fortress Press, 2000), 144.
30 Miroslav Volf, *Exclusion & Embrace: A Theological Exploration of Identity, Otherness, and Reconciliation* (Nashville: Abingdon Press, 1996), 15.
31 Ibid., 17, emphasis in original.
32 Ibid., 23.

ation. It is good news to the whole creation—to the whole earth and in fact to the cosmos."[33] Let us remember the words of Watson,

> Because Jesus was raised from the dead, we can trust his promises of *shalom*. Because Jesus was raised from the dead, the children of Auschwitz and Sudan do have an advocate. Because Jesus was raised from the dead, we can trust his word that the God of the cosmos is a parent God who will one day explain all our sufferings.[34]

Church Planting

It is obvious to most denominations that many, if not most, of their established churches are not prepared to cope with the vast issues globalization presents. They are steeped in tradition and do not necessarily see a need to change, or they realize they must change and either do not want to or do not know how to, so they move to a more comfortable setting for their members. We hear rumors and even exclamations that the West is moving into a post-Christian era. What can we do?

We believe the answer lies in planting new churches, churches that from the beginning are being creatively configured to reach out to a wide variety of ethnicities as well as to the postmodernists of our day. Many denominations are embracing church planting—some are more effective with their attempts than others—and there are many new churches springing up.

We are finding that denominationalism in our urban centers is not only not helpful, it is usually quite harmful. New partnerships in ministry must be formed with a view to reach whole cities for Christ. We not only want to see churches being planted, we want to see church planting movements, where churches are planting churches which, in turn, plant more churches. David Garrison helps us understand this better. "A Church Planting Movement is *a rapid multiplication of indigenous churches planting churches that sweeps through a people group or population segment*."[35]

In this section of our book we have essays by four authors. Chapter ten by John Algera describes exactly what we have been talking about—the beginning of a church planting movement in the New York City metropolitan area through

---

33 Escobar, *The New Global Mission*, 62, emphasis in original.
34 Watson, "The Mystery of Evangelism," 35, emphasis in original.
35 David Garrison, *Church Planting Movements: How God Is Redeeming a Lost World* (Midlothian, VA: WIGTake Resources, 2004), 21, emphasis in original.

partnership with a number of denominations. He then shares a case study of one denomination's efforts.

In chapter eleven Kyuboem Lee broaches a very difficult subject—that of cross-cultural church planting teams. We believe that church planting is often best accomplished by a team of leaders. It is always difficult to work as a team, but it is not only helpful, it also displays God's community to the people in the neighborhood. As difficult as teamwork can be, the issues are compounded when the team members are from different ethnic backgrounds. Lee gives us a candid look at the inner workings and principles behind ministering with such a team.

Chapters twelve and thirteen provide case studies of some very unique models. In chapter twelve John Leonard describes his missionary work in France and how hybrid church planting is a viable model for reaching North African Muslims. In chapter thirteen Manuel Sosa looks at church planting in South America through house churches. Sosa was the initiator of a program which has led to 500 small house churches spread all throughout the city of Guayaquil, Ecuador.

Leadership Development

When we think in terms of developing leaders, quite often the first thing we think about is formal training. Certainly theological institutions can be useful, but they can also be quite detrimental in this new age of postmodernism and pluralism. We need to challenge formal theological institutions to make changes in order to be more effective in training pastors for this new global church.

> All over the Western world, ministers are being trained and future theological scholars are being identified and taken to doctoral level and beyond without any idea of what the church of today, in which they are called to serve, is really like. The way that Christian thought is presented to them implies that it is a Western religion, or at least, if it did not start that way, it has now become one.[36]

We are forced to acknowledge that the influence of Christianity is declining in the West as postmodern secularism and pluralism pervade. Murray warns what will happen if theological institutions do not recognize this shift.

---

36 Andrew F. Walls, "Globalization and the Study of Christian History," in Craig Ott and Harold A. Netland, eds., *Globalizing Theology: Belief and Practice in an Era of World Christianity* (Grand Rapids, MI: Baker Academic, 2006), 78.

> *Training institutions* can resource missional movements. The Christendom mindset pervades many theological colleges and their influence will scupper progress unless they embrace this paradigm shift.
>
> ... On the threshold of post-Christendom, even a temporary shift is worthwhile; remaining in institutional mode will be disastrous.[37]

In chapter fifteen Timothy Witmer takes on postmodernism, a phenomenon touched upon by almost all authors who are looking at the West today (and increasingly in other places as well). Witmer reflects on emerging church leadership and how that leadership ought to be trained, focusing on a triangle of perspectives which should be utilized to produce well-rounded and biblically correct leadership for this new challenge to the church.

Walls warns us, "Neither the churches of the North nor those of the South have yet taken in the full implications of this major movement of the Christian heartland, the theological academy least of all."[38] Theological training needs to find ways to reach its global constituency. We ought to remember that *all* the continents should be represented in global theological education. One thing to be aware of is that "North American evangelical schools and their graduates can remain relevant only to the extent that they read, listen, and interact with believers from around the world... This means that students and educational leaders should be reading material developed by Christians from other cultures."[39]

Although technology is important,

> Theological education has globalized not only its healthy innovations but also its dysfunctions. Far too many programs are being driven by pragmatic concerns related to accreditation, funding, recruiting, and the expectations of constituencies. If we are ever to break out of this pattern of business as usual, creativity and intentionality are needed.[40]

---

37 Murray, *Church After Christendom*, 140-1, 145, emphasis in original.
38 Walls, "Globalization and the Study of Christian History," 77.
39 Pocock et al., *The Changing Face*, 14.
40 Lois McKinney Douglas, "Globalizing Theology and Theological Education," in Craig Ott and Harold A. Netland, eds., *Globalizing Theology: Belief and Practice in an Era of World Christianity* (Grand Rapids, MI: Baker Academic, 2006), 285.

To gain a perspective from the South, Jonathan Iorkighir, in chapter fifteen, looks first at clarifying what is meant by theological education in a global setting and then presents a challenge to think of a new way of doing it. He concludes his essay with a case study of his seminary in Mkar, Nigeria.

Chapter sixteen, takes a look at a non-formal mode of developing leaders, that of mentoring. Written by Pedro Aviles, it presents us with principles of mentoring intertwined with a case study of both how he was mentored and then how he, in turn, is mentoring others.

To conclude this section we should reflect on the words of Lois McKinney Douglas,

> If theological education around the world is to experience renewal, focusing on operational issues will not be enough. Commitments must be reexamined in the light of fundamental beliefs and values.... globalized theological education is rooted in *missio Dei*, celebrates spiritual formation, affirms the missional nature of the church, and emerges from hermeneutical communities.[41]

CONCLUSION

The authors represented in this volume are speaking from their own lives as they reflect on their grassroots experiences. My desire is that you find the rest of this book both interesting and informative, that you take to heart the need to see both positives and negatives in globalization, and that you apply what seems fitting for you from these essays. We need to continuously give God all the glory and honor as he works out his plan using globalization at this juncture of our history.

---

41 Ibid., 274, emphasis in original.

Section 1:

Globalization

.1.

Globalization:
How Should Mission Respond?

SUSAN S. BAKER

Most authors agree that the main definition of globalization has to involve global interconnectedness. Something happening in one part of the world affects events in many other locations. Although the Western world is considered to be the instigator of globalization, it is "not a one-way street, running from the West to the Rest. An interconnected world allows ideas and products from every part of the world to reach every other part of the world."[1] Speed of communication has brought about changed cultural values along with new hi-tech products. Consumerism/material-ism is rampant and is spreading around the world. "Globalization has created a world of opportunities and challenges, but it is at the same time oppressive and dominant."[2]

There are a number of key dimensions of globalization to which we should turn our attention. "The *economic* context of market capitalism is connected with *technological* changes, particularly in the area of telecommunications, and these have an impact on *political* interactions and on *cultural* influences."[3] All these dimensions have resulted in major movements—of people and their religions. This

---

1 Richard Tiplady, "Introduction," in Richard Tiplady, ed., *One World or Many? The Impact of Globalisation on Mission* (Pasadena, CA: Wm. Carey Library, 2003), 2.

2 Marcelo Vargas, "Can the global replace the local? Globalization and contextualization," in Richard Tiplady, ed., *One World or Many? The Impact of Globalisation on Mission* (Pasadena, CA: Wm. Carey Library, 2003), 209.

3 Warren Beattie, "Mission possible or impossible? Learning lessons from theology's engagement with globalization," in Richard Tiplady, ed., *One World or Many? The Impact of Globalisation in Mission* (Pasadena, CA: Wm. Carey Library, 2003), 214, emphasis in original.

essay reviews each of these areas with a view to bring missiological dialogue into each discussion. Beginning with technology, we will move to the economic/political realm and then culture. We will finish up with discussions on people movements and religious movements.

TECHNOLOGY

There is no question but that modern day globalization has been precipitated primarily through technological advances. This includes everything from cell phones, to ATM machines, to ever cheaper and more advanced computers, to the most important advance of all—the Internet. "Instantaneous information exchange facilitated by the Internet is a prominent feature of globalization. This exploded in the 1990s. Anyone from Azerbaijan to Zimbabwe can set up a Hotmail account and join the Internet at a village cyber café—even those who cannot afford a computer."[4] As with all other aspects of globalization, there are very definite benefits that come with technological advances as well as very devastating effects. We will first look at the benefits/deficits in general and then relate these to mission efforts.

When we talk about an interconnected world, the first thing we think of is technological advances. "Globalization has intensified the interchange between societies by way of technological advances and communications. It has lessened distances and has caused the fall of seemingly insurmountable barriers that separated the human race."[5] There is an abundance of information now available to virtually anyone with access to an internet connection. Thus, knowledge bases are spread in general and especially to those in specific fields, such as health, who can benefit from the research of others. Also, with a cheap web cam and a Skype connection, people can talk "face to face" with others in their field from around the world for extremely low costs. It has been said,

> If you have a bank account, a computer, a television, and a job, you are in the top 30 percent of the world's population and are considered "connected" in the process of globalization. For those who are connected, travel is relatively affordable, and opportunities exist to influence and be influenced by other cultures around the globe.[6]

---

4 Michael Pocock, Gailyn Van Rheenen, and Douglas McConnell, *The Changing Face of World Missions: Engaging Contemporary Issues and Trends* (Grand Rapids, MI: Wm. B. Eerdmans Publishing Co., 2003), 26.
5 Vargas, "Can the global replace the local?" 203-4.
6 Pocock et al., *The Changing Face*, 25.

However, there are real drawbacks to technological advances. For example, one aspect of all new technologies is speed which, in turn, affects the pace of life in general. Pocock et al. warn us that this speed could be "at the expense of relationships."[7] I recently went shopping with a teenager who spent much of our time together reaching into her purse to text message her friends. How often do we see people in public (or even members of our families at home) with ear plugs listening privately to their music while tuning out the rest of the world? How does this way of life affect us when even on vacation we take our computers to stay up on all the news and business we should be leaving at home and instead be spending time with our families? And how does this lessening of relationships help/hurt mission enterprise? Pocock et al. warn us,

> For all the efficiency of rapid communication and the enhancement of border-obliterating technology, personal relationships and simple acts of kindness may, in the end, constitute the best strategies—and they may have the most appeal in a postmodern era. We dare not let the existence of increasingly sophisticated communication technologies blind us to the continuing efficiency of simple presence and personal proclamation. At the same time, however, we must use available media and communication advances.[8]

As seen above, mission is usually built on the utilization of building relationships. Although God can use any and all means he desires, and certainly many have come to Christ through the use of media such as the *Jesus* video, the vast majority of evangelism which results in long-term maturing disciples of Christ will be done through one-on-one relationships. People in mission (and I use that word to mean both local and distant mission work) must resist the temptation of spending five to six hours a day in front of a computer monitor and relatively little time with people.

Another downside to speed is that "Technology is so focused on saving time that we have redefined quality to include the concept of speed. From a biblical perspective, this is a questionable value."[9] We must realize that not only does it take time to build relationships, it also takes time for our own character to develop, to effectively display the fruit of the Spirit. We have to take care with how we use our

7 Ibid., 304.
8 Ibid., 41.
9 Ibid., 303.

time since time is a precious resource and, as such, is in limited supply. We must be good stewards of it.

Air travel is still another issue related to speed. Unless we have very poor connections, we are seldom more than a day and a half away from any other part of the world. This allows missionaries to come home much more often than in the past. There are three missionary couples who came from our church and are now in Asia or Southeast Asia who have either had a baby or will be having one soon. All of them are taking a number of months from the field to have their babies back "home" in the U.S. In the past missionaries had their babies on the field and their adopted local community became a part of the process. Valerio puts it this way, the "proximity to the rest of the world now can create its own problems, with missionaries never quite "leaving home" and hence never committing fully and settling into their new place."[10] Pocock et al. explain, "Missionaries no longer step off a boat (or out of an airplane) and enter their new culture permanently. They now have a foot in each culture.... Will these jet-setters truly imbibe the local culture to the point at which they can effectively communicate the gospel? What message does their link to the home culture send to the people they are trying to reach?"[11]

Finally, Galadima warns us, "The fast pace of life in the global village is also creating a sense of disconnectedness, fragmentation, and homelessness... This person is everywhere but not at home anywhere."[12]

On the positive side, e-mail has proven to be a big help to missionaries. Whereas it is true that e-mail is another connection to "back home" and could be considered a negative, we find that e-mail has been a tremendous financial boon in terms of keeping donors up to date with praises and prayer requests almost instantaneously and virtually for free through sending a group e-mail. It also allows better communication between the missionaries and their mission agencies. Along with e-mail the use of ATMs has been a benefit. It not only allows missionaries to establish and have access to personal bank accounts in the U.S. into which their mission agency deposits their funding, but it also allows them to take advantage of lower exchange rates as ATMs usually have a lower rate than other venues.[13]

---

10 Ruth Valerio, "Globalisation and economics: A world gone bananas," in Richard Tiplady, ed., *One World or Many? The Impact of Globalisation on Mission* (Pasadena, CA: Wm. Carey Library, 2003), 23.

11 Pocock et al., *The Changing Face*, 303.

12 Bulus Galadima, "Religion and the future of Christianity in the global village," in Richard Tiplady, ed., *One World or Many? The Impact of Globalisation on Mission* (Pasadena, CA: Wm. Carey Library, 2003), 194.

13 Pocock et al. *The Changing Face*, 302.

Escobar relates yet another advantage, this time in terms of publications,

> In the field of Christian publishing, missionary linguists are working on the translation of the New Testament into an Indian language of Ecuador. A missionary aviation organization has flown the linguists to a remote village where they live and work. From there they will e-mail their drafts to their supervisor in Canada and discuss technical problems with him. When the manuscript is ready, the final layout of the book will be set by experts in Dallas, Texas, and then be sent by e-mail to Korea, where the books will be printed and later dispatched to Miami, the center from which they will be marketed in Ecuador.[14]

Concluding this section on technology, especially its use in mission work, we will once again turn to Pocock et al.

> Technology has facilitated missions in the areas of communication, distance learning, translation, and generally increased mobility. It has also introduced nontransferrable rather than appropriate technology, created tension between those who have access to certain capabilities and those who do not, and exposed Christian workers to workplace temptations they never had before the Internet. Appropriate technologies are those that can be used in a given context because they rely on locally available and affordable materials rather than on the ongoing resources or presence of outsiders.[15]

ECONOMICS/POLITICS

As we've seen, globalization can be a two-edged sword—maybe in no other arena as much as in that of economics and politics. A number of authors have succinctly mentioned the importance of the connection between globalization and economics. "The main patterns of globalization were shaped by the economic institutions and practices of free-market capitalism as well as the political alignments and agendas

---

14 Samuel Escobar, *The New Global Mission: The Gospel from Everywhere to Everyone* (Downers Grove, IL: InterVarsity Press, 2003), 56-7.
15 Pocock et al., *The Changing Face*, 11-12.

of the Western powers."[16] "Like an irresistible wave, the market is the main force behind this process of globalization."[17] These authors recognize that not only are economics at the root of globalization, it is a capitalist economic agenda coming from the West, primarily the U.S., with political ramifications.

For those of us born in the U.S. at the end of World War II and growing up in the Cold War era, it was impossible not to think of the world as being controlled by the two super powers of the U.S.S.R. and the U.S. This led us to view the world in terms of bipolar political relationships. All "Third World" countries were seen as aligning or being supported by one of the two super powers. When the world witnessed the relatively sudden collapse of the Communist State epitomized by the tearing down of the Berlin Wall, what occurred was a set of multi-polar political relationships.[18]

We must take note of a warning at this point. Economics is not a neutral dynamic—secularly or religiously. Extremes of wealth and poverty both within and between nations is now appalling. "The fuel that drives globalization is economic profit."[19] This produces a need for consumerism. In turn, "The new global environment and its structures encourage materialism and disrupt traditional ways of life, quickly eroding cultural structures. The primary drive of globalization is economics, and the goal of economics is profit. Morality is considered only if it has a bearing on profit-making."[20] This present consumer-centered system relies as much on creating need as it does in supplying need. How many times have you asked yourself the question, "How did I ever make out without having my PDA, or my computer, or my cell phone, etc. ?" We no sooner get a new program for our computers than it becomes old. Updates are available which, oftentimes, no longer support what we have, so we have to buy something new. Or we buy a PDA (already an almost obsolete term due to Blackberries and the Apple I-Phones), and when the batteries get low, we find out we can not just get a new battery; we have to buy a new and updated device. So many people now rely on cell phones that many homes no longer have a land line, or if they do, it's only for their computers so they can have high-speed internet connectivity. The danger of this is aptly summarized by Goudzwaard,

---

16 Howard A. Netland, "Introduction: Globalization and Theology Today," in Craig Ott and Harold A. Netland, eds., *Globalizing Theology: Belief and Practice in an Era of World Christianity* (Grand Rapids, MI: Baker Academic, 2006), 19.

17 Escobar, *The New Global Mission*, 56.

18 Netland, "Introduction," 19.

19 Galadima, "Religion and the future of Christianity," 194.

20 Ibid., 196.

Imagine what would happen if consumers began to show signs of satiation and satisfaction with what they have. Would it not threaten the foundations of growth for the whole economy and, in turn, threaten our economic and political power?

... The poor are in danger because the aim to create artificial scarcity will sooner or later prevent the alleviation of real scarcity. The resources and capital needed to feed and house the needy will no longer be available.[21]

Another aspect of the global system is explained by Vargas, "At the heart of the current world system is the free market, which is characterized by the continuous accumulation of wealth as an end in itself.... The idolatrous love of money is the beginning of all the evils that bind not only humanity but the whole of creation."[22]

Globalization and the Poor

Globalization has been catastrophic for the poor. To begin our discussion on the poor, we should understand who the poor are.

The poor are often thought of as those who are deprived of the basic objects which sustain life—adequate nourishment, housing, clothing and healthcare These criteria define poverty in terms of the *quantity* of goods and services available to people. The criteria which define life in terms of *quality*, realities which may be both the cause and result of material deprivation, are also vital. Among these are access to decision-making processes (which ensure that people are genuinely involved in deciding their own future), guaranteed redress in law against intimidation, violence and excessive bureaucracy, relevant and well-resourced education and training, useful and rewarding work and a healthy (pollution free) environment.[23]

Earlier we mentioned the "connected" ones which include about 30 percent of the world's population. But what about the other 70 percent? Many do not have phones in their homes which eliminates accessing the internet, at least from their

---

21 Bob Goudzwaard, *Globalization and the Kingdom of God* (Grand Rapids, MI: Baker Books, 2001), 32-3, emphasis in original.

22 Vargas, "Can the global replace the local?" 207.

23 J. Andrew Kirk, *What is Mission? Theological Explorations* (Minneapolis: Fortress Press, 2000), 97, emphasis in original.

homes. Cyber cafes are popping up in numerous places, but first of all, they could be quite a distance from large numbers of the people, and second, even though they are inexpensive the cost is prohibitive when a family is fighting for food to stay alive. Certainly many from the developing countries have benefited from the free-market system—just think of the times you have called for IT assistance and the person you reached to help you was living in India or Pakistan—however, we can not get away from the old adage that "the rich get richer and the poor get poorer." To understand this better, we turn once again to Pocock et al.

> Technological advances are growing by quantum leaps among wealthy nations, while poor nations, many of which are unable to feed their own populations, cannot afford to modernize and make use of increasingly complex, new technologies.

> There are a number of reasons for the growing gap. The cost to set up a digital infrastructure is significant. While one can easily create a single-access point using a satellite dish or other small-scale technology, the large bandwidth trunk lines that a nation must possess to deliver broadband Internet access require significant government commitment.[24]

Let's look at how power works to aggravate the situation in poorer countries. One aspect of this problem deals with how financial resources are used. Wealth comes from spending money on income-producing capital. However, poor countries must spend their finances for current consumption—they need to eat, be housed, get an education, and have access to health care. Kirk helps us understand how systems and structures can aggravate poverty.

> In the first place, a free-market economy operating through transnational businesses, with little accountability (beyond corporate shareholders) and ineffectually controlled, rewards the strong and punishes the weak. Secondly, there is the reality of international debt on an unprecedented scale. This means that there is a massive reverse flow of wealth from the main debtor countries, who are already destitute of capital reserves. In turn this results in these nations having inadequate resources to invest in healthcare, education and job-creation.... Thirdly, the world trade systems

---

24 Pocock et al., *The Changing Face*, 306.

operate to the disadvantage of those whose economies are weak through lack of diversification. Forced to a large extent to rely on the export of primary materials, the poor nations have never been strong enough to ensure a fair return for their crops or raw materials.... In spite of the rhetoric to the contrary, there are no level playing fields in world trade.[25]

Vargas, while appreciating the benefits of globalization, calls us to remember that "the law of globalization is the law of the strongest."[26] He continues by describing how social and economic inequality is growing, and how we are losing the fight against poverty. One of the issues at point is that capitalism is being imposed on countries through forms of domination and oppression. It is the old story that the American way (a foreign way) is the right way, regardless of another country's history, culture or context, and this is "degrading and unworthy."[27]

Before going into the implications for mission, we will listen to one more warning by Goudzwaard,

> This moment, at the turn of the millennium, appears to me to be one of the most critical points in human history. Powerful, untruthful, hypnotic ideologies corrupted societies and destroyed millions of people throughout the twentieth century. Yet none of them had the instruments of communication available to it to infiltrate the human mind the way the present ideology of limitless economic and technological expansion can do.[28]

What is the responsibility of Christians in the midst of all this?

Poverty and Mission

Jayakumar Christian correctly connects the issues of power and poverty. He challenges us to understand power and its relationship to the poor, as well as an appropriate church response to this, through three perspectives—that of the poor, that of the powerful, and that of the kingdom of God.

---

25 Kirk, *What is Mission?*, 99-100.
26 Vargas, "Can the global replace the local?" 204.
27 Ibid.
28 Goudzwaard, *Globalization and the Kingdom of God*, 33.

These three scenarios—from the perspectives of the poor, the non-poor and the throne of God—suggest at least three conflicting views of power evident in poverty situations. One is the deep-seated powerlessness of the poor... Second is the different expressions of power among the non-poor... Finally, for the church in mission among the poor, there is also the determining understanding of power as seen in the kingdom of God.[29]

He later implores Christians to address the injustices in this world. "From a Christian perspective the reality, causes and resolution of poverty are inseparable from the call for relationships of justice between individuals, communities and nations."[30] The reason for this plea is that "the basis for and the meaning of justice spring from the nature of the God who is. Justice is what God does, for justice is what God is."[31] Vargas warns us, "Without any real reference to social justice, we will only end up distorting good theology and the missionary task."[32]

It has been noted that the amount of money in this world that is controlled by Christians is around $10 trillion. They earn about one quarter of all the income in the world.[33] If Christians invested differently, they could certainly affect the economic distribution in our global economy. Ruth Valerio writes, "Globalisation's effects on the poor mean that social concerns must be at the heart of mission and the church."[34] One mistake made by Christians, whether personally or churches or para-church organizations or missions, is that they are overwhelmed by the needs of the poor and their conviction to meet those needs without presenting the gospel in all its fullness to the poor. Escobar warns us that "providing relief and service cannot be divorced from evangelism, because the world needs both their presence [their concern for the poor] and their proclamation."[35] Grigg recognizes that missions have a different stance in reaching the poor, usually through diaconal ministries, and reaching the middle class. In his words, *"But the church has given bread to the poor and has kept the bread of life for the middle class."*[36]

---

29 Jayakumar Christian, *God of the Empty-Handed: Poverty, Power and the Kingdom of God* (Monrovia, CA: MARC, 1999), 9.

30 Ibid., 103.

31 Ibid., 104.

32 Vargas, "Can the global replace the local?" 211.

33 See Goudzwaard, *Globalization and the Kingdom of God*, 10-11.

34 Valerio, "Globalisation and economics," 23.

35 Escobar, *The New Global Mission*, 151.

36 Viv Grigg, *Cry of the Urban Poor* (Monrovia, CA: MARC, 1992), 12, emphasis in original.

Another point to make is that "most of the members of Christian communities worldwide are themselves poor. The church, therefore, does not stand over against the poor. It does not even stand alongside or in the midst of the poor. The poor are in the Church or *are* the Church. Thus the Church has an immense interest in the transformation of their situation."[37]

We now turn to the unfortunate truth that mission agencies often mimic their home country's practices in their new homes, again bringing "foreign" ways into different contexts. Pocock explains,

> Transnational corporations tend to homogenize their cooperating part-
> ners in the name of efficiency and profit. Transnational mission agencies
> and the churches they establish in other cultures face the same set of is-
> sues. It is difficult to tell if one is really in another country when a church
> looks like, acts like, and sings like the churches in the West."[38]

There is a dire need for the church to be involved in justice. Here we need to make a distinction, "The practice of charity is not synonymous with justice, and to dispense justice would mean that much of the time charity would be unnecessary. The time is now favourable for the Christian community to apply the justice of the kingdom of God."[39]

We have been explaining how the West, at the helm of globalization, has run rough shod over many other countries. Valerio indicates, "It is imperative that those from poorer countries be heard and that those from more wealthy churches/mission agencies find the humility to sit at the feet of these others and let themselves be taught by them."[40] Pocock adds to this that "Mission agencies and missionaries must minister to both extremes—to the beneficiaries *and* to the marginalized losers of globalization."[41] This is an awesome task, one which will require mission agencies and missionaries to utilize all the creativity that comes from our all-creative and loving God in order to reach out to the two extremes for the glory of God.

---

37 Kirk, *What is Mission?*, 111, emphasis in original.
38 Pocock et al., *The Changing Face*, 27.
39 Vargas, "Can the global replace the local?" 210.
40 Valerio, "Globalisation and economics," 19.
41 Pocock et al., *The Changing Face*, 29, emphasis in original.

CULTURE

Often when we think of culture, we think of different ways people dress, different foods they eat, possibly different languages that they speak, and maybe even different religions they serve. And all this is certainly a part of culture. However, the underlying values and beliefs which formulate the worldview of a people are even more important, yet they are more difficult to ascertain. In this section we will explore how globalization has shaped values that affect all cultures yet do not eradicate any local cultures. Guthrie expresses it this way, "Culture... is the expression of the society's worldview. Worldview has been described as the way a people looks upon itself and the universe, or the way it sees itself in relationship to all else."[42] But how does globalization affect worldview? "Globalization... means a change of perspective on the meaning of life... the globe has itself become a platform for action, a point of departure and not just a destination."[43] Araujo gives us another perspective,

> In the realm of ideas—and more fundamentally, of worldviews—globalization means greater exposure to and less protective isolation from alien worldviews in local communities.... Globalization pressures us into withholding our convictions in order to co-exist with other value systems, for the sake of peace. It is in this realm of worldviews that the interaction of the church with the globalization phenomenon becomes particularly relevant.[44]

He continues,

> Globalization is more than a way of organizing how humans relate to each other as individuals and as societies; it is a framework for making sense of the universe and of our existence in it.... It is here that the church, the only effective alternative, needs to exercise its prophetic role.[45]

Araujo does not stop here. He goes on with even stronger words.

---

42 Stan Guthrie, *Missions in the Third Millenium: 21 Key Trends for the 21st Century* (Waynesboro, GA: Paternoster Press, 2000), 102
43 James W. Skillen, "Foreword," in Bob Goudzwaard, *Globalization and the Kingdom of God* (Grand Rapids, MI: Baker Books, 2001), 7.
44 Alex Araujo, "Globalization and the church," in Richard Tiplady, ed., *One World or Many? The Impact of Globalisation on Mission* (Pasadena, CA: Wm. Carey Library, 2003), 230.
45 Ibid., 233.

> Globalization, at the level of worldviews, is today's dominant manifestation of the "pattern of this world" to which the Apostle Paul refers, and it is aided by new and powerful instruments of technology.
>
> ... History is clear: the pattern of this world will always seem enticing and sensible. Resisting may at times look foolish.[46]

These words bring to mind Paul's words in 1 Corinthians 1:25, 27, "For the foolishness of God is wiser than man's wisdom, and the weakness of God is stronger than man's strength.... But God chose the foolish things of the world to shame the wise; God chose the weak things of the world to shame the strong." We, as God's children, need to be foolish for the Lord and aggressively attack this new worldview in order to bring shalom to the peoples of this world.

In our discussion of culture, we want to look at a number of areas. First, we will look at consumerism/materialism and its effects on worldview, especially that of the youth. Next we will look at how the postmodern mindset and plurality are undermining our concept of an authoritative God. After that we will do a short study on human identity and how globalization is presenting a view of that identity that is antithetical to the gospel. Finally, we will conclude with implications for mission.

Consumerism/Materialism

Netland informs us that "Although local cultural distinctives remain, disparate peoples and places are today increasingly linked by common cultural symbols, institutions, values and behavior."[47] We can find a McDonalds almost any place we go in the world. Popular (Western) music and movies are available through the internet so young people everywhere are tuning in. Western dress styles are infiltrating numerous localities, replacing traditional garb. In this tension between the local and the global (often termed glocal), "The local will always have a kind of priority over the global,"[48] but the global effects are huge.

This global consumerism leads to a pronounced hedonism.

> There are products, methods and stimuli for enhancing physical pleasure in all its forms. This search for pleasure has become a mark of contemporary life that, coupled with the hopelessness brought about by the

---

46 Ibid., 234, 235.
47 Netland, "Introduction," 21.
48 Ibid.

collapse of ideologies, becomes pure and simple hedonism. The media portrays this hedonistic way of life and thought, and propagates it across the globe. Incitement to expensive pleasure fills the screens of TV sets in poor societies, and young people especially crave for the symbols and instruments of a sophisticated, hedonistic West while lacking some of the basic necessities of life such as adequate housing and running water.[49]

Consumerism has become an ideology and is fleshed out by the overwhelming desire to continue buying and using.

We need to take heed of Escobar's warning.

An uncritical acceptance of modernization and globalization as supreme values would be similar to the uncritical acceptance of the imperial order... in the Constantine experience. They would become idols, *powers* regarded as almost superhuman forces that cannot be reined in or even challenged but are appeased or accepted as lords of our lives.[50]

Postmodernity and Pluralism

Although we will go more deeply into the movement of religions later in this essay, worldview is so intricately connected with religious beliefs that we will touch on it just a bit here. As Newbigin puts it, "We live in a pluralist society... pluralist in the sense that this plurality is celebrated as things to be approved and cherished."[51] This pluralism is associated with a secular society which questions all accepted beliefs and does its best to deny all sense of authority. This causes grave questions for the church as "the global values of pluralism, tolerance, and inclusivism pose a serious challenge to the Christian message. To preach an exclusive gospel is considered as intolerance."[52] This challenge has displaced Christianity to a large extent in terms of its central role in societies. This lends to the label of post-Christianity that Murray writes about.[53] However, as Escobar points out, "The renewed interest in all kinds of religions, including those that existed before Christian missionaries appeared, can better be described as a sign of postmodernity."[54] Whether we use the term postmodern or post-Christian, we are describing what is happening in much of the

49 Escobar, *The New Global Mission*, 75.
50 Ibid., 58, emphasis in original.
51 Leslie Newbigin, *The Gospel in a Pluralist Society* (Waynesboro, GA: Paternoster Press, 2004), 1.
52 Galadima, "Religion and the future of Christianity," 199.
53 Stuart Murray, *Church After Christendom* (Waynesboro, GA: Paternoster Press, 2004).
54 Escobar, *The New Global Mission*, 70.

West. Since Western ideology is spreading worldwide through the internet, media, etc., we are also seeing these trends in countries outside the West.

Johnson describes features of the emerging worldview coming from postmodernity.

- *Cynicism*, especially about authority, hierarchy, and "experts."...
- A strong emphasis on *personal relationships* and contacts, rather than organizational structures, to provide the networks for getting things done....
- An emphasis on *reality*, rather than truth....
- Desire for *hands-on involvement* and for *adventure*, which can in part be met by short-term mission experiences.
- *Insecurity* about the future....
- *Consumerism* and *customization*....
- *Materialism*.[55]

This is a new era for Christianity, one which will require innovative responses in order to grow as a healthy worldwide church. Hunter warns us, "The culture barrier between the churches and the unchurched [postmodern] people of Europe is the largest single cause of European Christianity's decline in this century.... The culture barrier is an even bigger problem for mainline American Christianity."[56]

Personal Identity

Human beings long for identity. Galadima expresses it this way, "Apart from the quest for food, shelter, and clothing, probably the next greatest human need is that of belonging. Human beings have a dire need for identity."[57] As Christians, when we speak of a person's identity, we must begin in Genesis and recognize who each person is as an image-bearer of God. The Fall brought damage to our humanity in a number of ways, but we never lost that basic reality of being created in God's image. We take that with us and no person and no phenomenon should demean that in any way. However, we are all so capable of hurting someone else's true identity through our own ethnocentrism and egoism—sometimes unintentional but often quite purposeful. Adeney describes how God used humankind to develop the cultures

---

55 Ros Johnson, "Cutting out the middleman: Mission and the local church in a globalized postmodern world," in Richard Tiplady, ed., *One World or Many? The Impact of Globalisaton on Mission* (Pasadena, CA: Wm. Carey Library, 2003), 244, emphasis in original.

56 George G. Hunter, III, "The Case for Culturally Relevant Congregations," in Howard A. Snyder, ed., *Global Good News: Mission in a New Context* (Nashville: Abingdon Press, 2001), 102.

57 Galadima, "Religion and the Future of Christianity," 198

of the world and how he also uses ethnicity to counterbalance the dehumanization of globalization—be it overt, as in including only the "chosen" to be a part of the economic world system, or tacit, as in how its reliance on "*virtual*" realities so that "we miss out on the real rhythms of nature and society."[58]

How do we affect personhood, whether for good or evil? Valerio indicates that "personhood arises precisely through being together in relationship" and "our relationships with one another are based on our understanding of each one being made in the image of God."[59] Globalization can have very serious implications for developing identity. Valerio continues, "Globalisation reduces humanity merely to consumers and robs us of our ability to relate fully, whether to God, to one another, or to the world."[60] Galadima adds to that,

> The fast pace of life and the wide dissemination of news and informa-
> tion make us conscious of other people and religions around the world,
> even when we do not want to be. They increase the range of options
> of how individuals can constitute themselves in the global village....
> Unfortunately, the global systems do not tell us how to make the right
> and the best choice between the myriad of options available.[61]

What are the implications for mission? First, the church has to answer the question of how it can utilize globalization to advance missions. One of the major ways, to be discussed in the next section, is that through migration God has brought all the peoples of the world into the West, so we must take advantage of that, in our churches, in our communities, and in our workplaces. Escobar warns us,

> The culture of globalization creates attitudes and a mental frame that
> may be the opposite of what the gospel teaches about human life under
> God's design. If mission simply rides on the crest of the globalization
> wave it might inadvertently change the very nature of the gospel.... [The
> phrase] "I think, therefore I am," [seems to be changed to]... "I buy,
> therefore I am." That is the spirit of the age, and we must be careful not

---

58 Miriam Adeney, "Is God colorblind or colorful? The gospel, globalization, and ethnicity," in Richard Tiplady, ed., *One World or Many? The Impact of Globalisation on Mission* (Pasadena, CA: Wm. Carey Library, 2003), 91-4, emphasis in original.

59 Valerio, "Gobalisation and economics," 28,30.

60 Ibid., 30.

61 Galadima, "Religion and the future of Christianity," 194.

to become prisoners of it, lest we accept that human nature and happiness are totally dependent on the market.[62]

We now revert to how we began this section and remember that culture affects all aspects of life and, therefore, it affects all aspects of mission. It is difficult for us to see beyond the confines of our own culture—to evaluate its strengths and weaknesses. "We do not see the subtle, and perhaps insidious, influence of culture on our beliefs and behaviour."[63] It is also difficult to recognize the goodness, yet differences, in other cultures. If we follow past trends of "Westernizing" other people groups in our attempts to bring Christianity to them, we will contribute to the dehumanization wreaked on other cultures. We must not do that. Nor should we blanketly accept another culture. However, "A saving revelation of God is possible in any culture. Every culture has enough to work with and the Holy Spirit makes up the difference, so the meaning of the Christian gospel can be communicated in any culture."[64] This is a question of contextualization which is beyond the scope of this essay, but it is important to at least mention it here.

POPULATION MOVEMENT

One of the movements most affecting the visible face of nations is that of people movements. The causes for population migration are primarily economic. However, "We are experiencing migration on a scale never equaled in history. Much of this is survival migration, refugees fleeing for their lives."[65] DeLung and Jones give us some statistics, "In 2002, over 40 million—16 million refugees and an estimated 25 million displaced persons—fled their homes because of persecution, war, and human rights abuses."[66] Although these figures tend to shock us, the reality is that the majority of migration is for economic reasons. On the one hand, those who live in poorer countries of the developing world will often migrate in order to find work just for survival. On the other hand, professionals from the developing world will often migrate for further education or in order to advance and excel in their chosen fields. In either case there is a tendency for these new migrants to move

---

62 Escobar, *The New Global Mission*, 59,60.

63 Kirk, *What is Mission?* 78.

64 Hunter, "The Case for Culturally Relevant Congregations," 105.

65 Howard A. Snyder, "Introduction," in Howard A. Snyder, ed., *Global Good News: Mission in a New Context* (Nashville: Abingdon Press, 2001), 18.

66 Jane DeLung and Becca Jones, "Executive Summary: International Migration" (2003): 4, http://www.prcdc.org/files/InternationalMigration.pdf (accessed 9/2/08).

back and forth with frequent visits to and sometimes relocation in their home communities.

As with other aspects of globalization, migration presents us with some positive and some negative ramifications. On the positive side, migrants have long been documented as sending back relatively large sums of money to their families in their often impoverished homelands. This alleviates some of the burden in these countries. Often, however, well-educated migrants are "seeking better pay and greater access to resources. This phenomenon is a contributing factor to 'brain drain,' with its crippling effects on the developing world. Rather than assisting in overall development, remittances tend to create financial and social dependencies, further complicating unequal global economic growth."[67]

Another positive facet emanating from the degree of migration going on in this global village of ours is that when people migrate to new locations, they are more apt to find communities of their own people already established. This greatly aids in the transitioning process which can be so difficult. It is beginning to be close to impossible to be homogeneous in many countries of the world, especially in urban areas, because it is nearly impossible not to rub shoulders with others unlike yourself. "Either through immigration, the forced displacement of peoples or the arbitrary setting of national boundaries, most nations today contain a multiplicity of different ethnic groups with different histories, customs, religions, languages and traditions."[68] Ortiz describes his own life in a Philadelphia neighborhood as follows,

> When I, as a Puerto Rican, wake up to the hustle and bustle of the African-American community in which I live, I realize that there are similarities and dissimilarities in our lifestyles, yet we live as neighbors. When I go to our favorite grocery store to buy ingredients to make our regular Puerto Rican meals, I discern that the owners are from an area not associated with Latin America—they are Palestinian. I go to the cobbler shop, and the man who tells me that my shoes will be ready by five o'clock is from Southeast Asia. The hardware store is close by, and I walk over to have an additional set of keys made. The owner speaks to me of her home in Seoul, Korea.[69]

---

67 Pocock et al., *The Changing Face*, 48.
68 Kirk, *What is Mission?* 79.
69 Manuel Ortiz, *One New People: Models for Developing a Multiethnic Church* (Downers Grove, IL: InterVarsity Press, 1996), 28-9.

How does this produce an impact on mission? One of the most wonderful effects of the movement of populations from country to country is that we no longer have to go abroad in order to reach all nations—we only have to minister to those next door. Since, as we have seen, there is movement between homelands and adopted homelands, we are in an era not dissimilar to what Paul faced as he witnessed the spread of the gospel through the journeys of first century "migrants." But this is not just a one-way street. "Migration also brings vibrant Christians from Africa or the Caribbean to post-Christian areas of Europe."[70] This is also true of the U.S. African churches in New York City are bringing renewal to communities whose churches had been stagnant.

RELIGIOUS MOVEMENT

We've already mentioned that the movement of people has brought about a movement in Christians. We are now going to focus on a number of areas regarding changing and moving religions. We will begin with a deeper analysis of the post-Christian phenomenon facing churches in the West. Then we will look at its counterpart and delve into the exploding Christian presence in much of the Two-Thirds World. From that we investigate the movement of non-Christian religions and how that challenges the Christian church. Finally, we will see how mission work is changing because of what is laid out in the first three sections.

The Post-Christian West

We begin this section with words from Lamin Sanneh, "Many writers argue that we live in a post-Christian West and that, thanks to irreversible secularization, we have outlived the reigning convictions of a once Christian society."[71] This phenomenon is lamented by Stuart Murray,

> The end of Christendom and transition into post-Christendom in Western culture is a paradigm shift. Many Christians are resisting this shift... But Christendom is fading. We may grieve or celebrate its passing, but we cannot revive, restore, or recover it. Post-Christendom is coming.[72]

---

70 Pocock et al., *The Changing Face*, 25.

71 Lamin Sanneh, *Whose Religion is Christianity? The Gospel beyond the West* (Grand Rapids, MI: Wm. B. Eerdmans Publishing Co., 2003), 1.

72 Murray, *Church After Christendom*, 7.

He later states,

> Church after Christendom, if we negotiate this transition, will be mar-
> ginal, in exilic mode, journeying towards a different way of being God's
> people in a strange new world. Discovering a new way of being church—
> not a revival of an old way—is the hoped-for future.[73]

How did we get to such a desperate place? Speaking for the U.S., we have always
been a nation of immigrants, but only certain immigrants have been welcomed or
acknowledged. This can be seen clearly in terms of how we respond to tragedies.

> The parochialism of Western public opinion is striking. When a single
> racial or religious-motivated murder takes place in Europe or North
> America, the event occasions widespread soul-searching, but when thou-
> sands are massacred on the grounds of their faith in Nigeria, Indonesia,
> or the Sudan, the story rarely registers. Some lives are worth more than
> others.[74]

Now we are not only faced with the very real possibility that within the next 30 to
40 years non-Hispanic whites will no longer hold a majority among the population
of the U.S. but we are also faced with the cynicism and skepticism of a postmodern,
secular society. Ethnocentric churches that either do not want to adapt or do not
know how to adapt to all these new people groups are couple with a watered down
theology that has lost its prophetic voice to speak into the culture. The Western
church seems impotent to change the tide. Rather than leading the world in recep-
tivity to the gospel, the West now struggles as it falls further and further behind
the rest of the world. Escobar bemoans, "If we take into account the secularization
of Europe and the paganization of North America, or the lack of depth in some of
the younger churches, it is debatable whether in the initial years of the twenty-first
century we are in a period of advance or recession."[75]

Is there any hope? Is there anything that can be done? Watson exhorts, "Our
North American congregations urgently need an inversion of their religious self-
preoccupation and ecclesial self-indulgence…. we find ourselves spending more

---

73 Ibid., 131.

74 Philip Jenkins, *The Next Christendom: The Coming of Global Christianity* (Oxford: Oxford University Press, 2002), 163.

75 Escobar, *The New Global Mission*, 35.

time talking about evangelism than doing it—a sure sign of self-preoccupation."[76] Murray also offers some advice, "Post-Christendom churches need a missional *ethos*, expressed in their core values and nurtured in their corporate life."[77] He calls the Post-Christendom church to make some drastic shifts: from maintenance to mission, from institution to movement, and from centre to margins.[78] The church in the West is far from dead, but it first needs to recognize and not deny or rationalize its current condition. It then needs to accept its marginality and not fight it, so that it can begin rebuilding anew. And third, it needs to encompass the Southern church, both in Western cities as well as in their own homes, as a gift from God to assist in the renewal process.

The Shifting Center of Christianity

As we move from the Post-Christian West to the Southern Christian explosion, we should understand the historical dynamics of Christianity. "The Christian story is serial: its center moves from place to place. No one church or place or culture owns it. At different times different peoples and places have become its heartlands, its chief representatives. Then the baton passes on to others."[79] Philip Jenkins follows the journey of Christianity's center beginning in the first century in the Near East with roots in Palestine. From there it moved to Syria, Egypt, and Mesopotamia and then traveled to the Eastern half of the Roman Empire, followed by Asia and North Africa, and didn't reach the West until approximately 1400 A.D. when the myth of Western Christianity was born. Now it is on the move once more, going to Asia, Africa, and Latin America.[80] To be clear, saying that the center of Christianity is on the move does not mean that Christianity was not to be found in the Two-Thirds World before, nor does it mean that Christianity is dead now in the West. Again, we are talking about Western Christianity moving to the margins while the center moves to the Two-Thirds World.

In order to buttress our analysis of this shift, let's look at some statistics compiled by *Operation World* at the beginning of the 21st century. Total population in this

---

76 David Lowes Watson, "The Mystery of Evangelism: Mission in an Age of Cosmic Discovery," in Howard A. Snyder, ed., *Global Good News: Mission in a New Context* (Nashville: Abingdon Press, 2001), 31.
77 Murray, *Church After Christendom*, 137, emphasis in original.
78 Ibid.
79 Andrew Walls, "The Mission of the Church Today in the Light of Global History," in Paul Varo Martinson, ed., *Mission at the Dawn of the 21st Century* (Minneapolis: Kirk House, 1999), 385, cited in Samuel Escobar, *The New Global Mission: The Gospel from Everywhere to Everyone* (Downers Grove, IL: InterVarsity Press, 2003), 36.
80 Jenkins, *The Next Christendom*.

world is increasing at a rate of 1.39%. That means to simply keep even with the population growth, Christianity should also be near that percentage, which it is—at 1.43%. However, if we break that down by continent we find the following:[81]

CONTINENT	CHRISTIAN GROWTH RATE
Europe	-.044%
North America	.066%
Pacific (Oceania)	.074%
Latin America	1.52%
Africa	2.83%
Asia	3.66%

We can now visualize this shift as Europe, the U.S. and Oceania are not keeping pace with the population growth rate while the Two-Thirds World continents are exceeding it.

To further understand the shift, Jenkins tells us, "In 1800, perhaps one percent of all Protestant Christians lived outside Europe and North America. By 1900, that number had risen to 10 percent, and this proved enough of a critical mass to support further expansion. Today, the figure stands around two-thirds of all Protestants."[82] What does that mean to the global church? Walls writes, "African, Asian and Latin American Christianity will become more and more important within the church as a whole and Western Christianity less and less so."[83] Sanneh adds, "The contemporary confidence in the secular destiny of the West as an elevated stage of human civilization is matched by the contrasting evidence of the resurgence of Christianity as a world religion; they are like two streams flowing in opposite directions."[84]

Authors, in analyzing these trends, have begun to use such terms as "world Christianity" or "global church" to express what is happening.[85] We conclude this section with some words from Pocock et al.

---

81 Patrick Johnstone and Jason Mandryk, *Operation World: When We Pray God Works*, 21st century ed., CD-ROM.

82 Jenkins, *The Next Christendom*, 37.

83 Andrew F. Walls, "Globalization and the Study of Christian History," in Craig Ott and Harold A. Netland, eds., *Globalizing Theology: Belief and Practice in an Era of World Christianity* (Grand Rapids, MI: Baker Academic, 2006), 77.

84 Sanneh, *Whose Religion is Christianity?* 3.

85 See Netland, "Introduction," and Pocock et al., *The Changing Face.*

As the body of Christ expands to include more and more peoples and nations, it is only natural that it shows great diversity. The church is an organism. It is not a corporation like McDonald's that seeks to deliver a uniform product with uniform quality in every outlet worldwide. Like so many things God makes, the body of Christ exhibits diversity in the way it worships, fellowships, passes on knowledge, organizes for tasks, and relates to cultures.... Christians differ from nation to nation, but as part of the body of Christ, they are a single entity with one Lord, one faith, and one Scripture.[86]

Religious Plurality

As the peoples of the world move from country to country, they bring their religions with them. Ramachandra writes, "The movement of forms of Hinduism and Buddhism around the world through the efforts of traveling gurus and monks is an important event in modern times that has taken place alongside the emigration of South Asians and South Asian culture."[87] Escobar adds, "In the streets of London, Madrid, Philadelphia or Los Angeles, mosques and Hindu temples increasingly fill the cityscape... as places of worship for communities that sometimes outdo Christians in their missionary zeal."[88] The U.S. has been affected more than many other nations as it "has become the religiously most diverse nation on earth.... Nowhere, even in today's world of mass migrations, is the sheer range of religious faith as wide as it is in the United States."[89] The growth of Islam in nations around the world certainly poses a difficult challenge for Christians. "Six million Muslims live in the United States, but only 30 percent of them are American born. Over 1 million Muslims live in the United Kingdom, and an additional 3.4 million live in Germany."[90]

So how do we handle the challenges presented to us from both a moving center of Christianity and religious pluralism. First, it is important for the West to listen to their brothers and sisters in the Two-Thirds World. The resurgence is happening there, and, again, we must take the position of sitting at the feet of this newer

---

86 Pocock et al., *The Changing Face*, 156.
87 Vinoth Ramachandra, "Globalization, Nationalism and Religious Resurgence," in Craig Ott and Harold A. Netland, eds., *Globalizing Theology: Belief and Practice in an Era of World Christianity* (Grand Rapids, MI: Baker Academic, 2006), 229.
88 Escobar, *The New Global Mission*, 81.
89 Diana Eck, *A New Religious America: How a "Christian Country" Has Become the World's Most Religiously Diverse Nation* (New York: HarperCollins, 2001), 4-5, cited in Netland, "Introduction," 23.
90 Pocock, *The Changing Face*, 81-2.

church, humble ourselves, and learn from them. Second, "It is important in a global world that the church be more informed about religious differences."[91] This is the subject of elenctics.

> When we speak of *elenctics* we do well to understand it in the sense
> that it has in John 16:8. The Holy Spirit will convince the world of sin....
> Taken in this sense, elenctics is the science which is concerned with the
> conviction of sin. In a special sense then it is the science which unmasks
> to heathendom all false religions as sin against God, and it calls heathen-
> dom to a knowledge of the only true God.[92]

The subject of elenctics should be taught in all seminaries at this time. It is important both for missionaries called to go abroad and for local churches thrust into the milieu of all these new religions. We cannot just sit by and ignore their presence; we must gather them into the kingdom of God.

Missions

Who is responding to all we have shared? Arias tells us, "In the last decade... a new pattern has emerged: missions from the Two-Thirds World.... today, approximately one-half of the total Protestant missionary force comes from non-Western countries."[93] Johnson adds, "Old categorizations, such as that of 'sending' and 'receiving' countries, have not just ceased to be relevant but become a barrier to understanding the diversity of what is now happening."[94]

What should we do now? It is time that Christians from the West and from the South start forming partnerships that are not paternalistic. Mission is not something we go to but something that is all around us no matter where we are. We are faced with new and interesting people with ways that seem strange to us, as our ways seem to others. We need to join together to reach this world for Christ.

---

91 Beattie, "Mission possible or impossible?" 220.
92 J. H. Bavinck, *An Introduction to the Science of Missions*, trans. by David H. Freeman (Phillipsburg, NJ: Presbyterian & Reformed Publishers, 1960), 222.
93 Mortimer Arias, "Global and Local: A Critical View of Mission Models," in Howard A. Snyder, ed., *Global Good News: Mission in a New Context* (Nashville: Abingdon Press, 2001), 62,
94 Johnson, "Cutting out the middleman," 243.

.2.

Contextual Theologies:
The Problem of Agendas

HARVIE M. CONN[1]

Mention the word "contextualization" in Reformed and evangelical circles and sooner or later another word pops up—syncretism. Why?

There are many answers to that question. Most certainly a basic one is our legitimate concern that the authority of the Bible will become lost in the plethora of localized theologies. If we start with our particular, historical situation, what will happen to the once-for-all character of the Bible as norm? In constantly taking account of the receptor cultures, isn't hermeneutic in danger of letting the medium become the message and the message become a massage? Will the "sameness" of the Bible get lost in a diversity of human cultures?

There are plenty of illustrations to confirm these fears. Liberation theologies often reduce the Bible from canon to paradigm. Korea's Minjung theology often sounds, through the voices of some of its advocates, to be more Korean than biblical.

My purpose in this essay, however, moves in another direction. I wish to suggest that there is still another cause for fears, and this among those committed to the full inerrancy of Scripture. It is not as obvious to us as is the expression of doubts regarding the authority of the Bible. In fact, we are only beginning to recognize its potential for creating trouble. I speak of our lack of sophistication about the circumstantial issues which all theologies, including evangelical and Reformed ones, address.

---

1 Reprinted with permission from *Westminster Theological Journal* 52(1990): 51-68, with minor editing.

To put it positively, I wish to underline the place of the historical context in rightly doing theology. I shall use several key figures from the early church to point out the liabilities of misjudging context and indicate how that misjudgment has affected our understanding of theology. And, finally, I shall make a few comments about how evangelicals in the two-thirds world are attempting to be more aware of this issue of context.

SHIFTS IN PERSPECTIVE

The basic purpose of theological reflection has never changed—"the reflection of Christians upon the gospel in the light of their own circumstances."[2] John V. Taylor, the missionary statesman of the Church of England, remembers the heartbreaking moment when his son decided to give up on the church. "Father," he said on one occasion as the two left church together, "the preacher is saying all of the right things, but he isn't saying them *to* anybody. He doesn't know where I am and it would never occur to him to ask!"

Relevance and irrelevance are the words we have used in the past to justify the dilemma placed before us by Taylor's son. Are our sermons and our theology scratching where the world does not itch? How can we live out and share the gospel in such a way that the cultures of the world will respond, "God speaks my language!"? "If Jesus is the answer, what are the questions?"

In recent years, however, that question of relevance and what we have called "application" has become more dominant. Much more attention is being paid now to how our context, our setting, is related to gospel response. Recent discussions in hermeneutics have underlined these questions in terms of "the two horizons."[3] The global agendas of missionary Christianity are reminding us that our Anglo-Saxon applications don't always fit in Uganda or Uruguay or Bedford-Stuyvesant. Evangelical cultural anthropologists are exploring this cultural terrain and questioning the ease with which we used to talk. Now, we speak not of application but of inculturation, not of relevance but of indigenization and/or contextualization.

Are John Taylor's remarks about Africa true of Asia and North America and the Latin world as well?

---

2 Robert J. Schreiter, *Constructing Local Theologies* (Maryknoll, NY: Orbis, 1985), 1.

3 Harvie M. Conn, "Normativity, Relevance, and Relativism," in Harvie M. Conn, ed., *Inerrancy and Hermeneutic* (Grand Rapids, MI: Baker, 1988), 189-94.

> Christ has been presented as the answer to the questions a white man would ask, the solution to the needs that Western man would feel, the Saviour of the world of the European world-view, the object of the adoration and prayer of historic Christendom. But if Christ were to appear as the answer to the questions that the Africans are asking, what would he look like? If he came into the world of African cosmology to redeem Man as Africans understand him, would he be recognizable to the rest of the Church Universal?[4]

In Japan, for example, the same problem can be illustrated another way. The word *tsumi* is used to translate the Christian worldview built into the word *sin*. But in a shame-oriented culture like Japan, *tsumi* comes closer to the English word *imprudent*. To the non-Christian Japanese it does not convey the idea of moral right or wrong or of sinning against God or even against duty. "The fearful thing about *tsumi* is rather the inherent potential of being discovered in the act and therefore shamed for being imprudent."[5] To the Christian, *tsumi* speaks of rebellion against God, lawlessness. To the non-Christian, *tsumi* points to the fear of being out of harmony with society and nature, of acts disapproved by humanity. How will the Christian cross this "culture gap" and still hold the gospel in his or her hands after passing over?

The average evangelical listening to this kind of example and this kind of question might easily respond, "This is a question of application." And, in a sense, this answer is still a useful one. On the simplest understanding of communication, this kind of response is good enough—if communication is understood simply as the strategic skill needed for gift-wrapping packages of information materials. But there is more to see and more to say than that.

Making the gospel relevant to the Japanese or a disillusioned young Englishman requires more than a "gift of words." It requires a "gift for cultural understanding." You can't fool a cultural Archie Bunker by changing words like "this" to "dis" and "moron" to "meathead." Behind Archie's judgments on Poles and Blacks and Jews and Jesus is a cultural world that informs him, a cultural agenda that must be seen, "dark glasses" worn by Archie that tell him what God and his next door neighbor are supposed to look like.

---

4 John V. Taylor, *The Primal Vision* (London: SCM Press, 1963), 16.

5 David Hesselgrave, *Communicating Christ Cross-Culturally* (Grand Rapids, MI: Zondervan, 1978), 268.

Biblically oriented theologizing is the work of a gospel optician who must assist the reluctant patient in trying on a new set of glasses. Words like *tsumi* are more than crossword-puzzle answers for the right number of squares in a verbal game. They are suitcases in which the user packs all his or her cultural luggage. They are glimpses through a window into someone else's cultural house. They are furniture arrangements that make the owner feel "comfortable" and "at home." They are cultural fences around a piece of property that say, "This belongs to me."

For theology to become theology, it must, at some time or other, rummage through those suitcases and be a Peeping Tom, looking through those windows. Reflecting biblically on what we find, on what we see, is called theology. It is what Bengt Sundkler called "an ever-renewed re-interpretation to the new generations and peoples of the given Gospel, a representation of the will and the way of the one Christ in a dialogue with new thought-forms and culture patterns."[6]

Theology, by this definition, is not a gentleman's hobby. Nor is it ever exclusively a Western, white gentleman's hobby. It is not simply the mental exercise of persons sitting on the high front balcony of a Spanish house watching travelers go by on the road beneath them.

> The 'balconeers' can overhear the travellers' talk and chat with them; they may comment critically on the way that the travelers walk; or they may discuss questions about the road, how it can exist at all or lead any-where, what might be seen from different points along it, and so forth; but they are onlookers and their problems are theoretical only.[7]

A biblically oriented theology is done by the travelers whose questions come from their involvement in the trip. They are questions that call not only for com-prehension but for decision and action. They ask not only, Why is this so? but also, Which way to go?

Theology is always theology-on-the-road. And, in this sense, it is not simply a question of relevance or of application. It is not a twofold question of, first, theological interpretation, and then, practical application. Interpretation and application are not two questions but one. As John Frame says, "We do not know what Scripture says until we know how it relates to our world."[8] Theology must always ask what

---

6 Bengt Sundkler, *The Christian Ministry in Africa* (Uppsala: Swedish Institute of Missionary Research, 1960), 281.

7 James I. Packer, *Knowing God* (Downers Grove, IL: InterVarsity, 1973), 5.

8 John Frame, *Van Til the Theologian* (Phillipsburg, NJ: Pilgrim, 1976), 25.

Scripture says. But it always asks in terms of the questions and answers our cultures raise. And to ask what Scripture says, or what it means, is always to ask a question about application.

Evangelical theologians in the two-thirds world seem more sensitive to all this than we do in the white, Western world. A 1982 gathering in Bangkok expressed their concern "that our hermeneutic should both be loyal to historic Christianity and arise out of our engagement with our respective situations."[9] The same conference report says with concern, "Churches of the Two Thirds world are in danger of bondage to alien categories. These do not permit them to meet adequately the problems and challenges of proclaiming Christ in our contexts."[10]

Later in the same year (1982) appeared the Seoul Declaration, sponsored by the Asia Theological Association and bringing together Asia's evangelical theologians. Again, in even more explicit language, Western theology, "whether liberal or conservative, conservative or progressive," was criticized for an agenda obsessed with problems of "faith and reason," for abstractionism from life. It was said to have capitulated to the secularistic worldview associated with the Enlightenment. The report charged that "sometimes it has been utilized as a means to justify colonialism, exploitation, and oppression, or it has done little or nothing to change these situations."[11] Orlando Costas comments that "this statement may lack precision. However it does articulate a well-known criticism of Western theologies."[12]

Where can we trace the origins of these alleged problems? And how does the agenda of the two-thirds world differ from ours? These are the questions we seek to answer now.

THE ROOTS AND FRUITS OF THE WESTERN AGENDA

Melba Maggay, a Filipino Christian, suggests where to begin.

---

9 Conference Findings, "Towards a Missiological Christology in the Two Thirds World," in Vinay Samuel and Chris Sugden, eds., *Sharing Jesus in the Two-Thirds World* (Grand Rapids, MI: Wm. B. Eerdmans Publishing Co., 1983), 277.

10 Ibid.

11 Third World Theological Consultation, "The Seoul Declaration Towards an Evangelical Theology for the Third World," in Bong-rin Ro and Ruth Eshenaur, eds., *The Bible and Theology in Asian Contexts* (Taichung, Taiwan: Asia Theological Association, 1984), 23.

12 Orlando Costas, "Evangelical Theology in the Two Thirds World," *TSF Bulletin* 9, no.1(Sept.-Oct. 1985): 10.

Christians in Asia and Africa are taught to answer questions raised by Greek sophists in the fourth century. While we live in a culture still very much awed by the Power that can be clearly perceived in things that have been made, we start from the supposition that we are talking to post-Christian men long past the age of the mythical and therefore must belabour the existence of a supernatural God. We defend the Scriptures as if we speak to the scientific rationalist, and not to men who have yet to see nature 'demythologised,' stripped of the wondrous and the magical.[13]

History also reminds us that the two-thirds world's struggles with "translating" the gospel into their own cultural setting is not unique. The church did not begin with a prepackaged gospel kit and do its theologizing through a kind of cultural circumcision. Against the challenge of accretions and distortions brought about by tradition and cultural consensus, the message of the gospel was shaped. Even in the early years of the church evangelism was never proclamation in a vacuum and theology was not what was done by someone talking in someone else's sleep. Situations have always shaped our confessions of faith.

The early church was not afraid of letting the culture set its gospel agenda, though it recognized the risks. Origen (c. 185-254) advocated what he called "spoiling the Egyptians," taking from pagan thought and culture all that is good and true, and using it in the interests of Christian thought. He was not the first to make these demands. A new cultural context was forcing new questions on the church. The physical persecution of the church was shifting to more subtle levels of attack. Intellectual assaults were being mounted. Legal charges demanded answering. The church was increasingly isolating itself from any earlier identification as a Jewish sect. What was its relation to the world Jewish community?

A pioneer and innovator in answering these questions was Justin Martyr (c. 100-165). To the urbane Hellenistic world, he heralded Christianity as "the only philosophy which I have found certain and adequate." The gospel and the best elements in Plato and the Stoics were seen as almost identical ways of apprehending the same truth. Between Christianity and Platonism "there is no gulf fixed so great that the passage from the one to the other is impossible or unnatural."[14]

The center of harmonization for Justin lay in his concept of the *Logos*. Using the Johannine vocabulary, Justin saw Jesus as the Logos inherent in all things and

---

13 Melba Maggay, "The Indigenization of Theology," *Patmos* 1, no. 1(1979): 1.

14 Henry Chadwick, *Early Christian Thought and the Classical Tradition* (New York: Oxford University Press, 1966), 11-12.

especially in the rational creation. All who have thought and acted rationally and rightly have done so because of their participation in Christ and universal Logos (*Apologia* 2.10.13). So both Abraham and Socrates were "Christians before Christ." Each rational being shares in the universal Logos. We possess a piece of this Logos, like a seed sown by the Divine Sower. Each philosopher speaks truth according to one's share of this seed, and according to one's ability to perceive its implications.

Without being critical at this stage in the argument, at least we must recognize now Justin's effort to communicate Christ according to the agenda of his hearers. His ultimate intention was not to carry out a kind of philosophical penetration of the Christian message and blend Plato with Jesus. It was to remove the impression that Christianity was just another religion. In view of its universality, it was able to embrace them all. His goal was evangelistic, that of presenting Christianity as the fulfillment of a longing and desire in paganism.

Others followed Justin, speaking also to a context that drove them to underline some of Justin's earlier emphases. The so-called Alexandrian school of this third century faced new antagonists who sought to push the church further into their Greek corner. Fifteen or twenty years after Justin, the Platonist Celsus wrote a blistering attack on Christianity. Celsus' arguments were an exact reversal of Justin's. He may in fact have been answering them directly.[15] The Greeks, he contended, did not borrow from the Hebrews. It was, in fact, the reverse. Jesus had read Plato and Paul had studied Heraclitus. Christianity is a corruption from the primordial truths enshrined in the ancient polytheistic tradition. How does one explain so many Christian deviations then? Replies Celsus, "The majority of Christians are stupid!" The dull-wittedness of the majority of Christians is no accidental fault to him and certainly not a virtue. It is symptomatic of the inherently irrational and anti-intellectual character of Christianity. Adding to this assault was the growing strength of Gnosticism, "a stepping stone from Plato to Plotinus." Obsessed with evil, it consisted essentially in a radical rejection of this world as being at best a disastrous accident and at the least a malevolent plot.[16]

Against this context, men like Origen and Clement of Alexandria (c. 150-215) shaped their presentation of the gospel. Philosophy for the Hellenistic world was *paideia*, the education of rational man. Greek culture was the pedagogue that prepared us for a new world culture. Clement, using Galatians 3:23 and its reference

---

15 Ibid., 132-33.

16 Henry Chadwick, "Philo and the Beginnings of Christian Thought," in A.H. Armstrong, ed., *The Cambridge History of Later Greek and Early Medieval Philosophy* (New York: Cambridge University Press, 1967), 166.

to the law as "the pedagogue," presents Christianity as fulfilling "this paideutic mission of mankind to a higher degree than has been achieved before."[17] Before the coming of Christ, he proposed, philosophy was necessary for the Greeks to obtain righteousness. Philosophy was their schoolmaster to bring them to Christ, just as the law was the schoolmaster for the Hebrews. In the philosophies of the ancient Greeks, the Logos revealed himself, though dimly and vaguely. In those philosophies, he prepared that world for the gospel which would be preached to it.

For Clement, there is only one true philosophy, "the philosophy according to the Hebrews." And since the Greeks have drawn from it, so we do also. This "true philosophy" has two streams, Holy Scripture and Greek philosophy. They are like two rivers, at whose confluence Christianity springs forth (*Miscellanies* 6.8).

It was Clement's successor, Origen, who systematized even further this effort at communicating. And like his predecessors, his purposes were evangelistic. Eusebius, the church historian, notes that "a great many heretics and not a few of the most distinguished philosophers, studied under him diligently... he became celebrated as a great philosopher even among the Greeks themselves." Origen asserts that he does not intend to deviate by a hairsbreadth from the teaching of the church. "We confess that we do want to educate all men with the Word of God, even if Celsus does not wish to believe it" (Contra Celsum 3.4).

How will we judge these early "borrowings from the Egyptians"? J.K.S. Reid, for example, sees Clement as roaming "round the rich intellectual world of his day with a far greater sense of mastery than Christian theologians had hitherto shown, fearlessly rebutting such elements as incongruous with the Christian faith, and just as eagerly putting others to apologetic use."[18] Henry Chadwick sees Clement seeking "to make the Church safe for philosophy and the acceptance of classical literature."[19] Before we dismiss Origen's work as "biblical alchemy," we need to remember that nothing for Origen was true simply because Plato said it. In *Contra_Celsum* and elsewhere he is occasionally prickly to the point of rudeness towards the classical tradition. For all these men, natural religion and natural ethics are not enough. There is salvation only in Christ and good works done before justification are useless. The soul of man is so weakened and distracted that it cannot be redeemed apart from the power and grace of God in Christ (*Contra Celsum* 4.19). Behind all of these formulations is the heart of the evangelist seeking to share Christ with his cultural world.

---

17 Werner Jaeger, *Early Christianity and Greek Paideia* (London: Oxford University Press, 1961), 60.
18 J.K.S. Reid, *Christian Apologetics* (Grand Rapids, MI: Wm. B. Eerdmans Publishing Co., 1969), 53.
19 Chadwick, "Philo," 180-81.

In short, the intentions of these men could not have been better. In the language of Michael Green, they sought

> to embody biblical doctrine in cultural forms which would be acceptable in their society. Not to remove the scandal of the gospel, but so present their message in terms acceptable to their hearers, that the real scandal of the gospel could be perceived and its challenge faced.... If Christ is for all men, then evangelists must run the risk of being misunderstood, of misunderstanding elements in the gospel themselves, of losing out on the transposition of parts of the message so long as they bear witness to him. Christians are called to live dangerously.[20]

Many of their mistakes, and many of ours, we can find understandable. What were they to say to pagan writers who charged that Christians promoted impiety to the gods, that they engaged in immoral practices, that their rejection of emperor worship was treasonable to the state? They answered by focusing on Christian ethics.

What gospel encouragement could they offer to a world fearfully aware of demonic activity and power? Celsus saw such demons as inferior subordinates of the great god. The Christians like Justin answered by focusing on Jesus' redemption as one that destroys the demons. "The power of exorcism lies in the name of Jesus," testified Origen (*Contra Celsum* 1.6). What answers could they give their critics who charged them with making blind assertions and giving no proof? They turned to an exposition of Christianity as "the true philosophy."[21]

At the same time, there were wrong turns taken and lessons to be learned of a negative sort also for us and for the two-thirds world. I suggest that at least one part of their mistake may have been made in perceiving their context. They shifted the attention of the church to a new target or receptor audience. About the middle of the second century, a large body of literature was aiming at the pagan majority of the population masses. But as the decades wore on, Christian writers spoke less and less to the illiterate masses. The Alexandrian School addressed people who read for the purpose of obtaining better information. They speak to the educated few, including the rulers of the Roman Empire. They address them individually as men of higher culture (*paideia*), who will approach such a problem in a philosophical spirit.[22] Thus

---

20 Jaeger, *Early Christianity*, 27.

21 Michael Green, *Evangelism in the Early Church* (Grand Rapids, MI: Wm. B. Eerdmans Publishing Co., 1970), 142.

22 Adolf von Harnack, *History of Dogma*, vol. 2-3 (New York: Dover, 1961), 209-24.

the presentation of the gospel was drawn deeper into the pull of a rationalistic orbit. Holistic balance was distorted by the magnetic attraction of a philosophical outlook that cuts up reality into an intricate series of related philosophical problems.

A second related problem was their failure to deal with their own preunderstandings in evaluating the gospel agenda. Their predispositions, the presuppositions they brought to the theological task of hermeneutic, were themselves captive to the same charms of rational speculation. Clement of Alexandria came to Christianity by way of philosophy. Could one expect such a man to see easily the Christian as anyone other than the "true Gnostic"? Origen was a professional philosopher. Like a dentist who looks at faces and sees mouths, he looked at Christianity and saw the *paideia* of humanity, Greek wisdom at the bottom line of divine providence.

And finally a third problem remained. The cultural agenda they chose to address showed sin's cracks and dents but no serious injury. Sin's side effects could be treated in an emergency room on an out-patient basis. There was no need for intensive care units. Culture was good "and not an evil," commented Origen. "In fact, it is a road to virtue. It is no hindrance to the knowledge of God." Rather it favors it (*Contra Celsum* 3.47, 49).

What of an antithesis between darkness and light? What of sin? Sin was the result of ignorance, not an inherited evil nature, argued Justin. With a highly optimistic confidence in human reasoning and free will, he fully expected that if the barriers of ignorance and misinformation were removed, the truth of Christ would shine in its own light. And if not, you could always blame the deceptions of demons. "The devils made me do it." Sin's darkness was no more apparent in the Alexandrian School. Clement was interested in free will, not inherited bondage or corruption of nature. And Origen reduced the fall to the state of preexistence, before the beginning of earthly life. Original sin became preoriginal sin.

Given these perspectives, accommodation became an easier way to deal with the cultural agenda issue than antithesis. But searching in good will for points of contact can become like falling on pitchforks in haystacks. Borrowing too many things from a neighbor, no matter how well intended, left the Western world with a very cluttered theological attic.[23]

Out of this came eventually a new understanding of how theology was formed. Theology saw itself as more and more an abstractionist task, a searching for essences untouched by the realities of the cultural context. The goal of theology became a

---

23 For amplification of this criticism, consult C. Van Til, *A Christian Theory of Knowledge* (Nutley, NJ: Presbyterian and Reformed, 1969), 109-18.

rational display of the Platonic ideal. The Latin Fathers, with their legal training, reinforced this perception. The Cappadocian Fathers, Basil of Caesarea and the two Gregorys, in the second half of the fourth century, carry it on. In the language of Werner Jaeger:

> Even in their high appreciation of Origen, to whom they often refer, they show that they, like him, think of theology as a great science based on supreme scholarship and as a philosophical pursuit of the mind. And this science is part of the entire civilization that is theirs and in which they feel at home.[24]

Out of this, we suggest, comes a confusion of the Bible as norm with theology as a neutral search for the rationally ideal, the "heavenly principles." True theology is seen as *sui generis*, the liberating search of the mind for essence, core, unhindered by any kind of historical, geographical, or social qualifier. Theological pursuits are freed to become the Platonic search for abstract, rational principles.

Anglo-Saxon evangelicals are today properly concerned over current attitudes to biblical authority. Is the history we have just sketched also part of the reason why they become more fearful that any thinking which explores the tentative nature of theology will lead to a downward slide to syncretism? Do they see the rational core "ideal" of theology being threatened? How much of that fear is biblically proper? And how much is controlled by a hidden agenda that assumes theology, wherever it originates, is a rational given ontologized out of reality? Has the evangelical in the two-thirds world seen this history better than we have?

THE AGENDA OF EVANGELICAL TWO-THIRDS WORLD THEOLOGIES

The emerging theologies in the two-thirds world share many things in common with Western models. (1) They are intentionally contextual and occasional, as is all theological effort. One will not always find great theological systems. But these systems have come late to the Anglo-Saxon world as well. The first centuries of church history did not produce a systematician like Calvin or Luther until there had been an Augustine writing on soteriology or an Anselm on the atonement to feed into the larger stream. In fact, there may be those who do not want to build

---

24 Jaeger, *Early Christianity*, 74.

such systems in the church of the two-thirds world. On the part of some, this could very well be a part of the criticism of the Anglo-Saxon world of theology. Some apparently might fear any theological system that appears to be timeless and culturally universal.

(2) There is also a sense that this occasional, local character of theology is crucial if Christianity is to survive in its particular settings. And this too is a feeling shared with Justin and the Alexandrian School. We are aware, for example, that we must Christianize Africa. The African theologian shares that commitment with us. But with it, there is another question. How will we Africanize Christianity? How will we move from Christianity for Africa to Christianity in Africa? If Christianity is to survive in Africa, it must be seen as more than a relic of the colonial period. It must be truly African; it must speak to actual African concerns with an authentically African voice. The authenticity of all theology, argues one evangelical, depends on two factors: its Christian integrity and its cultural integrity.[25]

(3) We share together as well an inability to break ourselves free from our cultural preunderstandings. The same weakened view of sin that encouraged accommodation to our Greek and Latin cultures often inhibits theology in the two-thirds world. Is this not a major flaw, for example, in liberation theology? In its necessary protest against a reduction of sin to the merely private, is liberation theology still encumbered with too shallow a view of sin? Are some of the richest descriptions of sin in the Bible blurred? Is liberation theology willing to see sin as such a state of corruption that the elimination of poverty, oppression, racism, classism, and capitalism cannot alter the human condition of sinfulness in any radical way?[26]

But, after we have admitted the similarities, we are still left with differences that may be pointing to more hopeful learning signs for the future of theology. It is a few of these signs I point to now in closing.

(1) There appears to be a more conscious awareness among two-thirds world theologies of the human, cultural context and contextuality as a key in the process of theologizing. These evangelicals appear to find it easier to admit that all theology has always been situational. It has always been a case of theology in context. At the same time, these evangelicals also distance themselves from those who argue that

---

25 Dick France, "Christianity on the March," *Third Way* 1, no. 21(November 3, 1977): 3-5.
26 For a fuller exposition of these problems, consult Harvie M. Conn, "Theologies of Liberation," in S. Gundry and A. Johnson, eds., *Tensions in Contemporary Theology* (Grand Rapids, MI: Baker, 1986), 404-18.

context takes precedence over text. Old doubts concerning the authority of the Bible can emerge again, they warn, under the cloak of an enculturated hermeneutics.[27]

But even admitting this, there is still a lesson for us to learn whether it be from Korean Minjung theology or American Black theologies of a liberal orientation. Theology cannot be done in an ontological vacuum. Theology speaks out of the historical context; and theology must speak to that context.

(2) There also appears to be in two-thirds world theologies a deeper appreciation of the social and cultural dimensions of the historical context than one finds elsewhere. These theologies have not made the mistake of the Alexandrian School and focused on the purely ontological and epistemological. Their setting does not seem to have allowed them that luxury. They have done their theologizing in a world of vast poverty, a world of oppressor and oppressed, a world of dependence and marginalization.

Where was theology to turn to respond to these issues? The agenda of inherited Anglo-Saxon theology did not speak to these issues. If theology was to speak to two-thirds world needs, it would need a new agenda. It would have to search for new answers. What does the Bible say about poverty and oppression? About nation-building and torture, racism and, dare I say it, sexism? The indexes of Anglo-Saxon theological texts yield little fruit for these kinds of questions.

(3) There also appears to be in two-thirds world theologies a deeper interfacing with non-Christian religions. The churches of Asia especially have found it necessary to make the growth of the great traditions of Islam, Hinduism, and Buddhism a central emphasis in their theological development. Again, there seems to be little help in meeting this challenge from contemporary Anglo-Saxon theologies. Our world has left behind the interest in pagan religions shown by Justin and the Alexandrian School. We live in a post-Enlightenment world where we must spend our energies on Anglo-Saxon secularization and antisupernaturalism. There are some who fear an escalating self-preoccupation even of evangelical theology with its own welfare.

In the Buddhist context of Sri Lanka and Thailand, by contrast, theology finds itself oriented to questions of the nature of suffering, of impermanence and the non-self, of enlightenment. In Africa the dialogue is with Africa's traditional religions. What is the connection, if any, between Christian theology and African religions?

---

27 Asian Evangelical Theologians, "The Bible and Theology in Asia Today: Declaration of the Sixth Asia Theological Association Theological Consultation," in Ro and Eshenaur, *Bible and Theology*, 9-12, and Third World Theological Consultation, "The Seoul Declaration," 23-24.

Can Africa's religions become bridges, points of contact, for the development of a distinctly African sound to Christianity?

Anglo-Saxon theology will have much to learn from these studies. As our countries become increasingly pluralistic in religions, we will have to ask the same questions. We are already doing it with Judaism. Now our study of Hinduism, Islam, and Buddhism must begin.

(4) Finally, there is a new recovery in two-thirds world evangelical theologies of the missiological nature of theology. That missiological dimension was present in the classical theologians we paid attention to at the beginning of this paper. But the results of their encounter led theology further away from that dimension. By contrast, this missiological dimension is being recovered in the two-thirds world theologies. In some settings, such as Asia or most of Africa, theology is forced to do its work without the benefit of the *corpus christianum*. In this setting theologizing has a more "missiological" sound to it. It is done with more consciousness that the non-Christian world is eavesdropping.

In settings like Latin America and among blacks in South Africa and North America, the church also sees itself as a marginalized minority. But in this instance their world is the world of institutionalized Christendom. But, either because of oppression or racism, they are forced to do their reflective work "from the under-side." In these contexts, they carry on their efforts in spite of the *corpus christianum* or directly to it. In both of these contexts, theology then sees itself as a witness of a prophetic sort. The theological tone is more "missiological." Theologians sound more like evangelists.

THE REAFFIRMATION OF "SITUATIONAL" THEOLOGIZING

The lessons from the early church and from the two-thirds world converge. Contextualization is not a new discovery; it has always been a characteristic of theology as such. Paul's "task theology" is a biblical pattern for our own theologizing. Adrio König puts it this way:

> All theology, all reflection about the Bible should be done contextually, i.e., taking into consideration the context or situation of the theologian and the church. Everyone who thinks systematically about the meaning and implications of the biblical message should deliberately take up his

own situation in his thinking. Theology is practiced in and from within a specific situation, but also in terms of and with a view to a specific situation.[28]

This is just saying that theology must be biblical but it need not be borrowed. Even evangelical theology will have a different look when it is shaped in a context where Confucius, not Kant is king.

So a different twist to theology seems to be developing in the two-thirds world. It is addressing questions not usually dealt with by evangelical mainstream theologians in the northern hemisphere—ancestor practices in East Asia and Africa, Buddhist worldviews oriented to suffering, Muslim misunderstandings of Jesus, political and economic issues. "It offers critical evaluations of western theology and affirms at the same time its shared commitment to the authority and integrity of the Bible. It fears bondage to alien categories and confesses its loyalty to historic Christianity. It does not ask for approval but for affirmation."[29] One will hear sounds from the evangelical of the two-thirds world that may appear strange at first to Anglo-Saxon ears tuned to a Reformation creedal history through which the two-thirds world has not passed. Why will it sound different?

After a lengthy study of the 1982 Bangkok and Seoul statements referred to earlier, Orlando Costas answers our question this way:

> Evangelical theologians in these parts of the world are appropriating the best of their spiritual tradition and are putting it to use in a constructive critical dialogue with their interlocutors in and outside of their historical space. For them the evangelical tradition is not locked into the socio-cultural experience of the West. They insist that they have the right to articulate theologically the evangelical tradition in their own terms and in light of their own issues.[30]

Is not that our common calling in every age and in every cultural setting? And from it will there not come ultimately perhaps the richest contribution of all to the task of theology—the reminder to us all of what theology truly rooted in biblical revelation and addressing our real contexts can offer us? The ultimate test of any

---

28 Adrio König, "Contextual Theology," *Theologia Evangelica* 14, no. 3(Dec. 1981): 37.
29 Harvie M. Conn, "Looking to the Future: Evangelical Missions from North America in the Years Ahead," *Urban Mission* 5, no. 3(Jan. 1988): 28.
30 Costas, "Evangelical Theology," 10.

theological discourse, after all, is not only erudite precision but also transformative power. "It is a question of whether or not theology can articulate the faith in a way that is not only intellectually sound but spiritually energizing, and therefore, capable of leading the people of God to be transformed in their way of life and to commit themselves to God's mission in the world."[31]

---

31 Ibid., 12.

.3.

Globalization, Africa,
the Church and Its Mission:
An Introduction

I.W. (NAAS) FERREIRA

INTRODUCTION

While globalization is the driving force that is busy changing the world we live in, globalism is the dominant ideology of our time.[1] Not only is it likely to continue changing the global economic environment we live in, but it is also going to decisively impact our personal lives, the lives of our young and also the lives of the church in ways that are seldom discussed in Christian forums.[2] Globalization was once believed to be the phenomenon that was supposed to save the world system and provide a framework for global equality and integration, but today this noble vision of a more egalitarian and less violent global order is challenged. It is even suggested that globalization in some instances breeds violence and conflict.[3] As to the influence of globalization on the continent of Africa, it can at this stage be concluded that the continent of Africa has minimal influence on this process, but suffers maximum

---

1 Manfred B. Steger, *Globalization: A Very Short Introduction* (New York: Oxford University Press, 2003), 113.

2 Tom W. Sine, Jr., "Globalization, Creation of Global Culture of Consumption and the Impact on the Church and its Mission," *Evangelical Review of Theology (ERT)* 27, no. 4(2003): 353.

3 Yash Tandon, "The Violence of Globalisation: Justice, Peace and Creation News," World Council Churches, *Echoes* 17(2000) http://www.wcc-coe.org/wcc/what/jpc/echoes/echoes-18-08.html, accessed 7/28/08.

consequences because of it.[4] When considering the implications of globalization for this continent, the following African proverb communicates Africa's wish, "No one likes to eat crumbs from a feast; everyone likes to sit at the table."

Meanwhile, is it "business as usual"[5] for the Christian church in such a changing environment? Has the Christian church (both in the Western world and in Africa) made a concerted effort to anticipate the impact of globalization on the church and its mission in this changing world?[6] And what about Africa? Is anyone paying attention to what Africa is saying about globalization? It is very interesting to note that a lot has already been said, but is anybody paying attention? The time is now. Since the center of Christianity is rapidly moving towards the south, the Western church, in cooperation with the church in Africa, should actively strive to anticipate the cumulative adverse effects of globalization on Africa. Only when the Christian church knows what is happening, by studying the effects of what is changing, can it really be relevant in its response towards what needs to be done. Within a global kingdom perpective the Christian church should anticipate God's movement in these times, and start moving with him.

This essay can only serve as a humble introduction to the subject at hand in order to stimulate urgent thought and discussion within the Christian church, both Western and African. May the Lord bless this essay and use it to the advancement of his kingdom.

WHAT IS GLOBALIZATION?

In the most basic terms, the globalization of the world is the integration of economies throughout the world through trade, financial flows, the exchange of technology and information, and the movement of people.[7] It is a multidimensional set of social processes that create, multiply, stretch and intensify worldwide social interdependencies and exchanges while at the same time fostering in people a growing awareness of deepening connections between the local and the distant.[8]

---

4 Peter J. Henriot, "Globalization: Implications for Africa," http://www.sedos.org/english/global.html, accessed 7/28/08.

5 Samuel Escobar, *The New Global Mission: The Gospel from Everywhere to Everyone* (Downers Grove, IL: InterVarsity Press, 2003), 90.

6 Sine, "Globalization," 353.

7 Address by Alassane D. Ouattara, Deputy Managing Director of the International Monetary Fund, at the Southern Africa Economic Summit sponsored by the World Economic Forum, Harare, May 21, 1997.

8 Steger, *Globalization*, 13.

The word globalization may be new, but the process of globalization has been going on for centuries. It is as old as humanity itself. The expansion of religion, the rise of empires, the triumph of technology and the internationalization of the world's economy have been the engines of globalization in history.[9] Although economics is at the heart of globalization and will be the organizing principle in the future,[10] globalization constitutes a set of processes that also have an effect on the political, cultural, technological and ecological dimensions of social life.

In the political dimension a transitional phase between the modern nation-state system and post-modern forms of global governance[11] is experienced. Globalization encourages decreasing national, but increasing outside control over the internal economy of a country. The World Trade organization (WTO), primarily an instrument of Northern governments and countries, is emerging as a very powerful actor in the globalization process.[12] The world is not only becoming a borderless community, but a totally new world order is being formed. In this sense it should be noted that globalization is not merely an objective process, but it also has a very distinctive ideological dimension. The basis for globalization is the neo-liberal ideology, an "economic fundamentalism" that puts an absolute value on the operation of the market and subordinates people's lives, the function of society, the policies of government and the role of the state to this unrestricted free market.[13] Globalization is therefore sustained and reconfirmed by powerful political institutions and economic corporations.[14] It was created by the dominant social forces in the world today to serve their specific interests and is not only capitalistic and imperialistic in character, but profit driven to the extreme.[15]

The cultural dimension of globalization is very strong and is clearly seen in an increasingly homogenized popular culture underwritten by a Western culture industry based in New York, Hollywood, London and Milan. It is a form of cultural imperialism and is sometimes called the Americanization or McDonaldization of

---

9 Ali A. Mazrui, "Pan Africanism and the Globalization of Africa: A Triple Process," revised version of the Second DuBois-Padmore-Nkrumah Lecture given in Kumasi under the chairmanship of Professor Ayim, Vice-Chancellor of the Kwame Nkrumah University of Science and Technology, Kumasi, on August 6, 2001. Copyright 2006 Institute of Global Cultural Studies.

10 Escobar, *The New Global Mission,* 56.

11 Steger, *Globalization*, 64.

12 Peter J. Henriot, "Globalization: Implications for Africa."

13 Ibid.

14 Steger, *Globalization*, 113.

15 Ruth Valerio, "Chainsaws, Planes and Komodo Dragons: Globalisation and the Environment," in Richard Tiplady, ed., *One World or Many? The Impact of Globalisation on Mission* (Pasadena, CA: William Carey Library, 2003), 15.

the world. The American political theorist Benjamin Barber calls it the formation of a new world called McWorld.[16]

Within the technological dimension a growing number of new forms of technology are flooding the world. Personal computers, fiber electronics, satellites, cellular phones, fax machines, e-mail and the internet are rapidly changing the world as we know it.

The ecological dimension of globalization is closely associated with rapid worldwide environmental degradation. Climate change, deforestation, the loss of biodiversity and shortages of clean drinking water is symptomatic of the effects of the process of globalization on the ecology of the world.

GLOBALIZATION IN AFRICA

When considering the influence of globalization on Africa, it actually represents the fourth stage of outside penetration of Africa by forces which have negative social consequences for the African people's integral development.[17] The first stage was the destructive period of slavery. From outside of Africa the people and the continent were exploited to the extent that the consequences are still felt today. The second stage was the time of colonialism which also left its permanent marks and scars on this continent of Africa. The third stage is called neo-colonialism. Although the independence struggles of Africa have brought local government rule to the many nations of the continent, it did not break the ties, subtle and not so subtle, that bound Africa's future to outside influences. Through such dynamics as trade patterns, investment policies, and debt arrangements, conditions were enforced that were not beneficial to Africans. After three periods of negative outside involvement in Africa, the fourth stage, the period of globalization, has arrived.

I don't think anyone will doubt the fact that Africa needs the benefits that the process of globalization can provide, but the question remains, can (should) Africa pay the price? As much as globalization is inevitable for Africa, its consequences for Africa are devastating. Maybe that is why some African commentators are saying, "We would rather be a king in the jungle, than a deprived and malnourished messenger somewhere in a city." Globalization is yet another process from the outside enforced on Africa.

---

16 Steger, *Globalization*, 73.
17 Peter J. Henriot, "Globalization: Implications for Africa."

The benefits of globalization[18] can be grouped into three main categories: communication and technology, the interlinking and opening up of the world, and products and services. Is this also true in regard to the African continent? Even if it can be concluded that Africa needs and can benefit greatly from globalization, there still is a lot of concern for Africa. Norbert Mao[19] uses an analogy to describe the way that Africa experiences globalization at this stage. He says that a donkey and an elephant cannot be yoked together to pull a plow, for they are not of the same size or strength. Yet this is what globalization has done to Africa. Due to differences in weight and size, the weaker side is struggling to keep apace while the stronger one reaps the benefits disproportionately. In this way globalization is an uneven process and is associated with inequality.

People living in various parts of the world are affected very differently by this gigantic transformation of social structures and cultural zones.[20] Large segments of the world population, particularly in the global South, do not enjoy equal access to thickening global networks and infrastructures. Today it is fashionable to speak of the global village, yet the Human Development Report 1999, published by the UN Development Programme (UNDP), indicates that not everyone is a full member of this village. The benefits of globalization have largely gone to the wealthiest nations. Only the rich can cross borders freely, and advanced information technology is scarcely available in parts of the developing world. This is especially true for Africa. Of the 174 nations the UNDP report ranks according to its "human development index," the 22 lowest are African.[21] It is said in Africa that capital is a cowardly bird. It flies to safer places where it expects to earn better returns. It is indeed sad that while 300 million people in privileged communities guzzle Coke, 700 million struggle to find clean drinking water every day.[22]

Poverty does not simply exist but is created by the manner in which a region is integrated into the global economy. It is more by design than by accident that poverty has become a major institution in Africa despite this continent's stupendous resources. There is an unequal exchange between what the region contributes to

18 Fiona Wilson, "Globalisation from a Grassroots, Two-Thirds World Perspective: A Snapshot" in Richard Tiplady, ed., *One World or Many? The Impact of Globalisation on Mission* (Pasadena, CA: William Carey Library, 2003), 180.

19 Norbert Mao, "Has globalization dealt Africa a bad hand?" Yale Center for the Study of Globalization, YaleGlobal Online, 3 November 2003.

20 Steger, *Globalization*, 13.

21 United Nations Development Fund, "Human Development Index," *Human Development Report 1999* (New York: United Nations Development Fund, 1999), 133-167.

22 Escobar, *The New Global Mission*, 63.

the global economy and what it gets in return. Tandon[23] speaks of the violence of globalization because it is nothing but a new order of marginalization of the African continent. He says it is legitimated by the ideology of the free market. Behind the myth of the free market are big monopolies and oligopolies that control the markets—from diamonds to beef to Microsoft software. The violence of globalization is rooted in the region's continued impoverishment by the system.

Wilson[24] also speaks about the negative aspects of globalization for Africa. She did a survey and reported the results. The words that are used to describe the people's feelings are quite enlightening. On a global level the power of the giants made the people on the ground feel *strangled* by the economic plan, their businesses were being *sunk* by multinationals, entrepreneurs were *driven* from the markets, local markets were *invaded* by small arms, and local industrial initiatives were *killed.* In the agricultural sector there were reports of agriculture being *abandoned*, farmers being *impoverished* due to the drop in agricultural commodity prices, and the environment being *degraded.* On a national and cultural level globalization has brought about a loss of cultural identity with a decline in moral standards, the rise in crime and the growth of individualism. This decline in moral values has spread into the family and the church where all relationships were starting to break down. Africa and the different communities were not able to cope with the seemingly forceful entry of globalization into their everyday life. While experiencing this, the following question should be asked, is the fourth stage of outside involvement in Africa doing the same as the previous three?

African commentators are adamant that the asymmetry of power and interests of the member states of the global village, as well as the lopsidedness in the rules of the game there-in, cannot benefit Africa and her people. The reason? They are convinced that globalization is a new order of marginalization and recolonization of the African continent in a "neo-neo-colonial fashion."[25] It appears that the positive benefits of globalization are only for the economically advanced countries of the global North.

---

23 Tandon, "The Violence of Globalisation."
24 Fiona Wilson, "Globalisation from a Grassroots, Two-Thirds World Perspective," 181-2.
25 S.T. Akindele, T.O. Gidado, and O.R. Olaopo, "Globalization: Its Implications and Consequences for Africa," *Globalization Archives* 2, no. 1(Winter 2002), http://globalization.icaap.org/content/v2.1/01_akindele_etal.html, accessed 7/25/08.

THE CHURCH AND ITS MISSION IN A GLOBALIZING WORLD

We are currently living through one of the transforming moments in the history of religion worldwide.[26] Over the past century the center of gravity in the Christian world has shifted to Africa, Asia and Latin America. There are now many more Christians in Africa, Asia and Latin America than in Europe and North America. This is the beginning of the so called "Third Church,"[27] and is a sign of the new age of Christianity.[28] In the future Christianity will be defined in terms of what is happening outside of the Western church within this new formation called the Third Church. It will thus be crucial to understand the context wherein the new center of Christianity will have to operate. Apart from everything that was already identified as the negative effects of globalization on Africa, the following important issues will have to be faced.

The Global Culture of Consumption

The reasons for the numerical decline and changing patterns of involvement in the Western church include changing demographics, but Sine[29] is convinced that one of the major causes, which is seldom discussed in the church, is the growing influence of the values of modern western culture and economic globalism on Christians everywhere. The church is facing a new world, with new values, the world of one economic order. The architects of this new *McWorld* are eager to have the entire world's people become part of a global labor pool and eager consumers in the global macro-mall.[30] This is about more than global consumerism. There is compelling evidence that the marketers of *McWorld* aren't just selling products. They are consciously at work seeking to persuade the world's consumers to become part of a homogenized culture of consumption. In the beginning of the modern age Descartes said, "I think, therefore I am." It seems that the contemporary paraphrase at this time of globalization is, "I buy, therefore I am."[31] This very competitive new

---

26 Philip Jenkins, *The Next Christendom: The Coming of Global Christianity* (New York: Oxford University Press, 2002), 1.

27 Escobar, *The New Global Mission,* 15. According to Bühlman, the first 1000 years of Christian history was connected with what happened in the Eastern Church, the next 1000 years focussed on the history of the Western Church. The Third Church will be called the Southern Church.

28 Ibid. Walls speak about this time as the new age of Christianity.

29 Sine, *Globalization,* 358.

30 Ibid., 357.

31 Escobar, *The New Global Mission,* 60.

global economy wants more of our time and more of our lives. These trends mean less time for family, prayer, scripture and church. It is very clear that this culture of globalization creates attitudes and a mental frame that is the opposite of what the gospel teaches about human life under God's design. This new culture of consumption is not only creating a crisis in the western church but will spread to the entire church in the very near future. It could undermine the vitality of the church in the two-thirds world as it is doing in the church in the one-third world. The church should urgently focus on ministering spiritual values that will transform lifestyle priorities in order that people's lives will no longer be defined by their income levels or the aspirations of the global consumer mall but by the values of God's kingdom.[32]

Poverty and HIV (AIDS)

The gap between rich and poor on both the global and national levels increases with the spread of globalization. The 1992 Human Development Report of the United Nations Development Fund documented that the richest 20% of the world's population receives 82.7% of global income, while the poorest 20% receives only 1.4%.[33] This gap is continuing to grow, having doubled over the past thirty years. Of the 45 countries listed in the "low human development" category in the 1997 Report, 33 are in sub-Saharan Africa.[34] More statistics of a rapidly worsening situation are available, but is anybody interested in them? Is somebody doing something about them? The church and mission leaders have been largely naïve about the effects of globalization and the emerging cultures.[35] When the critical issue of the HIV-AIDS pandemic in sub-Saharan Africa is included in the scenario, the picture of Africa's future is indeed looking very bleak. Who is going to help? The new global economy is an asset-based economy that works much better for those with assets than for those without.[36] In the very competitive global race to the top, a number of Western countries are trying to find ways to reduce the drag on their national economies by cutting back spending on foreign aid abroad and social programs at home. This means that the church and private sector will increasingly be asked to address the growing physical needs of those left behind in this new global economic order. In

---

32 Sine, 367.

33 United Nations Development Fund, *1992 Human Development Report* (New York: United Nations Development Fund, 1992).

34 Peter J. Henriot, "Globalization: Implications for Africa."

35 Sam George, "TerrorCulture: Worth Living for or Worth Dying For" in Richard Tiplady, ed., *One World or Many? The Impact of Globalisation on Mission* (Pasadena, CA: William Carey Library, 2003), 50.

36 Sine, *Globalization*, 367.

many places in the twenty-first century Christian compassion will be the only hope of survival for victims of the global economic process.[37]

SUMMARY

Globalization and Africa

The following quotation that focuses on the negative aspects of globalization is very important.

> Even as its proponents speak of increased prosperity and investment confidence, the process of globalisation breeds violence and conflict when it continues to produce inequality, poverty, environmental destruction and unprecedented concentration of economic power for a few while the majority are marginalised and excluded. Africa is a victim of this sad phenomenon of globalisation. The cumulative adverse effects of globalisation on Africa require careful and deep analysis which go beyond the contemporary ideology of the free market and the "blame the victim" syndrome.[38]

The wholesale acceptance of globalization as a savior of the developing countries, particularly those in Africa, has been likened to that of a moving train with which Africa and Africans must keep pace, regardless of whether the latter has a similar destination in mind. It is said that Africa has no choice but to run along even if it can not keep up with the pace. If it has no choice, it surely has something to say about it. Careful attention should be paid to what is being said in Africa about what is happening in Africa. To really understand what globalization is all about we should not merely focus on what is intended and expected to happen, but we should also carefully listen to what is experienced. The Western optimism about what globalization is going to achieve is not shared within a continent that has again (for the fourth time) been "invaded and scarred" by outside forces.

The New Age of Christianity

While the center of gravity of the Christian church is shifting to the southern hemisphere, the Christian church is also moving into a post-Christendom period.

---

37 Escobar, *The New Global Mission*, 66.
38 Tandon, "The Violence of Globalisation."

In this period the church is moving from the center of society to the margins. The traditional (inherited)[39] Western church must face the fact that Christianity in the future will be defined by what is happening and being experienced in the Third church.[40] A church that lives comfortably in the post-Christian West is unable to respond to the pain and spiritual need of postmodern generations.[41] It will be challenged by the poverty and injustices of a new economic world order. It will be called to demonstrate social responsibility and Christian compassion. The inherited Western church also faces the enormous challenges that are brought about by the paradigm shift of the post-Christendom period. This is a daunting task if the inherited church still wants to have a future in the post-Christendom period. Acknowledging the fact that it is now moving to the margins of society is a matter of honesty, not defeatism.[42] The global Christian church is called to face the challenges of a modern world in order to be faithful and obedient to the Lord our God.

The Mission of the Church

According to Galadima, globalization gives tremendous opportunities for advancing the cause of the gospel.[43] In the regions where Christianity is growing (Africa, Asia and Latin America), Christianity has the unique opportunity to participate in reconstituting church and society. Believers in these regions should be empowered to develop a new spirituality that is not Western, but biblical. This new and emerging post-Christendom Christianity should reshape the Christian church for a changed and changing context and should also recover authentic ways of being church that were damaged, distorted or compromised during the Christendom era.[44] Eventually these non-Western churches will be able to send a new and fresh message of Christianity to the church in the Western world. This honest engagement response[45] wants to engage globalization's challenges in the light of the eternal truths of the Christian message. It must be accepted that the church after Christendom,

---

39 Inherited church is a term used by Stuart Murray to describe the traditional Western church of the Christendom period. The new church that is "evolving" in the post-Christendom period is called the emerging church.

40 See note 27.

41 Escobar, *The New Global Mission,* 69.

42 Stuart Murray, *Church after Christendom* (Waynesboro, GA: Paternoster Press, 2004), 48.

43 Bulus Galadima, "Religion and the Future of Christianity" in Richard Tiplady, ed., *One World or Many? The Impact of Globalisation on Mission* (Pasadena, CA: William Carey Library, 2003), 200.

44 Murray, *Church after Christendom*, 125.

45 Galadima, "Religion and the Future of Christianity," 210. This honest engagement response to globalization's challenges is contrasted with the rejection response (fundamentalist) and the acceptance response (liberal type of response).

living in a globalized world, will be marginal, in exilic mode, journeying towards a different way of being God's people in a strange new world.[46] In this way the new Southern church will be an authentic witness and a biblical example to the post-Christendom Western church.

Africans can well ask, "Please explain it to me (for the fourth time): How can I benefit if I am carrying the load?"

---

46 Murray, *Church after Christendom*, 131.

.4.

Post-Christianity and Renewal in London

MICHAEL EASTMAN

EXCITING TIMES

London is in ferment. People and faiths from around the world co-exist in areas such as east London. Along with this mix is the overarching changes caused by this area's transition into a post-industrial district and connections with other global cities. New entrants have changed the face of this district so that over half the population is black. We find immigrants, refugees and asylum seekers from the Caribbean, Asia, and Africa all bringing with them their own culture, beliefs and life-styles. Describing his own backyard Colin Marchant, who has lived and ministered in London, puts it like this,

> Names, languages and people groups tell the story. Names: Ambedkar
> International Mission, The Church (World-wide Inc.), French African
> Church. Languages: Filipino, Tamil, Urdu, French, Punjabi, Kiswahili.
> People groups: Afro-Caribbean, Asian, and African break down into
> Jamaican, Barbadian and Trinidadian, Sri Lankan, Filipino and South
> Indian; Kenyan, Congolese and Ugandan. In the Primary Schools of
> Newham Muslims (32%), Hindus (6%), Sikhs (4%) have combined with
> Buddhists and Taoists (4%) to leapfrog the Christians (43%).[1]

---

1 Colin Marchant, "New Signs in the City" in John Vincent, ed., *Faithfulness in the City* (Hawarden: Monad Press, 2003), 209.

Where there used to be cathedrals, now we find mosques, Hindu temples, and Sikh *guruwaras*. These new faiths are challenging the traditional religious education in schools as well as the morality of British life. We find people from these religions are avid missionaries as they bring their faiths into their workplaces, such as local minicab drivers, and openly "evangelize."

Christian theologies are confronted and tested by these new faiths and by the post-modern Western milieu. How will the church answer needs for signs and wonders? How will it compete with the relativism that is rampant in society? It will no longer be able to merely hand down church traditions and assume they will be accepted. Muslims prioritize prayer and classes in the Koran. How will the church compete? Is co-existence a good compromise? No matter how we look at what is going on, we must accept that cultural and religious tensions are with us and will continue to be so.

A "MART OF MANY NATIONS"

It all began with the Romans! Following the sacking of Londinium by Queen Boudicia in 61 CE the city was rebuilt and gradually took over from Colchester as the Capital of Britannia. By 200 CE it was a thriving metropolis of 45,000 populated by those from all over the Roman Empire. London was cosmopolitan from its earliest days. "The wide mouth of the Thames estuary seems to have sucked in people from other countries for as far back as history records."2 By 730 CE the Venerable Bede could write of London as "the mart of many nations resorting to it by land and sea."3

After the Norman Conquest a parish church was built to every three acres giving a place of worship for each 300 of its 40,000 inhabitants. In 1510 CE the population was 50,000 rising to 85,000 in 1565 CE and on to 120,000 by 1580 CE. The seventeenth century began with the population at 155,000 in 1605 CE, a trebling in a hundred years.

By 1750, when the beginnings of the Industrial Revolution started to be felt, the population stood at 650,000, and by the time it was in full swing the 1801 Census put the figure at 958,865. It was 2,363,000 in the 1851 census and 4,536,000 at the 1901 census. Peter Ackroyd notes that "in each of five successive decades of the 19th

---

2 Irene Howat and John Nicholls, *Streets Paved with Gold* (London: Christian Focus Publications, 2003), 219.
3 Felix Barker and Peter Jackson, *London: 2000 Years of a City and Its People* (Oondon: Cassell, 1974), 16.

century the population would increase by 20%."[4] Just prior to the Great War it stood at 7,000,000 in 1911 and prior to World War 2 at 8,600,000. The decline from this peak at the end WWII left 6,908,000 inhabitants in 1945. Today the population is rising again at 7,477,300.

WHERE DID THEY COME FROM?

Like a restless sea, ebbs and flows of people have characterized London. Who were they? Peter Ackroyd tells us that in Tudor England

> The new arrivals came from every area of England, Cornwall to Cumberland (it has been estimated that one sixth of all Englishmen became Londoners in the second half of the sixteenth century) and the number of foreign immigrants rose at an accelerating pace, making the city truly cosmopolitan. So high was the mortality, and so low the birth rate, that without the influx of traders and workers the population would in fact have steadily declined. Yet instead it continued to expand, with brewers and bookbinders from the Low Countries, tailors and embroiderers from France, gun makers and dyers from Italy, weavers from the Netherlands and elsewhere. There was an African or 'Moor' in Cheapside who made steel needles without ever imparting the secret of his craft.[5]

Ackroyd continues,

> London has always been a city of immigrants. It was once known as "the city of nations" and in the mid-eighteenth century Addison remarked that "when I consider this great city, in its several quarters or divisions, I look upon it as an aggregate of various nations, distinguished from each other by their respective customs, manners and interests." The same observation could have been applied in any period over the last 250 years.[6]

John Nicholls tells us that at the end of the 1970s "of London's 6.6 million population, 382,000 were from Europe, 296,000 from Asia, 170,000 from Africa, 168,000

---

4 Peter Ackroyd, *London the Biography*, (London: Vintage, 2001), 519.
5 Ibid., 105.
6 Ibid., 701.

from the Caribbean and 69,000 came from the Mediterranean countries. One in every six of the capital's population was born outside of the United Kingdom."[7] By 2006 one third of London's population was born outside the U.K.[8]

Why did they come? To seek refuge like the Huguenots "who began arriving in Elizabethan times. The extent of their influx varied with their treatment in France. The peak was reached after the Revocation of the Edict of Nantes in 1685, when over a hundred thousand, most of them destitute, made their homes in England."[9] Forty thousand refugees from the French Revolution arrived at the end of the eighteenth century and settled in a newly built inner suburb.[10]

Not all fared well. Ackroyd charts the up and down story of the Jewish migrants from the eleventh century onwards. Bermant tells the changing story of his own people as well as of the Irish. The arrival of Pakistanis and Bangladeshis in the 1960s changed the East End yet again. "The Samuels and the Cohens have given way to the Selims and Kahns ... The Hebrew lettering on the facias have given way to the Bengalis."[11]

THE EMPIRE STRIKES BACK

Others were economic migrants. "At its height the British Empire alone boasted 390 million people through its colonisation of some fifty two nations, all interlocking across the globe."[12] They all looked to London. The Commonwealth still links them. Those from the Caribbean, recruited by the government and Ugandan Asians forced out by Idi Amin turned up with British passports. Upheavals in Zimbabwe are resulting in new arrivals from another Commonwealth country. Free movements of people across the European Union's 25 Nations brings Poles, 500,000 at the latest count, and Portuguese, 300,000 of whom are in the U.K. Many turn up in London. In round numbers there are now 300 mother tongues in this polyglot city. Ten percent of London's population are Muslim who for the first time, in 2006, marked the end of Ramadan with a big rally in Trafalgar Square. Earlier in 2006 the Durga Puja, Bengali Hindus' biggest Hindu festival, was celebrated with a parade culminating in

---

7 Howat and Nicholls, *Streets Paved with Gold*, 219.

8 Per phone call to the Office of National Statistics in reference to the *2001 Population Census*.

9 Chaim Bermant, *London's East End: Point of Arrival* (New York: Macmillan Publishing Co., 1976), 31.

10 Barber and Jackson, *London: 2000 Years*, 246.

11 Ackroyd, *London the Biography*, 249.

12 Laurie Green, *The Impact of the Global: An Urban Theology* (Sheffield: New City Special, 2001), 51.

candles floated on the Thames which accompanied the effigy of the goddess Durga, sculpted in mud from the Ganges, in her journey down the river.

GLOBAL FLOWS

Globalisation has accelerated this flow of people. Heathrow airport is a crossroads for the nations. Tourism brings people in their millions. It's a major overseas currency earner. Globalisation has intensified the phenomenon of neighbours who are strangers. Space is contested for schooling, work and housing. The rising resentments of an older white population is played upon. The British National Party with its Fascist roots and world view make gains in local elections. The terrorist bombings on the underground fuel fear and uncertainty. Trafficking in people and drugs has increased. Wealth has grown alongside poverty. London gets older and younger at the same time. The elderly are trapped in the 19th Century tenement buildings originating in Victorian initiatives to deal with the slums. Housing Estates (called projects in the U.S.) built in the immediate post-war period have become places of alienation. Andrew Davey writes of global cities in terms of networks and flows of which cities are nodes in a new interconnectedness.[13] Driven by capital, "globalism—a new global culture" has emerged in which there are winners and losers. "Cities articulate the global economy, link up information networks, concentrate the world's poor. They become 'command centres.'"[14] This is true of London. The forces making for convergence "also strangely encourage localisation, which may issue in tribalism, nationalism, anti-capitalism ideologies and anti-Western religious fundamentalism all driving for strengthening of local identity against those dominating Western values."[15] All this is apparent in London.

CHRISTENDOM'S DEATH THROES

These cross currents and contradictions are occurring as post modernism has taken hold. The increasing pluralism of our society means that no metanarrative shapes our culture. This has occurred as 1000 years of Christendom has come to an end. Whilst there are signs that the accelerating decline in church attendance, noted by

---

13 See Andrew Davey, *The Urban Challenge – The Eleventh Bishop Williams Memorial Lectureship* (Sherbrooke, Quebec: The Bishop Williams Memorial Fund Committee, 2005).
14 Ibid., 78.
15 Laurie Green, *The Impact of the Global*, 9.

Peter Brierley in "The Tide is Running Out,"[16] is now lessening,[17] a secular world view predominates. This in turn is challenged by militant Islam and vibrant other faith communities. Questions about multi-culturalism and multi-faith communities are mixed with the stuff of politics.

Whilst religion is back in the public square, it is not necessarily Christianity. Christendom has been re-placed by "Culture Christianity" dubbed as "Christianism" by some. It doesn't translate into church going. It is paralleled by "non observant" Judaism. Plans have been submitted to build a huge 55,000 capacity Mosque in London's East End near the site of the 2012 Olympics ironically on the site occupied for several centuries by Lanthorne Abbey. At the same time an African church, whose site is being compulsorily purchased for the Olympics, is seeking to build a 12,000-seat building also in East London. Public debate about Muslim women wearing the veil and a British Airways staff person wearing a cross make headlines. Religion is in the news. The Christian People's Alliance now has three local Councilors in the East London Borough of Newham. The local M.P., a government minister married to a Malaysian, is himself a member of a newer local church, founded by a West Indian.

Archbishop John Sentamu, himself an Ugandan, has spoken of Christianity being unfairly squeezed out of consideration alongside other faith communities. Competing faith claims vie for attention much as they did in the Athens of the first century CE where Paul argued his case before the Areopagus (Acts 17).

ECHOES OF THE PAST

The mainstream denominations responded to the rapid growth of Victorian London and other industrial cities by building churches.

> The first Church census in 1851 shocked Victorian England in showing that just about half the nation did not go regularly to church. The largest section to stay away was the urban working class and the urban poor.[18]

---

16 Peter Brierly, *The Tide Is Running Out: What the English Church Attendance Survey Reveals* (London: Christian Research, 2000).

17 See Peter Brierly, *Pulling Out of the Nose Dive: A Contemporary Picture of Churchgoing: What the 2005 English Church Census Reveals* (London: Christian Research, 2006).

18 David Sheppard, *Built as a City: God and the Urban World Today* (London: Hodder and Stoughton, 1974), 113.

£35 million... was spent (by the Church of England) on Church building programmes. The Free Churches spent even more in those years on
buildings. The Baptist founded more churches in London in the 1860s
than at any other time.[19]

The legacy of this building program of 150 years ago is evident in massive
Anglican churches built in Victorian gothic, crumbling brick-built free churches
and church buildings taken over as warehouses, some converted into apartments
or offices. Many have been remodeled and adapted. Newer ethnic churches have
restored and recycled buildings. Others have become mosques or temples.

Colin Marchant maps other layers and waves of the Christian response to the
tides of industrialisation which put London in the vanguard of urban mission
enterprise.[20]

City Missions came first, adapting the models used for "overseas" missions to the
industrial city. The London City Mission founded in 1836 is going strong today.[21]
"*Agencies* proliferated in the Victorian era, the YMCA, Shaftesbury Society and
Society of St Vincent de Paul, all started in 1844."

Kathleen Heasman in Evangelicals in Action shows that 70% of all the work
undertaken to tackle the poverty and destructive effects of rapid urbanisation in
the nineteenth century was undertaken by evangelicals. "The *Armies* [were] apparent first in London. William Booth launched the Salvation Army in 1865,"[22] to be
followed later in 1852 by the Church Army. Both are still going strong. *Settlements*
began in London and are still there. Public Schools (i.e., private!) and universities
were behind them. "The Methodist *Central Halls/Missions* took Methodism Urban
Concern to the heart of the U.K cities and large towns."[23] My own grandfather, a
baker by trade in East London, was superintendent of the huge Sunday School of
Methodism's East London Mission on the Commercial Road.

Industrial Mission emerged after WWII. Following the riots in cities across
the U.K. in 1981, notably in the Brixton area, which exposed the raw underside
of an alienated and disenfranchised largely black community, the Archbishop's
Commission on Urban Priority Areas was established. After two years of intensive

19 Ibid.
20 See Colin Marchant, "The Story of Urban Mission in the UK" in Michael Eastman and Stevie Lathan,
eds., *The Urban Church: A Practitioners Resource Book* (London: SPCK, 2004), 1-2.
21 See Howat and Nicholls, *Streets Paved with Gold.*
22 Colin Marchant, course notes for M.Th. in Applied Theology, "The Story of Urban Mission in the
U.K.," London: Spurgeon's College, 1994.
23 Ibid.

work it issued, in 1985, the ground breaking Faith in the City report[24] which in time gave rise to the Church Urban Fund. Marchant summarises, "The U.K. was the first nation to face the Industrial Revolution and the consequent industrialisation and urbanisation. The Victorian wave of response is matched by the 1960-1990 wave."[25] All are still evident in London.

THE HOLY SPIRIT'S SURPRISE

Black majority churches began to appear following the wave of migration, begun in the 1950s, of people from the Caribbean, recruited to make up the labour shortage in post-war Britain. They received a cold shoulder by white congregations.

> Post war British History tells us that immigrant communities' reaction to racism and other prejudices was often quick, organised and successful. Blacks developed the "pardoner" system: pooling resources together to buy property.... Black Pentecostalism comforted the weary soul, offering a place of sanctuary, a place in which to wail. This welcome refuge from the cold world outside—including the established "white" churches—gave birth to a generation. Second-generation black Christians are still coming to terms with their identity in this distinctive and complex community.[26]

In turn the black majority churches have given rise to the Afro-Caribbean Evangelical Alliance.[27] Now on any given Sunday there are more non-white than white worshippers in churches across London. Black Baptists, Methodists, and Anglicans, the products of denominational mission agencies like the Baptist Missionary Society and the Church Missionary Society also swelled the congregations of their mother churches in London. Attendance by ethnicity in 2005 is given by Christian Research for Inner London[28] as White 42%, Black 44%, others 14%. For Outer London it is White 69%, Black 18%, others 13%.[29]

---

24 Ibid.

25 Ibid.

26 Richard Springer, "Search for Roots: Power and Powerlessness: in Michael Eastman and Stevie Latham, *Urban Church: A Practitioner's Resource Book* (London: SPCK, 2004), 90.

27 See Mark Sturge, *Look What God Has Done: An Exploration of Black Christian Faith* in Britain (Bletchley: Scripture Union, 2005).

28 Brierley, *Pulling out of the Nosedive*, 108.

29 Ibid., 106.

GLOCALISATION

Fueled by the drive for economic growth in a world shrunk by means of rapid, instant communication, the free flow of goods, services, labour, ideas and people accelerate as the world's population increases exponentially, doubling from 3 billion to 6 billion in the last 30 years. Refugees, asylum seekers, economic migrants criss-cross the globe, tourists come and go. As nation states lose their significance people seek their means of belonging in more ancient tribal and ethnic roots. "Glocalisation," the effects of these global tides within the local communities, is uncomfortably apparent. Crime, exploitation, corruption is internationalised along with hunger, poverty, want and conflict. Multi-ethnic, multi-faith, and multi-cultural neighbourhoods increased. For the churches, within a lifetime, missionary outreach to those geographically and culturally distant has needed to refocus to those geographically close but culturally distant. Daughter churches of the missionary movement of the 19th and earlier 20th centuries have in turn generated their own mission agencies sending their own nationals seeking to re-evangelise the West. Ethnic churches have mushroomed. Christian agencies and networks have multiplied.

Under the new London plan the metropolis is set to grow to over 10 million or more over the next 20 years, with major brown field development East and South and growth along the corridors to Stanstead, Heathrow and Gatwick as well as along the Thames Gateway. Cities increase mobility and choice for those with the means to take advantage of these opportunities as well as creating communities of the left behind. Different forms of human association multiply, based on neighbourhood, work, recreation, leisure, interests, age, politics, religion, ethnicity, and family. Individuals experience a variety of relationships, some more transitory than others. Churches are seen as one form of association among many, another club to join and leave as needed. Communities of interest overlay communities of place.

RESPONDING AND REACHING

The cross currents arising from these and other underlying forces shaping our culture have an impact on the churches resulting in a variety of responses and reactions.

Preservation
A defensive strategy aimed at retaining the legacy of the past and recapturing and promoting a previous era is evident in some ways of doing and being church.

It provides security for those whom change and changes threaten to overwhelm. Maintenance sets the agenda.

Adaptation

Many churches go with the flow seeking to adapt and modify their programme to meet felt needs expressed in the congregation and the communities in which they are placed.

Innovation

Some churches introduce new forms of music, worship, and communication, which are brought to bear upon the functions of Church.

Re-creation

New forms of Church starting from scratch have been developed tailored to the language, thought forms and life styles of a post-modern era.

Replication

Forms of Church pioneered elsewhere are transplanted into situations where they have not existed before.

Insulation

Such is the corrosiveness of our culture that strategies are developed to shield Christians, particularly the young, from the debilitating effects of a world increasingly antipathetic to Christian values and outlook. This has led to creating Christian sub-cultures where Christians feel safe.

Penetration

These strategies have as their purpose Christian infiltration of the institutions of our society—schools, hospitals, prisons, the world of business and commerce, the professions and industry—whereby Christian people acting as salt, light and leaven have a transforming effect. These take many forms including chaplaincies, cell groups, projects and some of the Catholic Orders.

Alleviation

Churches have a good and generally recognised track record in caring for the casualties of our self-centred and competitive culture. This ministry is expressed in a multitude of forms. It gives the Christian community the right to raise questions about the causes and challenge those in power when their decisions adversely affect the vulnerable and powerless. Christians find themselves making common cause with others including those of other faith communities.

Contextualisation

As our society becomes more fragmented and diverse, forms of church are forged that fit the needs, language, aspirations and lifestyles of particular churches and sub-cultures. This strategy, historically pioneered by missionary endeavour, resulted in a dazzling array of churches in Africa, Asia and the Indian sub-continent. These strategies developed for over there are being applied back here.[30]

SHAPES AND KINDS

A descriptive analysis of churches mostly on the East side of London notes,
New Churches are appearing, older churches are changing:

- **The Estate Churches** - Classic incarnation, showing and sharing the weakness of a Local Authority area.
- **Parish Churches** - Servicing the civic good in a geographical area.
- **International Churches** - Different cell congregations from different ethnic groups.
- **Power Churches** - Individualistic, enabling immigrant poor to make good.
- **Ethnic Churches** - First generation immigrants reaching out to others of same origin.
- **Multi-cultural Churches** - Leadership white but "non-cultural."
- **Pioneering Churches** - New experiments with small teams and a radical life-style.
- **Alternative Churches** - Disillusioned and disenfranchised Christians coming together. High Tech churches using electronic media.
- **Political Churches** - Entering the public arena.
- **Teaching Churches** - Providing grounding in the Christian faith.
- **Project Churches** - Arising from a particular project, e.g., with homeless people or drug abusers.
- **Global Churches** - Expression of mother churches of other countries which have more links outside U.K. than within.

---

30 For a summary of the recent literature see Stuart Murray, *Church After Christendom* (Exeter: Paternoster, 2004).

- **City Churches** - Spanning and networking across the whole city.
- **Specialist Churches** - Arising through work with a particular client group, e.g.,youth churches.
- **Left behind Churches** - Faithful remnants maintaining the flame with potential for life.[31]

RE-IMAGINING CHURCH

A group of urban church leaders mainly ministering in London when reflecting on these changes identified the following ten significant characteristics of urban ministry:

1. The wide variety of forms requires networking skills based on *relational* rather than I institutional means.
2. Expressions of Church are *uncontrollable* like waves and cross-currents; such unpredictability requires responsiveness, prophetic openness, adaptability, celebration of failure and discontent.
3. Appropriate approaches to creating a *catchumenate* and developing training are needed.
4. The intensity of urban living, both a living of the past and the living of the future, requires space; thus the importance of the *contemplative* and direct experience of God.
5. The significance of *smaller* forms.
6. *Anonymous god seekers* don't go to church but are there in the community.
7. Mission and ministry requires *involvement in the community.*
8. Preaching should be an experience of *encounter with God.*
9. *Visionary leaders* with realism should pace themselves for the long haul rooted in the neighbourhood.
10. Churches drawing their *source of hope* from the "end times" keep hope alive in their communities and neighbourhoods.[32]

---

31 From paper presented by Rev'd Dr. Steve Latham at the Network of Urban Evangelicals Annual Consultation in East London, October 2000.
32 See Evangelical Coalition for Urban Mission, *Wineskins for the City: Report of Network of Urban Evangelicals (NUE) Annual Consultation* (London: Evangelical Coalition for Urban Mission, 2000), 2.

NEW FORMS OF ASSOCIATION

A marked feature of the current church scene is the emergence of a variety of coalitions and networks to mobilise Christian people and individual congregations in regard to one or another aspect of mission and ministry. Some of these are short lived, others longer standing with an ebb and flow in their size and significance. This means of relating tends to be informal, organic and non-institutional and is paralleled more widely in society.

Key people and agencies enable crossover and linkage to occur. The e-mail, internet and mobile phone are making these ways of connecting and interacting more pervasive. Christian solidarity is increasingly expressed in these ways, by-passing older intermediary forms of councils, associations and alliances. People connecting with people for a purpose is their hallmark.

FACING THE CHALLENGES

In "Hope from the Margins"[33] the authors describe eight new congregations and five projects. They explore some challenges which arise from these initiatives. All are faced in post-Christendom London.

- **A Challenge to the Concept of Gathered Churches** - In a context where belonging precedes believing "a dynamic model for people on a journey is more liberating than a static model that separates believers and unbelievers."
- **A Challenge to Denominationalism and Ecumenism** - The arrival of "post-denominational churches" and the impetus to innovate require a new way of expressing Christian togetherness which is relational and organic. "Grassroots action, small groups and networking are preferred ways of relating and operating." Diversity should be celebrated.
- **A Challenge to the Ways of Celebrating Communion** - In the smaller more intimate expressions of Christian community meals together assume greater significance. Communion is integral to these settings. Being lay led and non-liturgical is a growing feature.

---

33 Stuart Murray and Anne Wilkinson-Hayes, *Hope from the Margins: New Ways of Being Church, Grove Evangelism Series, No. 49* (Cambridge: Grove Books Limited, 2000), 4.

- **A Challenge to Leadership** - Many of the newer initiatives are "lay" led rather than clergy led and with shared leadership, participation and consensual government. Forms of training to meet the needs of "non-professional" leadership are springing up.
- **A Challenge to the Focus of Church Life** - "What does Church begin to look like when we put those on the margins into the centre?"
- **A Challenge to our Language** - "... the word 'Church' is vested with too many preconceptions and too much baggage."
- **A Challenge to our Priorities** - Robert Warren concludes that the essential nature of Church requires worship, mission, and community cohering around a shared spirituality. To focus on one without the others limits the full expression of Church.
- **A Challenge to the Christendom Mentality** - In an "environment where the church is increasingly marginal and Christianity but one of many options in a pluralistic society.... [it] is unlikely that the privileges churches enjoyed under Christendom will be sustained forever..."[34]

LIVING WITH TENSION

In the light of this kaleidoscopic picture a group of Christian leaders noted a number of tensions in the current urban church in London and elsewhere. The following *gains and losses* should be weighed.

1. Hidden churches don't feature in the local landscape. The tension between maintaining a recognisable visible presence and a tendency to impermanence and invisibility.
2. The tension between engagement in the life of the community and maintaining Christian distinctiveness without creating an irrelevant Christian sub-culture.
3. The need for transcendence recognised in time honoured forms and traditions contrasts with the informal and immediate.
4. Small or large? Mustard Seed or "Mac World "?
5. Starting from scratch with new planting or renewal of the old?

---

34 Ibid., 14-18.

6. Independence on the edges or institutions and structures in tension with the need for accountability to others.

7. Going for the long haul or the short-term project ?

8. Experimentation in the inner city in contrast with settled churches in suburbia and rural settings.

9. Emphasis on the margins where there is creativity or at and from the centre?[35]

UNDERSTANDING THE TIMES

They went on to identify the following significant issues for the urban mission agencies in London.

1. Transformation of fractured and deprived situations requires the transcendent to break in with loss of place, loss of visible presence, loss of minister. Where are the markers that give meaning and identity?

2. What is appropriate and authentic? The post modern outlook gives credence to experience. Evident lived-out experience of God carries weight. What works counts. Stories matter.

3. People have multiple relationships. Internet interactions raise questions of how, to whom and to what people belong. Dimensions of mystical experience beyond the mundane assume greater significance. Children's spirituality embodies the importance of "now." The Millennium Dome's Faith Zone resonated with the spiritual within all humankind.

4. Institutional decline and congregational life exist together. Ours is a time of fireworks, flux, flows and waves which are impossible to predict or to chart.

5. Following Jesus is to incarnate mission in concrete, community-rooted ways.[36]

---

35 Evangelical Coalition, *Wineskins*, 3.
36 Ibid.

NEW WAVES

Into this potent mix has come the impact of the African Diaspora. Jehu J. Hanciles estimates that there are 3 million African Christians in Europe.[37] Many are refugees. Others are economic migrants. Those who are English speaking make for the U.K. and, as with so many in the past, London is their entry point. In the last ten years this new presence has made itself felt. These newly arrived Christians are the products of the massive and sustained missionary enterprise of the 19th and early 20th centuries. "Darkest Africa" captured the Victorian church's imagination. The churches formed through their endeavours, often at great human and material cost, have themselves generated mission agencies. Arriving freshly in "Christian England" African Christians are shocked by the decadence and godlessness of our culture and the weakness and defensiveness of the churches. Coming from churches which are the outcome of missions, these new arrivals see London as a mission field. Bringing their missional experience to bear on London they are establishing new churches and injecting fresh energy, vision and enthusiasm to existing congregations! Baptists in London currently number 26,000, five thousand of which are accounted for by two African-led churches—Calvary Charismatic in East London and Trinity in South of the river. Each claims to be the biggest Baptist church in Europe! Calvary Charismatic has thirty-four nations represented among its 2,500 membership and has established seven daughter churches.

However, of thirty newer Baptist Churches in East London, only five of the ministers are formally accredited through the denominational processes. The others have been called out and recognised by their congregations. This raises new and challenging questions about how ministers are recognised and trained in such contexts.

THINKING BIG

Kingsway International Christian Centre, headed by Pastor Matthew Ashimolowo, a dynamic and visionary Nigerian, when faced with compulsory purchase of their site for the 2012 Olympics, put in a daring bid to build an Olympic stadium which would be used as the base for their main church after the event. This was not possible "because of rules linked to the post-Olympic public ownership of facilities."[38] People come from all over London to Kingsway ICC. In 2006 they completed the

---

37 Jehu D. Hanciles, "Migration, and Mission: Some Implications for the Twenty-first Century Church," *International Bulletin of Mission Research* 27, no. 4(Oct. 2003): 150.
38 *Friends of KICC: News and Information for our International Network of Friends* 2(Aug., 2006): 2.

modernisation and refurbishment of two other buildings, one of which is a redundant cinema but a Grade II listed building in Walthamstow which has resulted in the "careful preservation and refurbishment of the original interior décor and features of the Cinema and (created) a lovely new 1,200 seat church."[39] At the same time work has been proceeding on the refurbishment of KICC premises in Hackney which is the 1,000 seat church where the KICC was based before it bought and created the present 4,000 seat arena. In 2006 their International "Gatherings of Champions" brought 160,000 people from 40 different countries for eight days to Hackney, one of London's most deprived inner boroughs contributing an estimated £4 million to the local economy. Their mission statement is bold:

> KICC Vision – Grow Up – Grow Big – Grow Together. Be a place where the hurting, the depressed, the frustrated and the confused can find love, acceptance, help, hope, forgiveness and encouragement. Share the Good News of Jesus Christ with the 11 million people resident in London. Develop people to spiritual maturity. Equip every believer for a signifi-cant ministry by helping them discover, develop and deploy the gifts and talents God gave them. Be a church where every member is an evange-list, where every worker is a warrior.[40]

RENEWING THE OLD

Samuel and his family arrived in London some fifteen or more years ago from Nigeria. As an accountant he soon became treasurer of a small inner city Baptist church and master-minded a multi-million pound scheme to refurbish the Victorian Sunday School building as a community facility. He cut the ribbon at the official opening in the fall of 2005. As he and his family prospered, he moved to an outer London Borough on London's East-side and in 2006 along with another Nigerian was elected to the Board of Deacons. This church which had experienced decline from 600 to 250 in membership over a 25-year period is growing again. For the first time in its history an international evening was held as part of Harvest Thanksgiving in the fall of 2005. Twenty nationalities were represented with those from Africa prominent—Ghanaians, Zimbabweans, Kenyans, Nigerians and South Africans.

---

39 Ibid., 1.
40 Ibid., 4.

Alex from Ghana recently came into membership of this church. His father had sent him to a mission school established 125 years ago by a Swiss Presbyterian mission in a country area which became the site for a hydro-electric scheme. At this primary school he heard the stories of Jesus, and when he went to secondary school, he came to a living faith through the Scripture Union Group formed amongst the students. A renewal movement had swept across Ghana through these secondary school S.U. groups. Working in Accra he joined Accra Baptist Church and came to London to study human resources management. Not wishing to be culturally confined to Ghanaian churches, of which there are a number in London, on a visit to Romford he noticed the Baptist church and sensed that this was where God wanted him to be based. He brought with him the expectancy and vision and experience of being part of a 6,000-member church in Accra which has two youth congregations and programs for all ages including marriage guidance and parenting skills. He is an enthusiastic advocate for the church to develop similar programs here.

UNEXPECTED LIFE

For many years, as churches declined in London, older white congregations, which have maintained a presence, often with an increasingly elderly remnant, have prayed for renewal and revival, longing to recapture the days when churches were full. They have been taken by surprise. God is renewing this church in London first through the growth of black majority churches from the 1950s onwards and now by the Africanisation of the church.

Peter Brierley, in analysing the results of the 2005 English Church Census, notes, "the Evangelical growth in Greater London is largely due to the enthusiasm of the black diversity churches in both church planting and seeing individual congregations increase in size."[41] He also notes, "The growth in Greater London (of the Afro-Caribbean churches) represents four fifths, 81%, of the entire Pentecostal growth in England between 1998 and 2005."[42]

Alongside this are other ethnic-based churches and congregations—Portuguese-speaking and Filipino congregations, Korean churches, Chinese churches. Some are housed in the same buildings as the older congregations; others are revitalising redundant buildings. Now the newer tides of people from Eastern Europe are

---

41 Brierley, *Pulling Out of the Nose Dive*, 60.
42 Ibid.

making their mark. Just recently Lithuanian Elim Church has opened in London's East End!

Colin Marchant describes these new signs of God working in new ways.

> Signals flash from a spectrum of sources, shop-front presence, changing buildings, numerical growth, diversity, clustering of congregations, creative projects, world faiths and an incredible range of 'visuals.'

> Shop front 'presence' takes many forms. The Word of God International Worship Centre, Signs and Wonders hairdresser, His Grace Cosmetics Beauty Centre. It is Well (in our city); Amazing Grace has a mini-market and an International Worship Centre, a training, counselling and prayer unit. Buildings are converted! One garage has become the Calvary Charismatic Church, another a Muslim Mosque. A clothing store now houses the Glory Bible Church and another shop has become Street Narayan Guru Mission.

> Growth can be phenomenal. An initial "church plant" of 40 Ghanaian Christians grows to 700 in five years, across in Hackney the Highway Church claims 5,000 members. New buildings set aside for religion have nearly doubled every decade since 1970 (1970s-19; 1980s-25; 1990s-50).

> Diversity is Kaleidoscopic. Colombian Fathers and Coptic Church, Faith Temple Mission and Mayflower, St. Matthew's and Tehillah Prophetic Ministries, Centres, Shops, Churches, Fellowships, Missions, Units, Ministries, Chaplaincies, Assemblies and Programmes.

> Clustering of congregations is everywhere. Some community centres have 6 churches using their premises. The Baptist Church where I belong has two new churches following on from our morning service and two others use our adjacent halls. World Faiths are with us in strength—25 Muslin organisations, 15 Hindu, 4 Sikh and 2 Buddhist. We have 3 Interfaith and 2 Multi-Faith groups alongside the Bahai and Jewish people.

> Visible signals flash. Bible carrying Pentecostals and white-capped Muslim boys, Buddhist flags and all night Christian prayer meetings, murals and mini-vans, projects and lit-up crosses.[43]

This reflects reverse missionary flow. Churches in Africa are sending their missionaries back into the docklands areas of London from where British missionaries embarked to take God's Good News to Africa in the nineteenth century. African pastors of congregations in London also continue to pastor churches in their countries of origin.

NEW WINESKINS

A 1998 listing of Pentecostal/Ethnic churches notes fifty-seven new churches in the one Borough of Newham.[44] Marchant reports that these have increased to ninety-three in 2006.[45] In different degrees this is happening across London, at an accelerating rate. The challenge now is how links of support and common enterprise are to be built in London between older white churches and new ethnic churches in order to work together for the re-evangelisation of one of the most cosmopolitan of global cities.

Peter Brierley concludes, "Greater London is different in its church life from almost any other part of England, in terms of local environment, the number of larger churches, the growth in its congregations, the size and vibrancy of the ethnic majority churches, the size of its churches, the skills of its leaders, the age of its attendees." He raises the question of whether the churches of London can work together for

> the 2012 Olympic Games which will provide an immense opportunity for mission to the thousands of competitors and millions of visitors who will attend... Such a collaboration (if it happens) could well be a model which other groups throughout the country could follow. *Greater London's* uniqueness in church life could then perhaps become a *Springboard by which its input could be felt across the whole of England.*[46]

---

43 Marchant, "New Signs in the City," 208.
44 Colin Marchant, unpublished research, University of East London Center for Institutional Studies.
45 Ibid.
46 Brierley, *Pulling out of the Nosedive*, 260.

Section 2:

Reconciliation

.5.

Commitment to Reconciliation:
The Cost and the Future[1]

MANUEL ORTIZ

When the apostles were faced with the truth of the ascended Christ and the selection of the twelfth apostle, they came to the Lord and said, "Lord, you know everyone's heart. Show us..." (Acts 1:24). God is the *kardiognosta*, the heart surgeon, the heart searcher.

What truly is in our hearts? We are called to be honest and intentional with the issues that continue to plague our country and Christian institutions—racism, ethnocentrism, and the lack of justice and race reconciliation—subjects which we have learned to live with as bed partners, keeping them alive and healthy in our Christian community. We have learned to separate truth from justice without flinching a muscle. We have separated knowing from doing, and it is okay and even common. As Dr. Gaede tells us, "Evil is cagey."[2]

Art Gay once referred to a World Relief conference as "the last opportunity the Bible-believing church in the United States will have to bring reconciliation between two races. This will be a fine beginning," he notes, "with much work to be done." There have been many conferences on this important subject. They usually turn out to be gatherings where Christians come with high expectations but will ultimately settle for the fellowship and verbal dialogue—and no more.

---

1 This is an edited version of a lecture presented by Manuel Ortiz at a World Relief conference in Chicago, Illinois, on January 6-7, 1995.

2 S. D. Gaede, *When Tolerance Is No Virtue: Political Correctness, Multiculturalism & the Future of Truth & Justice* (Downers Grove, IL: InterVarsity Press, 1993), 51.

We have become biblical tourists, visitors, and then we are off to do what we have always done in the past. We must go beyond tourism and become obedient to the truth of his Word.

OUR ATTEMPTS

As we enter this new century, we have probably said all there is to say about racial reconciliation, and I am not sure we can say it any better than those who have shared in this struggle in the evangelical community. We honor the voices of our prophets who are now with the Lord, people like Tom Skinner, Orlando Costas, Bill Bentley, and Clarence Hilliard who, along with many others, have endured this battle. In 1974 Dr. Bentley reflects,

> We felt that while racial prejudice and discrimination are not the only social issues that plague America and her churches, it is the one above all others that colors all others. In America it determines more than anything else where a man shall live, whether or not he shall work, and the quality of education he will have the opportunity to obtain.[3]

Clarence Hilliard, in his treatise of the Funky Gospel, says,

> [T]he gospel we discovered may not get you on the list to speak at the President's prayer breakfast; it can, however, get you on the more "colorful" list in circulation in high places today.[4]

Samuel Escobar also reflects,

> [O]ur evangelical rank and file... are not ready for some truth at all. It is not only that a huge dose would prove to be fatal, but that just a drop will be too much.... A step is a step.... During a convention some time ago, a missionary friend of mine told me that evangelicals have come to the point of having as part of their program an act of masochism. They let radical

---

3 William H. Bentley, "Reflections" in Ronald J. Sider, ed., *The Chicago Declaration* (Carol Stream, IL: Creation House, 1974), 136.
4 Clarence L. Hilliard, "The Funky Gospel," unpublished paper, 1976, 1.

speakers come and talk, and after an adequate dose of verbal abuse which they stoically accept, *they then carry on their business as usual.*[5]

There are a score of others working overtly and silently in evangelical institutions for the cause of Christ and his Kingdom. Many of us have become vulnerable, publicly expressing our pain and rage for all to examine and touch, with many concluding, "That was a nice testimony." Many of us have joined numerous small group discussions, and we have been asked to participate as advisors for church and para-church organizations on the subjects of racial reconciliation and multi-ethnicity. We are on committees developing a theology appropriate for reconciliation, with the hope, the biblical kind of hope, that the organization will buy it and move towards healing and wholeness with a capital W. Let me be candid with this subject.

It is always confusing taking this approach of developing a committee to write out our theology for racial reconciliation and then spend years trying to refine it as though we are ignorant and need proof that being racist or participating in an exclusive institution as Christians was against the will of God. It seems more like smoke than fire, or an intelligent Christian response. We request money from funding organizations in order to more fully approach this subject. We determine that we need long and exhaustive meetings in some fashionable hotel.

I think it is not that we do not know what to do—it is what we do not want to do that is before us. It is a Pauline dilemma, "For what I do is not the good I want to do; no, the evil I do not want to do—this I keep on doing" (Romans 7:19).

In my opinion, we have not had the right heart to pursue justice, for the cost seems so insurmountable. I believe we are buying time and hoping to get by with minimal pain and change, nurturing the "good old boy" syndrome hoping that we won't have to give up much before our lives are swept up in glory and the task is on our children's shoulders. I am afraid that we will leave this work to the generation to come, and we will be held accountable for our lack of commitment to acting on divine revelation. My concern is that *we have left our children stewards of bad theology, a dysfunctional ecclesiology.*

Is it not that justice and truth have become empty terms that are meaningless to us? "To determine what is just, one must have a rather clear idea about what is right and wrong."[6]

---

5 Samuel Escobar, "Reflections" in Sider, *Chicago Declaration*, 120, emphasis added.
6 Gaede, *When Tolerance Is No Virtue*, 38.

OUR SITUATION

It was J. M. Blaut who stated,

> [T]he dominant racist theory of the early nineteenth century was a biblical argument, grounded in religion; the dominant racist theory of the period from about 1850 to 1950 was a biological argument, grounded in the natural science; the racist theory of today is mainly a historical argument, grounded in the idea of culture history or simply culture. Today's racism is cultural racism.[7]

Today, in universities, we have racism but few racists.

> Slavery, broken treaties, immigration policies, disfranchisement all testify not only to past sins but to the fact that our institutions were originally designed with overt discrimination in mind.[8]

While we have done something about overt racism, and it may seem that it has been reduced, underground racism continues. Gaede indicates, in agreement with Blaut, that since institutions spring from culture and even though it seems that overt racism has lessened, institutional racism continues because many of the assumptions of these institutions have not changed.[9]

Many of us are exhausted with the ongoing discussions and board meetings but feel a sense of obligation. Often we are called to attention, "Aren't you the ones that wanted change and documentation in order to bring healing to the Body?"

Yes, but to be honest, the process is questionable and the options are limited as to how we might get to the cause and how we might bring transformation to what this dreadful sin has done to the body of Christ.

OUR JOURNEY

Our journey into this mine field has brought about many hardships, doubts, suspicions and cautions. There is no neutral ground on this subject. We cannot stay as formalists or continue to talk about process. No, we have to admit our failure

---

7 J. M. Blaut, "The Theory of Cultural Racism," *Antipode* 24, no. 4 (1992): 290.

8 Gaede, *When Tolerance Is No Virtue*, 42

9 Ibid.

in being God's people in this American context. We have to again say that we have at times been too American and not enough Christian. Repentance has been intellectualized and has not come down to concrete forms that move us towards wholeness and reconciliation. "If we are not on the side of both truth and justice, we are not on God's side."[10]

We cannot write about denouncing racism but never have to do anything about it—no cost at all. We cannot speak or attend meetings like this one and think for one moment that we can ignore the call of God to justice and delegate this responsibility to someone else. We can have a collection of diverse people in a congregation or in our institutions that looks like reconciliation has taken place—multi-cultural-ism—but never have to do anything significantly about racism. We can give and get advice about this illness and never have to do anything about it. "The authenticity of the knowing is demonstrated in the actions.... real understanding leads to changed behavior."[11] "Lying can never save us from the lie."[12]

We can no longer speak of multi-culturalism as a goal, inclusivism for our institutions as an end, and not come to grips with the goal of justice. You see, inclusivism can never be a goal; it is only a means to justice and righteousness. Being sensitive is honorable, but it cannot be a goal; it is a means towards reconciliation. Nor can we continue to harp on the problem, which in reality reinforces the gap and places those on either side in a profound entrenchment. Criticism without action is self defeating.[13]

WHAT WILL IT COST US, AND WHAT IS THE FUTURE?

Reconstruction of the Past

We must correct the past in the present. "He who fears facing his own past, must necessarily fear what lies before him.... Falsifiers of history do not safeguard freedom but imperil it. Truth liberates man [and woman] from fear."[14]

---

10 Ibid., 51-2.

11 Ibid., 52.

12 Arthur M. Schlesinger, Jr., *The Disuniting of America: Reflections on a Multicultural Society* (New York: W. W. Norton & Company, 1992), 52.

13 Os Guiness, *Fit Bodies Fat Minds: Why Evangelicals Don't Think and What to Do About It* (Grand Rapids, MI: Baker Books, 1994), 20.

14 Schlesinger, *The Disuniting of America*, 52.

We must tell the story truthfully. The testimonies of our organizations, churches and mission movements have been too *innocent* and not sufficiently Christian. We might read, "He was a segregationist," and yet "mightily used of the Lord" on the following page. This is outrageous, but, as we know all too often, it is true that we allow sin to be condoned publicly. "As a second-century writer commented, error must clothe itself in truth in order to have power."[15]

It is remarkable how we can tell the old, old story without truth. We are confused as we hear and read about our side-stepping of racial reconciliation while we boldly move towards world evangelization and relief. There must come a time when we close the fourth century, where Constantinianism, popular Christianity, must come to an end.

"A new future requires a new past."[16] As long as we do not correct the past we will insure our children, even permit them, to pursue the violence and illness of racism. Havel tells us, "Honest history is the weapon of freedom."[17]

Honesty, admitting, a truth-disclosure of what we have done and will *not* continue to do by the grace of God, must be revealed. This is what we refer to as "repentance." The call to repentance is not a matter of feeling sorrow, but rather of having a change of direction. And if we have repented, then where is the beef, the new direction? It is also not individualistic, something that occurs in one's closet, alone, between you and God. No, it is corporate. "If one part suffers, every part suffers with it; if one part is honored, every part rejoices with it" (1 Cor. 12:26). God is calling us to a biblical demonstration of repentance.

Dr. Orlando Costas reminds us,

> The new order of life demands a radical change. There can be no reconciliation without conversion, just as there can be no resurrection without the cross, much less new life without birthpangs. Hence Jesus came not only announcing the kingdom, but calling for repentance and faith (Mk. 1:15).

> On a personal level this implies a change of attitude and values, the appropriation of a new relationship with God and neighbors, and a new commitment to the messianic cause. The Kingdom demands a transfer

---

15 Justo L. González, *Mañana: Christian Theology from a Hispanic Perspective* (Nashville: Abingdon Press, 1990), 45.
16 Schlesinger, *The Disuniting of America*, 50.
17 Ibid., 52.

from "self" to "other," from an individualistic and egocentric consciousness to one communally and fraternally oriented."[18]

Signs of Repentance - A New Direction - There are a number of signs that demonstrate repentance. First, we must cease to separate knowing from doing and
come to theological grips that this separation is not right. We are, as Gaede says,
"knowledge consumers, *not responsible knowers*."[19]

Second, our constituencies cannot determine the future of our organizations.
We say that we are in a Catch 22. We can not write, denounce or promote aspects
of justice in our journals, publications, or denominational quarterlies, because
our constituency will not approve. We are not in a Catch 22; we are in Relativism
22, or, as Paul speaks about it, "Am I now trying to win the approval of men, or
of God?" (Gal. 1:10). "When I saw that they were not acting in line with the truth
of the gospel, I said to Peter in front of them all, 'You are a Jew, yet you live like a
Gentile and not like a Jew'" (Gal. 2:14).

I remember asking an editor why his publication was not publishing matters of
race, justice and reconciliation and articles written by authors who were not the
norm for that publication. The answer came back, "It is because our constituents
will not read such a journal. We leave that to those folks such as *Sojourners* and *The
Other Side* magazine." It is a matter of marketing, what is often called "Protestant
marketability," and ultimately not truth but capital that drives our institutions.

Finally, we must not attempt to hide truth concerning justice by saying that we
will have people of color in our organization, or have curriculums that are sensitive to minorities, as much as I appreciate that. It must begin with our institutional
discussion concerning truth and justice.

If there is one term that we have left out of our dialogue and deployed to our
friends at *The Other Side*, it is justice. It seems as though justice is too much to the
left and not enough to the right for us. I am afraid we are misdirected.

When we do not implement justice, we become educators, sociologists, writers
and theologians without truth, or what Os Guinness calls, "cultural imitators."[20]

---

18 Orlando Costas, *Christ Outside the Gate: Mission Beyond Christendom* (Maryknoll, NY: Orbis Books,
1984), 92.
19 Gaede, *When Tolerance Is No Virtue*, 52, emphasis added.
20 Guiness, *Fit Bodies Fat Minds*, 14.

Reconstruction of the Present For the Future

Some time ago I attended a conference on Latin America at Eastern Baptist Theological Seminary, and a paper was presented on "The Political Significance of the Protestant Presence." The author of this paper stated,

> One of the clearest examples of "Protestant Marketability" took place in Chile during the Pinochet dictatorship. When the Catholic Church began to protest against Pinochet's unjust policies, the dictator used the moral reputation of Chilean Evangelicals, primarily Pentecostal, to his advantage. Evangelists like Luis Palau were more than eager to share the gospel in "presidential (... "dictatorial") prayer breakfasts," even at the expense of trading off their moral "capital" to a corrupt or oppressive government in exchange for the privilege of sharing the gospel.[21]

How do we respond to this trade-off? Again, the government in Mexico discovered great support from evangelical leadership during unjust action by inviting 600 Protestant leaders to the presidential residence for breakfast. Some responded that Salinas "was one of the greatest presidents of all times in the concert of the nations."[22]

In Jim Wallis' book, *The Soul of Politics*, he notes, "When religion becomes conformed to the culture, it can no longer provide a reliable path to spirituality, and our public life loses its moral compass."[23] He indicates that "Polarized leaders have behaved much like the politicians they have allied with."[24]

Signs of Reconstruction of the Present

Again we need to look for signs, this time for signs of reconstruction of the present. The first sign is reconstruction of personal and institutional involvement. Our discretion on how we get involved with others and for what reasons is important. If our motivation is for personal and institutional ambition, we must deter from being involved. If the participation does not enhance the kingdom of God and justice, we again must evaluate our motives for involvement. Often a call to be with one of the super-star evangelicals or a high authority along with a round-trip

---

21 Author Unknown, "The Political Significance of the Protestant Presence," paper presented at Eastern Baptist Theological Seminary's conference on Latin America, October 7, 1994, 11.

22 Ibid., 12.

23 Jim Wallis, *The Soul of Politics: A Practical and Prophetic Vision for Change* (Maryknoll, NY: Orbis Books, 1994), 36.

24 Ibid., 37.

ticket and comfortable lodging will be too seductive for us to handle—even if we are UNEQUALLY YOKED. When it comes to organizational engagement, we buy in without sufficient reflection and even enjoy it.

The second sign is missiological reconstruction. We must consider a missiological imperative to serve together in both foreign and domestic challenges. This sign of the kingdom is appealing because it is fundamentally biblical. The "I Have Need of You" calling, the high priestly prayer evangelism strategy in John 17, will do more for world evangelization than all the statistics we compile and all the strategy we devise. Missiological reconstruction needs to find its place in biblical authority rather than in pragmatism.

The third sign is celebration reconstruction. What is my point here? We cannot quickly celebrate freedom from apartheid in South Africa if we do not move to liquidate the sin of racism in our church and Christian context. Martin Luther King said, "Injustice anywhere is a threat to justice everywhere."[25] No one is free until all are free.[26]

> The Second World War gave the Creed new bite. Hitler's racism forced Americans to look hard at their own racial assumptions. How, in fighting against Hitler's doctrine of the Master Race abroad, could Americans maintain a doctrine of white supremacy at home?[27]

During the civil rights movement the discussion would often center on the idea of exclusion because of color and race. One could not eat at a counter in a downtown restaurant or enter a clothing store because he or she was the wrong color. To speak of solidarity means that if my brother or sister is not invited, I am not invited. I cannot sit down at the counter and eat as though nothing is wrong while they wait outside. This is more than a political agenda, it is the justice motif of the Scriptures.

At Lausanne II in Manila, I realized that my African-American brothers and sisters were not represented in the American caucus. Those who were able to come came on their own frequent flyers. Shall we enter evangelical conferences and participate as key note speakers recognizing that our brothers and sisters were left

---

25 Manuel Ortiz, "An Assessment of William Bentley's Commitment to Christian Community: A Hispanic Perspective," an unpublished paper, 1995.

26 Ibid.

27 Schlesinger, *The Disuniting of America*, 39-40.

"outside?" Many of us decided not to attend the sessions. I had to ask myself, how did the Hispanics on that committee respond to that exclusion?

It is difficult to participate in such a conference in that I must stand where I believe God stands. I cannot please someone because of friendship, employment, or relationship. Some want me to be hard; some want me to be soft and pleasant. In Joshua 5 Joshua requests that the Lord take a stand, "Are you for us or our enemies?" and the response comes back, "neither." Our foremost call is that we stand with the Lord.

Reconstruction of our Reconciliation Boundaries

We must extend the boundaries of reconciliation. Racism is when one group decides to prevent another from the necessities of life, success, prestige, and power on the basis of who they are, and then they blame the victim. "It is because you are Black, Hispanic, Asian, or a woman" that you will be replaced or will not receive the income due you.

Racism in this country, and I imagine throughout the world, is an illness of all sinners. We all have been touched with this dreadful sickness. The Hispanic church here in the U.S. is growing, and Hispanics will soon be the largest minority in the U.S. What will we do as Hispanic Christians when another group is limited in recognition and financial resources on the basis of demographics? What will we do when we also realize that the dominant society continues to stratify the poor and pits one minority against the other?

Dominga Zapata states,

> Blacks and Hispanics share closely the lot of the oppressed. Our neighborhoods are the same or next to each other. We compete for the same low-paying jobs and the high-rental housing. Our children sit next to each other in the domesticating educational classrooms. We share the roots of Christianity handed down by our colonizers. We are in need of an old word become new, solidarity. Unity is often associated with sameness.[28]

We must bend the lines of reconciliation and consider for one moment how we have been too exclusive and even sometimes too superior in our ethnic discovery and celebration.

---

28 Dominga Zapata, "What is the Place of Holistic Community Development in Hispanic Liberation Theology," unpublished paper, 1982, 1.

Reconciliation Boundaries

Evaluation – Serious evaluation is needed of our commitment to reconciliation as it relates to other ethnic groups. We have been fighting on one front for too long, and we have not considered that exclusivism, racism exists in our own backyard. As one of my brothers from Boston stated, "Black people don't like Black people." Racism exists in my community among Hispanics, and God is not pleased. In El Paso where Hispanics dominate, and as one of the young bloods once told me, "This is wonderful—to see our people in charge." How will we, in the distribution of power, be just? Will we, the oppressed, become the oppressor?

Solidarity Strategy – We must develop a strategy for solidarity among other ethnic groups. In some ways we have not learned how to be ethnic without being ethnocentric. How can we form a networking link that will help African Americans, Hispanics, Asians, Native Americans, and other groups to form a means of working in mission together, of sharing information and resources as needs arise?

Building – Can we learn from each other and with each other? I was pleased when I noticed the reference work in one of John Perkins' books. He had used Dr. Orlando Costas as a key resource. I noticed in his volume that the writings of a Hispanic encouraged and enhanced his own work. We know so little about each other. And as long as we do not know, we do not grow in our perspective of who this multilingual God is.

CONCLUSION

As I review all these pieces required for true racial reconciliation, I find much comfort in the closing statements of Orlando Costas' book as he preached from Hebrews 13:12.

> Jesus died outside the gate, and in so doing changed the place of salvation and clarified the meaning of mission. No longer can I see God's saving grace as an individual benefit, a privileged possession, or a religious whitewash that enables me to feel good and continue to live the old way because my bad conscience has been soothed and my guilt feelings washed away. On the contrary, because salvation is to be found in the crucified Son of God who died outside the gate of the religious compound, to be saved by faith in him is to experience a radical transformation that makes me a "debtor" to the world (Rom.1:14) and

calls me forth to share in the suffering by serving, especially, its lowest representatives: the poor, the powerless and the oppressed. Nor am I allowed to use the cause of evangelism to build ecclesiastical compounds that insulate Christians from the basic issues of life and impede them to follow Jesus through the crossroads of life.... Let us not sell our missional birthright for the mess of pottage of a cheap social activism but, rather, let us be prophets of hope in a world of disillusionment and false dreams, pressing forward to the city of God—the world of true justice and real peace, of unfeigned love and authentic freedom. Amen.[29]

---

29 Costas, *Christ Outside the Gate*, 194.

.6.

Chinese American Protestant Christianity: A History on the Margins[1]

JEFFREY K. JUE

In the introduction of his book, *New Spiritual Homes: Religion and Asian Americans*, David Yoo recounts one of the greatest industrial achievements in the history of America. On the nineteenth of May 1869, a group gathered at Promontory Point, Utah, to observe and celebrate the completion of the transcontinental railroad.[2] Begun in 1863, the railroad symbolized the triumphal spirit in America, when many believed that this country was destined for prosperity and greatness. A photograph was taken capturing this historic moment with men opening champagne bottles and shaking one another's hand. As one observer noticed the last rails being laid by Chinese and European immigrant workers, he recorded, "here, near the center of the American continent, were the united efforts of the representatives of the continents of Europe, Asia and America—America directing and controlling."[3] Contrary to these eyewitness reports, no Chinese laborers appear in any of the photos taken at Promontory Point. The absence of the Chinese in these photographs demonstrates how they were no longer needed and thus relegated to the margins of obscurity by their new adopted home; this was confirmed by the passing of the Chinese Exclusion Act in 1882. However, to tell the story of the transcontinental railroad and omit

---

1 Research for this essay was first presented at the August 2006 U.S. and Chinese Christian Scholars Dialogue in Lafayette Hill, PA.

2 David K. Yoo, "Introduction: Reframing the U. S. Religious Landscape," in D. Yoo, ed., *New Spiritual Homes: Religion and Asian Americans* (Honolulu: University of Hawai'i Press, 1999), 1-2.

3 Ronald Takaki, *Strangers from a Different Shore: A History of Asian Americans* (Boston: Penguin Books, 1989), 87.

the Chinese contribution is to have an impoverished understanding of this history and a part of America's identity.

Thankfully, this understanding of American history is slowly being corrected. Beginning with Ronald Takaki's pioneering work, *Strangers from a Different Shore: A History of Asian Americans*, to the more popular volume authored by the late Iris Chang, *The Chinese in America: A Narrative History*, the history of the Chinese in America has been given more and more attention. With the flourishing of ethnic studies programs in American universities in the past fifteen years, the historiography of American history is being revised to account for the history of minorities which played a crucial role in many important events: the completion of the transcontinental railroad, the outcomes of two World Wars, monumental scientific and medical advancements, just to name a few. However, the revision is not complete. There continue to be fields of American historical studies that neglect the contribution of American minorities, and specifically Asian minorities.

In recent years the scholarly interest in the history of American Protestant Christianity has reached unparalleled heights. The substantial works of Mark Noll, formerly of Wheaton College and now at the University of Notre Dame, and E. Brooks Holifield of Emory University continue to add to the growing literature in this field.[4] However, even a cursory reading of these latest studies reveals the perpetuation of a historiography that either crudely stereotypes or marginalizes the religious histories of American minorities.[5] Minorities are either classified as perpetually foreign (and thus non-American) or assimilated (with no distinguishable cultural characteristics). Addressing the religious history of Asian Americans, Timothy Tseng, director of the Institute for the Study of Asian American Christianity, comments,

> To assert that American religious historiography has viewed Asian Americans through Orientalist lenses is to suggest that Asian Americans have been perceived as innately foreign or completely assimilated....
> In other words, whatever it is that makes Asians different from what is considered American is construed as something that is permanent or something to be erased.[6]

---

4 Mark Noll, *America's God: From Jonathan Edwards to Abraham Lincoln* (Oxford: Oxford University Press, 2002); E. Brooks Holifield, *Theology in America: Christian Thought from the Age of the Puritans to the Civil War* (New Haven: Yale University Press, 2003).

5 An older example of this historiography is Sydney Ahlstrom, *A Religious History of the American People* (New Haven: Yale University Press, 1972).

6 Timothy Tseng, "Beyond Orientalism and Assimilation: The Asian American as Historical Subject," in F. Matsuoka and E. S. Fernandez, eds., *Realizing the America of Our Hearts: Theological Voices of Asian*

Past studies have conformed to this reading that Tseng describes. Consequently, this historiography must be challenged in light of more recent scholarship.[7]

In the global era, characterized by massive ethnic and cultural diversity in the major urban centers, as well as a momentous population shift within Christianity from the Northern to the Southern hemisphere, it is important for American historians to recognize the roots of these changes which date back to the early nineteenth century.[8] In an effort to add to these newer studies and challenge the earlier historiography of American Christianity, this essay will begin with a general overview of the history of Chinese Protestant Christianity in America, from the mid-nineteenth century to the present. Next, this essay will address how that history intersects with the history of United States immigration policy, sociological issues of racialization, and the theological character of the Chinese church in America. Finally, special attention will be made to show how the history of Chinese American Protestants supplements and complements the broader history of American Christianity, which is so carefully investigated by previous historians of religion.

A BRIEF HISTORY OF CHINESE AMERICANS AND CHINESE AMERICAN PROTESTANT CHRISTIANITY

The earliest Chinese immigrants arrived in California in the late 1840s.[9] Most of these early immigrants emigrated from Guangzhou (Canton) in the southern province of Guangdong.[10] They labored in gold mines, dug ditches for agricultural growth, fished, and of course constructed railroads. The great majority were men who left wives and families in China and set out to make their fortunes on Gold Mountain (California). But labor became competitive by the 1880s and white workers began to accuse the Chinese of stealing jobs by undercutting wages. Propaganda was fierce against the threat of the so-called "yellow peril" and public opinion castigated the Chinese as unwanted foreigners. In 1882, Congress passed the Chinese Exclusion

---

Americans (St. Louis: Chalice Press, 2003), 58.

7 One example is Henry Yu, *Thinking Orientals: Migration, Contact, and Exoticism in Modern America* (New York: Oxford University Press, 2001).

8 Discussions of global Christianity include Philip Jenkins, *The Next Christendom: The Coming of Global Christianity* (Oxford: Oxford University Press, 2002) and Lamin Sanneh, *Whose Religion is Christianity?: The Gospel Beyond the West* (Grand Rapids, MI: Wm. B. Eerdmans Publishing Co., 2003).

9 Takaki, *Strangers*, 31.

10 Ibid., 32.

Act, denying citizenship and further immigration from China. This was legislation directly discriminating against a specific ethnic group.

After 1882 the Chinese who remained in the United States huddled together in Chinese ghettos, which became known as the Chinatowns, the largest in New York City and San Francisco. In spite of their harsh living conditions, these communities began to thrive as they opened restaurants, laundries and "exotic oriental" gift shops.[11] Although new immigration was technically illegal, many Chinese still arrived in America through creative means. The great San Francisco earthquake and fire of 1906 destroyed the city records office, along with the immigration records. Subsequently many Chinese arrived with false papers. These "paper sons and daughters" claimed relations with families already residing in America prior to 1882.[12]

The Chinese Exclusion Act was repealed in 1943, but this did not improve the immigration situation. A quota system was enforced that allowed only 105 individuals to emigrate each year from China. This was extremely disproportionate to other European countries.[13] But all of this changed dramatically in 1965. The Immigration and Naturalization Amendment Act of 1965 abolished the annual quota system and granted 20,000 immigrants from each country in the Eastern hemisphere.[14] This drastically increased the number of Chinese in America. In 1860 there were 34,933 Chinese in America; in 1940 there were 117,629. By 1970 there 383,023 and the 2000 census recorded over 2.8 million.[15] The post-1965 wave of immigration included Chinese from Taiwan, Hong Kong, Southeast Asia and China. Likewise a greater socio-economic diversity characterized these newer Chinese immigrants. Fenggang Yang writes, "Most of the post-1965 Chinese immigrants, like other Asian immigrants but in contrast with early Chinese immigrants, are characterized by their urban background, high educational achievement, and professional occupations before immigration."[16] Thus the stereotype began to shift from viewing Chinese as "perpetual foreigners" to the "model minority," given the ability of professional Chinese (both newer immigrants, Overseas Born Chinese or OBCs, and the second/third/fourth generations of earlier immigrants, American Born

---

11 Ibid., 239-257.

12 Ibid., 235ff.

13 Ibid., 378.

14 Ibid., 419.

15 Fenggang Yang, "Religious Diversity among the Chinese in America," in P. G. Min and J. H. Kim, eds., *Religion in Asian America: Building Faith Communities* (Walnut Creek, CA: AltaMira Press, 2002), 73. Timothy Tseng, *Asian American Religious Leadership Today: A Preliminary Inquiry* (Durham, NC: Duke Divinity School, 2004), 8.

16 Yang, "Religious Diversity," 72-73.

Chinese or ABCs) to assimilate into middle-class America without massive racial tensions, like the Civil Rights movement.[17]

Interwoven in this history of Chinese in America, is the history of Chinese Protestant Christianity. Protestant missionaries arrived in China in the early nineteenth century. Of course, it is often difficult to separate their missionary message from the agenda of Western imperialism and expansionism. Nevertheless the missionary zeal of the nineteenth century led to the establishment of the first Chinese Christian Church in the United States. With support from the Presbyterian Board of Foreign Missions, William Speer founded this church in San Francisco, California, in 1853.[18] This church was quickly followed by other denominational works, including Methodist, Baptist, Congregationalist and Episcopalian churches, by 1870, and by "1892 eleven denominations had established ten Chinese churches (including three in Canada), ten Chinese Christian associations, and 271 Chinese Sunday schools and missions in thirty-one states."[19] Such rapid growth is a demonstration of the concentrated mission efforts of the major denominations and the significant acceptance of Christianity within these immigrant communities. While it is important to recognize that many of these early Western missionaries expressed racist and paternalistic attitudes toward the Chinese, in many ways the Chinese American church became a central social institution that provided language classes, social services and a cultural community.[20] These early churches provided a support network and a legitimate "Western American" institution within which to participate in the broader culture.

By the 1930s interest in ministry efforts directed at Chinese Americans began to wane. Mainline denominations were embroiled in their own theological and cultural disputes. The modernist-fundamentalist battles occupied the attention of American Protestantism at large, while the majority of Chinese Protestant churches labored quietly with modest growth.[21] In the aftermath of these struggles, Chinese American churches maintained their associations with mainline denominations, although theologically the majority of these churches were very conservative. During the 1950s the landscape began to change. Second generation Chinese

---

17 See Mia Tuan, *Forever Foreigners or Honorary Whites: The Asian Ethnic Experience Today* (New Brunswick, NJ: Rutgers University Press, 1998) and Frank H. Wu, *Yellow: Race in America Beyond Black and White* (New York: Basic Books, 2002), 39-78.

18 Fenggang Yang, *Chinese Christians in America: Conversion, Assimilation, and Adhesive Identities* (University Park, PA: Penn State Press, 1999), 5.

19 Ibid., 5.

20 Yu, *Thinking Orientals*, 19-30.

21 Yang, "Religious Diversity," 87.

American pastors, with more extensive seminary educations, began to serve and assume influential leadership roles.[22] Many of these pastors began to organize their churches along non-denominational or inter-denominational lines. Likewise they continued to maintain a theological conservativism that situated these churches within the growing American evangelical movement of the twentieth century.[23] The 1960s brought some activism within the mainline denominations, where Chinese American pastors encouraged a greater representation and voice within denominational hierarchy.[24] However, the majority of Chinese churches remained single-ethnic and carried with them an independent attitude with an evangelical conservative theology. Since the 1960s Chinese churches have grown at a steady rate. In 1952 there were sixty-six Chinese Protestant churches in America, and by 2000 there were 819.[25] Most of the churches are located on the East or West Coast, but with growing Chinese American communities in Chicago and cities in the southern United States, like Dallas and Houston, Texas, and Atlanta, Georgia, we can expect to see a growth in churches in other locales as well.[26]

What accounts for this growth in the Chinese American church? Two factors should be mentioned. First, with the continual influx of immigrants from Asia, the Chinese church continues to serve as a social and cultural center that assists many Chinese with their transition to America. It is likely that many of these newer immigrants are not in fact new conversions but established Christians who are part of the global shifts in Christianity.[27] Subsequently they would naturally seek out Chinese-language churches upon settling in America.

The second factor that accounts for the growth of the Chinese American church is the popularity of evangelical university para-church ministries. Groups like InterVarsity Christian Fellowship and Campus Crusade for Christ have seen an

---

22 Ibid., 87.

23 Yang, *Chinese Christians*, 6-7. For a history and assessment of evangelicalism, see George Marsden, *Understanding Fundamentalism and Evangelicalism* (Grand Rapids, MI: Wm. B. Eerdmans Publishing Co., 1991); Mark Noll, *The Scandal of the Evangelical Mind* (Grand Rapids, MI: Wm. B. Eerdmans Publishing Co., 1994); and D. G. Hart, *Deconstruction Evangelicalism: Conservative Protestantism and the Age of Billy Graham* (Grand Rapids, MI: Baker Books, 2004).

24 Tseng, *Asian American: Religious Leadership Today*, 14.

25 Yang, "Religious Diversity," 88.

26 Paul Tokunaga, *Invitation to Lead: Guidance for Emerging Asian American Leaders* (Downers Grove, IL: InterVarsity Press, 2003), 162-163.

27 See Jenkins, *The Next Christendom*, for global shifts. For a useful, but somewhat biased account of the recent history of Christianity in China, see David Aikman, *Jesus in Beijing: How Christianity Is Transforming China and Changing the Global Power Balance* (Washington D.C.: Regnery Publishing, 2003).

astronomical increase in Asian American students, especially Chinese Americans.[28] Rudy Busto writes,

> The perception that Asian American students are currently dispro-portionately involved in InterVarsity and Campus Crusade for Christ appears to be well founded. *Christianity Today* reports that InterVarsity's seventeenth triennial conference on missions, "Urbana '93," noticed a "fundamental change in the makeup of the delegates" with nearly two-fifths of the seventeen thousand or so attendees ethnic minorities. Asian Americans represented more than 25 percent of the conferees.[29]

At the University of California, Berkeley, it is estimated that in the three larg-est Christian fellowships (InterVarsity, Campus Crusade for Christ, and Asian American Christian Fellowship), ninety-eight percent are Asian Americans. Tim Stafford comments, "At Berkeley, California's premier public university, 'evangelical Christian' and 'Asian American' are almost interchangeable descriptions.[30] An im-portant characteristic of these Asian American Christian students is their devotion to an evangelical tradition of Protestantism. Of course, Asian American cultural values which prioritize education have contributed to the increased representation of Asian Americans at major American universities. Likewise some have suggested that these cultural values complement traditional evangelical Protestant values and thus facilitate another form of assimilation.[31] In any case, Chinese students who participate in these college fellowships often maintain ties to the Chinese American churches during and after their university years.

Thus far we have surveyed briefly the intersecting history of Chinese Americans and Chinese American Protestant Christianity. It is a story that needs to be included in American history given its longevity (over 150 years) and significant contributions. But it needs to be told for another reason. The legacy of institutional and socio-cultural racism casts a dark shadow over the history of Asian Americans, including

---

28 In fact, InterVarsity is targeting Asian Americans for leadership positions. See Tokunaga, *Invitation to Lead*, 146. Also see Rebecca Y. Kim, "Negotiation of Ethnic and Religious Boundaries by Asian American Campus Evangelicals," in Tony Carnes and Fenggang Yang (eds.), *Asian American Religious: The Making and Remaking of Borders and Boundaries* (New York: NYU Press, 2004), 141-159.

29 Rudy V. Busto, "The Gospel According to the Model Minority?: Hazarding an Interpretation of Asian American Evangelical College Students," in D. K. Yoo, ed., *New Spiritual Homes*, 174.

30 Tim Stafford, "The Tiger in the Academy: Asian Americans populate America's elite colleges more than ever – and campus ministries even more than that," *Christianity Today* (April 2006): 70.

31 Busto, "The Gospel," 178-180.

Chinese Americans. This can not be ignored, yet the effects of this legacy must be examined and re-assessed in order to identify properly these past degradations and change our attitudes and understanding of Asian American Christians. Such an evaluation will contribute to the necessary historical revision of the history of Christianity in America.

THE PERPETUAL FOREIGNER

Racialization has had two major effects on the perception of Asian Americans, and Chinese Americans in particular. The first effect has been labeled the "perpetual foreigner" perception. The groundbreaking work of the late Edward Said describes the misguided and biased attitudes of the West towards the East and the postulation of an inferior exotic Orientalism against a superior Eurocentric civilized culture.[32] This postulation led to the exercise of Western imperial power in order to dominate the East and subjugated the evaluation of Eastern history and culture to the supposed normative values of the West.[33] Said's observations are consistent with the attitude of American sociologists in the 1950s who were pioneers in the study of race relations in the United States. However, their studies contributed to the "Oriental Problem," as Henry Yu describes,

> Unlike European immigrants who blended into whiteness, Asian Americans, like African Americans, have been both valued and denigrated for what was assumed to be different about them. Always tied to some other place far away, and marked with the desire for and abhorrence of the foreign that suffuses any use of the term "Oriental," Asian Americans still struggle to define themselves as part of the American social body.[34]

Chinese Americans never could be culturally American enough, no matter how fluent they were in the English language or how many generations were born in the United States.

The American church was not immune from the "perpetual foreigner" mentality. In fact many of the sociological case studies from the 1950s that Yu examines were conducted by Western missionaries who were working in Chinese American

32 See Edward Said, *Orientalism* (New York: Vintage Books, 1978).
33 Ibid., 11.
34 Yu, *Thinking Orientals*, 11.

ministries.[35] Likewise the continual presence of a single-ethnic Chinese American church exemplifies the persistence of this "foreigner" mentality. While language issues can be claimed as an important factor for maintaining a single-ethnic church, eventually all immigrants, or their children, will learn English. We have noted already that the trend in Chinese American churches tended towards an independent/non-denominational ecclesiastical polity. Still many Chinese American churches are affiliated with major denominations like the Southern Baptist Convention, United Methodist Church and the Christian and Missionary Alliance.[36] Within these Chinese churches there are fourth and fifth generation ABCs, yet they remain distinct in their denominations, often times still viewed as "other." Mia Tuan comments,

> I am skeptical that within a few generations Asian-Americans would *automatically* be absorbed into the mainstream. Generations of highly acculturated Asian ethnics who speak without an accent have lived in this country, and yet most white Americans have not heard of or ever really seen them. They are America's invisible citizenry, the accountants who do our taxes, engineers who safeguard our infrastructures and pharmacists who fill our prescriptions. Nevertheless, over the years they have continued to be treated and seen as other.[37]

Other "white" ethnic groups within the same denominations are not required to retain such distinctions because they have, what Timothy Tseng calls, "white privilege," the option whether to identify themselves ethnically or not.[38]

Recognizing the "perpetual foreigner" discrimination within American society is important for the wider evangelical church. The latest ministry trend is to establish multicultural or multiethnic churches.[39] But before this trend can be endorsed, it must take into account implications from the past, including the marginalization of Chinese American churches. What are some of these implications? Tseng argues that "racial thinking still colors our society and church, and is wrong. Thus, Asian Pacific American congregations organize along racial lines to testify to the real-

---

35 Ibid.

36 Tseng, *Asian American Religious Leadership Today*, 18, emphasis in the original.

37 Tuan, *Forever Foreigners*, 159.

38 Timothy Tseng, "Asian Pacific American Christianity in a Post-Ethnic Future," *American Baptist Quarterly* XXI:3 (September 2002), 289.

39 See Manuel Ortiz, *One New People: Models for Developing a Multiethnic Church* (Downers Grove, IL: InterVarsity Press, 1996) and Michael Pocock and Joseph Henriques, *Cultural Change & Your Church: Helping Your Church Thrive in a Diverse Society* (Grand Rapids, MI: Baker Books, 2002).

ity of racism."[40] A place for the single-ethnic Chinese American church may still be needed as a witness to the past, while engaging the wider dialogue within the broader evangelical church.

Likewise the definition of multiethnic must be critiqued in order to avoid perpetuating the same white dominant discourse that Said first alerted us to. Ministries with a multiethnic focus are often seen as a noble attempt to unify specific ethnic groups. However, invariably the categories are defined along racial and not ethnic lines. In the major denominations multiethnicity is usually some combination of White and Black, White and Hispanic, or White and Asian (and sometimes Native American). One denomination's position paper on multicultural ministries describes diversity in America in these exact terms.[41] Such distinctions are racial and not ethnic, and the failure to distinguish this reveals the persistence of a paternal and authoritative white position that possesses the power to define others accordingly. If a Chinese American church extended its ministry focus to include other Asian ethnic groups (like Japanese or Korean Americans) that would be technically multiethnic. However, according to the wider and more accepted definition of multiethnicity, adopted by many mainstream evangelical churches, such an effort would not qualify. Dispelling the "perpetual foreigner" myth will help to address remaining vestiges of discrimination that persist in the evangelical church.

THE MODEL MINORITY

Henry Yu writes,

> Asians have been understood in American social thought in two major ways—as a racial "problem" and as a racial "solution." From the time Chinese arrived in the mid-nineteenth century, migrants from Asia were considered a threat to white labor and American society. Categorized as Orientals, these immigrants were demonized as exotic and non-American. From violent lynchings through the internment of Japanese Americans during World War II, Asian Americans were treated as a problem. Since the 1960s, they have seemingly become the opposite, sanctified as the "model minority" solution to racial and economic ills. This new notion about Asians, however, still depends on an exoticization

40 Tseng, "Asian Pacific American Christianity," 291.
41 "Ministering Among the Changing Cultures of North America," *Mission to North America, Presbyterian Church of America* (October 2005): 20-21.

of them as somehow not American, and it traces a theoretical lineage to early sociological studies about the importance of race and culture in the United States.[42]

Co-existing with the "perpetual foreigner" perception of Chinese Americans is the "model minority" conception. Frank Wu describes this in detail,

> "You Asians are all doing well anyway" summarizes the model minority myth. This is the dominant image of Asians in the United States. Ever since immigration reforms in 1965 led to a great influx of Asian peoples, we have enjoyed an excellent reputation. As a group, we are said to be intelligent, gifted in math and science, polite, hard working, family oriented, law abiding and successfully entrepreneurial. We revere our elders and show fidelity to tradition. The nation has become familiar with the turn-of-the-century Horatio Alger tales of "pulling yourself up by your own bootstraps" updated for the new millennium with an "Oriental" face and imbued with Asian values.[43]

The "model minority" has been used to classify Chinese Americans (and other Asian Americans) as the new paragon of American success. Chinese Americans are seen as industrious, hard working and have easily attained the status of upper middle-class without the visceral protests exhibited by other racial groups. Thus, Chinese Americans are considered the model of assimilation for all other non-Asian minorities.

What is presupposed in the myth of the "model minority" is a theory about racial assimilation that adheres to the so-called "melting pot" analogy.[44] America is depicted as a cultural melting pot, where immigrant groups slowly abandon their culture and assimilate into the dominant Western white American culture. Arthur

42 Yu, *Thinking Orientals*, 7.

43 Wu, *Yellow*, 40-41.

44 David Hollinger writes, "Uncertainty about the character of ethno-racial groups and their place in the larger American society was displayed even in constructions of the melting pot. As it was first construed in the early twentieth century, the melting pot—a figure of speech introduced into the American lexicon by Israel Zangwill's 1908 play of the same name—served to transform not only immigrants, but everyone... Yet in Zangwill's time this figure of speech also became associated with an antithetical, conformist impulse to melt down the peculiarities of immigrants in order to pour the resulting liquid into pre-existing molds created in the self-image of the Anglo-Protestants who claimed prior possession of America," Hollinger, *Postethnic America: Beyond Multiculturalism* (New York: Basic Books, 1995, revised 2000), 91-92.

Schlesinger supports this theory and speaks of a past "Anglocentric domination," which employed a process of "ingesting other cultures."[45] Following the melting pot understanding, Chinese Americans are seen as the prime example of an immigrant group that has melted into upper middle-class American life, with significant ease. But the irony is that the melting pot never quite dissolves all the distinctions for Chinese Americans. With China's astounding economic and military growth, America is faced for the first time since the end of the Cold War with a legitimate geo-political rival. This potentially casts a cloud of suspicion over many Chinese Americans who are working in sensitive scientific/engineering fields and defense research. A case in point was the failed prosecution of physicist Wen Ho Lee, a U.S. citizen, who was accused of espionage.[46]

Once again the evangelical church in America is not immune to assumptions drawn from the melting pot paradigm. This is most pronounced in the previous histories written about Asian American Christianity, which followed an assimilationist historiography. The success of mission efforts targeting Asians and the growth of the Chinese American church reinforces the "model minority" perception. Chinese Americans, who joined the church, were viewed as simply assimilating into the established "Christian American commonwealth."[47] Tseng comments,

> Protestants retreated to a more comfortable view that the assimilation (and eventual Christianization) of Asian Americans was a natural and gradual process. By helping to shape the ideology of assimilation, Protestants inadvertently contributed to the merging development of the Asian American "model minority" thesis.[48]

The unique experiences and contributions of Chinese Americans to the growth and development of Christianity in America were completely marginalized. Consequently, in commenting on Chinese and Japanese Americans, Sydney Ahlstrom assumes that "ethnic religious commitments have not figured prominently in their self-consciousness as peoples."[49] Ahlstrom wrote these words in 1972, and this historical interpretation needs to be challenged today.

---

45 Arthur Schlesinger, Jr., "The Return to the Melting Pot," in Ronald Takaki, ed., *From Different Shores: Perspectives on Race and Ethnicity in America*, 2nd ed. (Oxford: Oxford University Press, 1994), 295.
46 Wu, *Yellow*, 175ff.
47 Tseng, "Beyond Orientalism," 68.
48 Ibid., 68.
49 Ahlstrom, *A Religious History*, 1051.

Moreover the "model minority" myth has also influenced some of the theological assessments given by major evangelical theologians. David Wells, of Gordon-Conwell Theological Seminary, recently published the last of a four volume series on American evangelical theology entitled *Above All Earthly Pow'rs: Christ in a Postmodern World*. In this final installment, Wells details the changes in American culture that are dramatically impacting Christianity in America. He masterfully describes how postmodern philosophy, new age spiritualities, consumerism, materialism and aberrant theology are all changing the landscape of Protestant Christianity.[50] But he goes on to add that religious diversity is another powerful force. He writes,

> Through the changed immigration law of 1965, America has become a truly multiethnic society and perhaps the most religiously diverse one in the world. The exotic religions from faraway places that once only filled pages of *National Geographic* may now be next door. Mosques, landmarks that once seemed confined to the Middle East, can now be seen side by side with churches in America, though much of the practice of Islam is also invisible to most people... The arrival of old, non-Christian religions in America and the emergence of more recent spiritualities that are not religious, and often not institutionalized, are a new circumstance.[51]

Wells relates the account of the history of immigration. He argues that prior to 1965 immigration was primarily a European phenomenon. Subsequently, these European immigrants arrived with their various religions: Catholic, Protestant and Jewish. However, over time the "rough edges" became smooth and the "pointed disagreements" were resolved between these three faiths. Their shared core beliefs were emphasized and a unifying "national faith" emerged.[52] This account fits well with the "melting pot" theory, where disparate ethnic groups were formed into a new race, "a people without its own particular ethnic memory, one with no inherited ideas or beliefs, and one in which immigrants were expected to shed the particularities of their past in order to become *Americans*."[53] Prior to 1965, according to

---

50 David Wells, *Above All Earthly Pow'rs: Christ in a Postmodern World* (Grand Rapids, MI: Wm. B. Eerdmans Publishing Co., 2005).
51 Ibid., 5.
52 Ibid., 102.
53 Ibid., 93, emphasis in the original.

this account, America reflected a Western European cultural and Judeo-Christian religious hegemony.

But all of that changed with the abolishment of the National Origins Act of 1924 and the new Immigration and Naturalization Act which significantly raised the immigration quotas for Asian, Middle-Eastern, African and South American countries. Consequently, from 1965 to the present, America has become one of the most ethnically diverse countries in the world. Likewise, Wells comments, "and what we have yet to see is whether the pot will once again melt these immigrants together."[54] As massive immigration from non-European countries continues, likewise, for the first time, new religious traditions were introduced into the wider American culture.[55]

What does this all amount to for the church? Wells writes, "[t]he reality... is that America is the world's most religiously diverse nation now and from a Christian point of view it is as fully a mission field as any to which churches now are sending their missionaries."[56] Gone are any notions of a Christian America; instead the church is faced with the challenges of ethnic and religious diversity alongside of new spiritualities and the postmodern mentality. Clearly, Wells is adding another chapter to the melting pot narrative. In essence he is arguing that the pot has over-flowed and can no longer contain and melt the cultural ingredients. But again in employing this historiography, Wells has marginalized the histories of American minorities, and their contribution to the church in America, prior to the revision of immigration laws in 1965.

Consequently, the model minority depiction is no longer adequate for describing Chinese American Christians.[57] The distinct history and contribution of Chinese American Protestants must be recognized and not relegated to the margins of histori-cal accounts. Of course we must not privilege the Chinese American history, and replace a white dominant discourse with a yellow one, but other minority histories need to be retold as well. The melting pot analogy must be replaced, possibly with a mosaic that reflects all the various cultural and ethnic hues and shapes. Only then can we abandon the previous historiography and begin to write a revised history of Christianity in America.

---

54 Ibid., 97.

55 Ibid., 106.

56 Ibid., 108.

57 Even in the context of corporate business, human resource specialists are recognizing the unique-ness of Asian American employees. See Jane Hyun, *Breaking the Bamboo Ceiling: Career Strategies for Asians: The Essential Guide to Getting In, Moving Up, and Reaching the Top* (New York: HarperBusiness Publishers, 2004).

CONCLUSION: MOVING FORWARD IN THE GLOBAL ERA

Correcting historical fallacies is important, but what does this really amount to for the Protestant church in America? How does the Chinese American church contribute to the ongoing life of the Christian church in America? Perhaps understanding the history and experience of the Chinese American church will help Christians in evaluating and assessing the inevitable global shifts that Christianity is experiencing in the twenty-first century. Philip Jenkins' important work in this area describes the rapid expansion of Christianity on the continents of South America, Africa and Asia.[58] Jenkins writes, "Over the past century... the center of gravity in the Christian world has shifted inexorably southward, to Africa, Asia, and Latin America."[59] Moreover, Jenkins contrasts this rise of Christianity in the southern hemisphere with the decline of Christianity in the West. He states,

> Over the past five centuries or so, the story of Christianity has been inextricably bound up with that of Europe and... North America. Until recently, the overwhelming majority of Christians have lived in White nations, allowing theorists to speak smugly, arrogantly, of "European Christian" civilization... Many of us share the stereotype of Christianity as the religion of the "West" or, to use another popular metaphor, the global North. It is self-evidently the religion of the haves. To adapt the phrase once applied to the increasingly conservative U.S. electorate of the 1970s, the stereotype holds that Christians are un-Black, un-poor, and un-young. If that is true, then the growing secularization of the West can only mean that Christianity is in its dying days.[60]

If Jenkins is correct, then the future of Christianity in America is indeed grim. But immigration from the Southern hemisphere continues. Chinese immigrants continue to arrive and they bring with them a vibrant faith that fuels and sustains the Chinese American church. Fenggang Yang writes, "Third World experiences of the immigrants before coming to America and immigration experiences as racial minorities in the United States have intensified the desire for religious interpreta-

---

58 Philip Jenkins, *The Next Christendom*.
59 Ibid., 2.
60 Ibid., 1, 2.

tions about the meaning of life and world events."[61] Subsequently, because of these experiences, the Chinese American church can be an important instrument in combating the advances of secularism in the West, and help the wider Protestant church in maintaining a witness in America.

Additionally, the Chinese American church can assume a greater role in teaching the Protestant church in America how to better minister in a multicultural context. The Chinese American church has the advantage because Chinese Americans are more aware of wrongly imposing a Western racialized paradigm. Moreover, bicultural existence is a universal fact of life. But where do you begin? Some Chinese American Christians have seized this opportunity by first establishing pan-ethnic ministries which first incorporate other Asian Americans. This is an easier transition since most Asian Americans, regardless of ethnicity, share similar values and experiences. Russell Jeung has provided a helpful study of Asian American pan-ethnic churches in northern California.[62] Jeung writes,

> If Asian American communities invest in the exploration of their heritage, interpret their experiences through scriptures with both the eyes of the privileged and the marginalized, and share their resources and talents in the promotion of justice, then they do have something to offer that is distinct and authentic... As Asian Americans lead Pan-Asian and multiethnic congregations, they want to avoid tokenizing other ethnic groups and [they are] sensitive to patronizing multiculturalism.[63]

Pan-ethnic Asian American churches exemplify an authentic effort for advancing multicultural ministries.

Yet this Asian American emphasis also plays an important role in helping the Protestant American church address issues of reconciliation. In mainstream American churches, racial reconciliation usually refers to the need for black and white reconciliation. However, the Asian American church provides a positive third voice in these racial reconciliation efforts. The 1992 Los Angeles riots were fueled by African American anger and frustration in the wake of the Rodney King incident, where white Los Angeles police officers brutally beat an African American. The rioters burned and looted many local stores, including many Korean American

---

61 Yang, "Religious Diversity," 89.
62 Russell Jeung, *Faithful Generations: Race and New Asian American Churches* (New Brunswick, NJ: Rutgers University Press, 2005).
63 Ibid., 165.

businesses. Yet, in the aftermath of the riots it was the specific partnerships between Korean American and African American churches that encouraged healing in the broken community of South Central Los Angeles. It is significant that the Korean American church played a unique and vital role in bringing racial reconciliation to the city of Los Angeles.

Moreover, while many non-Asian church leaders are often unable to discern ethnic differences between Asians, they do exist; and as a result Asians are not immune from ethnic prejudices. Amongst certain Asian Americans (particularly within the first and second generations) there is still a deep-seated resentment towards the Japanese because of atrocities committed by the Japanese army during World War

II. Likewise there is often a subtle social discrimination against less-educated Asians or those who have immigrated to the United States more recently. Pan-ethnic Asian American ministries provide a unique and almost exclusive context for pursuing reconciliation amongst Asians.[64] Thus, for the church, understanding the past is important for the present, and this is an ongoing project. But, perhaps with greater knowledge and opportunity, Chinese American Christians, as well as other Asian American Christians, will move out from the margins and reflect their uniqueness within American Christianity.

---

64 Reconciliation efforts between Korean and Japanese Americans were part of the 2006 InterVarsity Urbana Missions Conference. See Inguina Shieh, "Japanese and Koreans See Reconciliation," *Urban Today* (Dec. 31, 2006): 14.

.ז.

"If You Want Peace, Work for Justice": Reflections on the Ministry of Reconciliation[1]

MARK R. GORNIK

"The effect of justice will be peace"
Isaiah 32:17 (Jerusalem Bible)

There is an unmistakable order in the words of the prophet Isaiah. In order to have the experience of what the Scriptures call shalom, a foundation of justice must be in place. God intends the world, as Isaiah puts forward here and throughout his oracles, to be a "togetherness" of peace and justice, reconciliation and wholeness. Shalom, which means salvation, health, wholeness, integrity, joy and the complete restoration of what God intended, is the gift of reconciliation. As the saying goes, "If you want peace, work for justice."[2]

If we are going to speak rightly of working for justice and reconciliation, witnesses and exemplars are required. Manuel Ortiz is just such a witness, proclaiming in his life the Spirit who brings goods news to the poor. It is through such a witness, rooted in his experiences within Spirit and Truth, that we might be formed in the ways of Christian discipleship.

Appropriately, this essay is written on the ministry of reconciliation and its relationship to justice. In our world, marked by globally inscribed divisions of

---

1 My thanks to Dr. Susan Baker for her suggestion of this topic and Hansen Law for reading and commenting on this essay.
2 This statement is attributed to Pope Paul VI, but of course has a much wider currency in the Christian community.

persons and communities, the topic is crucial.[3] Paul's enjoining to a ministry of reconciliation in 2 Corinthians 5:17-20 calls for a deep engagement in the brokenness of our world.

The claim I will explore is that justice is among the most prominent themes of reconciliation in Scripture, and crucial for any desire to see healing in our world today. I seek to construct this argument on theological grounds, imagining a form of reconciliation and justice that puts shalom at the center. In Reformed fashion, my argument aims at the underlying structures of our world. But following the pastoral witness of Ortiz, it begins at the grassroots.

JUSTICE AND INCARNATION

Nicholas Wolterstorff, in his highly esteemed discussions on justice, traces his own personal engagement in the topic to hearing the cries of the poor and oppressed. For Wolterstorff, thinking and writing about justice started with hearing the voices of the marginal in South Africa and Palestine. The subject moved a potentially abstract topic of philosophy to a personal encounter. One can hear this story and feel its impact on his writing in his *Until Justice and Peace Embrace*[4] (1983) and more recently *Justice: Rights and Wrongs*[5] (2008).

I cannot offer a complete description of his arguments and emphases, but let me highlight some key elements. Justice, as Wolterstorff offers an account, follows inherent rights grounded in respect for persons. In his narrative of justice, God is central. "Bestowed worth" is the basis for justice, Wolterstorff explains.[6] "Once one has said that God has worth, that that worth grounds God's right to worship and obedience, and that human beings likewise have worth, it proves impossible not to continue in this line of thought and hold that human beings have rights on account of their worth."[7] As the argument flows, it is the image of God in persons that bestows worth that accounts for justice.[8]

Wolterstorff traces inherent rights to both the Old Testament/Hebrew Bible and the New Testament. Here God's concern for justice is linked to God's care for the

---

3 The United Nations Millennium Development Goals, which offer a benchmark, can be found at http://www.un.org/millenniumgoals/.

4 Nicholas Wolterstorff, *Until Justice and Peace Embrace* (Grand Rapids, MI: Wm. B. Eerdmans Publishing Co., 1983).

5 Nicholas Wolterstorff, *Justice: Rights and Wrongs* (Princeton: Princeton University Press, 2008).

6 Ibid., 356-360.

7 Ibid., 95, cf. 130-131.

8 Ibid., 342-361.

widows, orphans, resident aliens, and the poor, those at the bottom of the social hierarchy.[9] In the New Testament, Jesus brings the reign of the justice of God, but does so as he suffers injustice.[10]

The moral vision that Wolterstorff is getting at comes from having first listened to the voices of the oppressed, those who lack justice. I am sure others have similar stories, a personal encounter leading to a new way of seeing and ultimately a change in life course.

Urban ministry is grounded ministry that begins not in power but vulnerability. This is a Pauline vision found in 1 Corinthians 2:1-5 (NRSV),

> When I came to you brothers and sisters I did not come proclaiming the mystery of God to you in lofty words or wisdom. For I decided to know nothing among you except Jesus Christ, and him crucified. And I came to you in weakness and in fear and in much trembling. My speech and my proclamation were not with plausible words of wisdom, but with a demonstration of the Spirit and of power, so that your faith might not rest on human wisdom but on the power of God.

The movement into ministry is not feigned humility, but complete vulnerability. The model is Christological, as Paul explains elsewhere in Philippians 2:1-11.

Ministry begins and ends with people, relationships, and bonding with the community. The knowledge and love of God is expressed in relationship to the neighbor. "'He judged the cause of the poor and needy; then it was well. Is not this what it means to know me?' says the Lord" (Jer. 22:16, NRSV).

Like in the ancient days of the prophets, the city can press justice concerns to the forefront of ministry (Isa. 1:16-17). In the major U.S. cities we encounter the daily impact of racism and urban inequality. There is injustice in the school system, in economic inequality, in lack of access to health care, and in the paucity of decent and affordable housing. The structures of racial and economic exclusion are factors. These are justice issues and pastoral issues of the first order.

Pastoral practice is not rooted in an office or theological texts, but in the streets, in homes, and in public settings. To a degree continually undervalued in many pastoral formation traditions, it is the experience of working in a community that most profoundly shapes ministry. Pain, suffering, and the cries of the oppressed

---

9 Ibid., 75.
10 Ibid., 113.

should give rise to the concerns of justice and shape the pastoral life. Solidarity, not academic achievements, carries importance.

TRUTH AND RECONCILIATION

Out of claims for justice emerge questions of reconciliation. How does the church break cycles of violence, distrust, and division? How is God's concern for right relationships related to the embrace of the cross?

For good reason, many recent approaches to this topic begin by telling the story of the Truth and Reconciliation Commission in South Africa. Chaired by Archbishop Desmond Tutu, the commission looked at human rights abuses during the apartheid era.[11] At the heart of this confrontation with violence and injustice was a theology of reconciliation. As John deGruchy and others point out, reconciliation is about bridge building in pursuit of overcoming conflict; it concerns crossing borders in the work of building a new social order.[12] The process of the commission sought to provide a context for the truth about the past to be told in order to build a future.

While the overall impact of the commission is debated, few argue against its being a unique attempt to bring forth national reconciliation.[13] Still, the legacy of apartheid hangs heavily over South Africa. As Tutu comments, "In South Africa the whole process of reconciliation has been placed in jeopardy by enormous disparities between the rich, mainly the whites, and the poor, mainly the blacks. The huge gap between the haves and have-nots, which was largely created and maintained by racism and apartheid, poses the greatest threat to reconciliation and stability in our country."[14]

God's justice in Christ, as Paul explains in Romans, is crucial for reconciling diverse groups and the church's call to work for justice (12:3-21; 14:1-15:13). Yet it is the "vertical" reconciling work of God that creates such new "horizontal" relationships (1:16-17; 3:1-20).[15] In the biblical story, reconciliation is addressed to relationships between persons and all of creation; it is as expansive as the impact

11 See Desmond Tutu, *No Future without Forgiveness* (New York: Doubleday, 1999) and John Allen, *Rabble-Rouser for Peace: The Authorized Biography of Desmond Tutu* (New York: Free Press, 2006).
12 John W. de Gruchy, *Reconciliation: Restoring Justice* (London: SCM Press, 2002).
13 Charles Villa-Vincencio and Wilhelm Verwoerd, eds., *Looking Back, Reaching Forward: Reflections on the Truth and Reconciliation Commission* (Cape Town: University of Cape Town Press/London: Zed Books, 2000).
14 Tutu, *No Future Without Forgiveness*, 273-274.
15 For a review of recent issues in scholarship, see Luke Timothy Johnson, "Reading Romans," *Christian Century* (January 15, 2008): 32-36.

of sin on our world. Colossians presents a cosmic and social picture of Christ's work (1:15-20). Because of the work of Christ, working for justice—a vision of right social and economic relationships within the creation—is not an optional addition or sometime consequence to proclaiming reconciliation, but stands at its very center.

COMMUNITIES OF RECONCILIATION

As John Howard Yoder reminds us, "Medium and message cannot be divorced."[16] Matters of economics, justice, and social concern are to mark the church because the church is a sign of the kingdom. The church is a new humanity, a model and witness for wider society. Put another way, there is a political dimension to the church.

There is a hunger and thirst for churches that cross barriers of race and class. This can be an important sign of the kingdom. In many ways, it feels like a paradigm shift has taken place over the past three decades, moving away fears of failure to being compelled by theologies of reconciliation. Ortiz is in the vanguard of this movement, and recognizes the nuance of church configurations in his important *One New People: Models for Developing a Multiethnic Church*.[17]

When I think of a community loving its neighbors, when I want to glimpse Christians pursuing justice and reconciliation, I turn to New Song Community Church in the Sandtown neighborhood in Baltimore. When I explain that this was my church and home for many years, you may find reason for my discussion. I acknowledge that this is perhaps true, but my experience is that of a witness.[18]

In 2008, New Song Community Church celebrated its twentieth anniversary. Beginning as a tiny house church, New Song went on to pray into a vision of a new community. The social, spiritual and economic challenges were enormous in a part of Baltimore that provided the setting for *The Wire*. Through the development of a community-based school, jobs and economic development initiative, health center, and housing initiative, New Song shared in the rebuilding of its neighborhood. For example, as a result of New Song's housing initiative, community residents now own some 300 homes. Against the backdrop of exclusion in housing and access

---

16 John Howard Yoder, *Body Politics: Five Practices of the Christian Community Before the Watching World* (Scottdale, PA: Herald Press, 1992), 11.

17 Manuel Ortiz, *One New People: Models for Developing a Multiethnic Church* (Downers Grove, IL: InterVarsity Press, 1996).

18 This is one way I think of my reflections on Sandtown, *To Live in Peace: Biblical Faith and the Changing Inner City* (Grand Rapids, MI: Wm. B. Eerdmans Publishing Co., 2002).

to capital, this is justice. Young people in Sandtown are now going to college, the result of a school focused on developing the potential of its students. Against the backdrop of systemic failure in the educational system, this is justice.

Instead of "programs," these efforts aim at challenging the underlying injustices that have so harmed the community, creating a cycle of hope. To seek the peace of the city requires working for justice, which means changing social structures and overcoming a history of exclusion. I understand this to be part of how New Song performs the ministry of reconciliation.

What remains powerful, as I reflect on Sandtown, is the way in which the church is central yet finds its identity and life within its community. The gospel has the power to save, to heal, and to redeem in the city. It is a witness that goes forth by way of the cross.

Crossing racial and economic lines requires a commitment to a way of life, an intentional way of being church. From the experience of New Song in Sandtown, the idea of an inter-racial or a multi-ethnic church in inner city America must be grounded in a commitment to justice. A commitment to doing justice belongs to a group of practices that include economic sharing, fellowship, community ministry, and leadership development. Prayerful discernment by the body of Christ is a crucial element of putting into practice a local response to injustice.

A theory or theology of justice is important but not sufficient to such a task. Too often in the Reformed tradition, for example, there is a stress on theory but a weak link to practice. The same is true of worship. It is worship that is the "wild space" of God's kingdom and reconciliation. Emmanuel Katongole makes clear the importance of worship for learning reconciliation.[19] But only when a new imagination is focused on rebuilding community will the bodied activity of the church fully reflect the kingdom. Put another way, a commitment to a new identity expressed in worship but not given flesh in working for justice is materially problematic. In the Scriptures, fasting is linked to justice, right worship to care for the poor (Isa. 58:4-9).

For such reasons I think doing justice should be considered a social practice, something that must be learned in a community of grace and discipleship. Ultimately of course, a justice that restores and overcomes conflict is a process and gift, never a completed product.[20]

19 Emmanuel Katongole, "Greeting: Beyond Reconciliation," in Stanley Hauerwas and Samuel Walls, eds., *The Blackwell Companion to Christian Ethics* (Malden: Blackwell, 2004), 68-81.

20 See the reflections of Gladys Ganiel, "Is the Multiracial Congregation an Answer to the Problem of Race? Comparative Perspectives from South Africa and the USA," *Journal of Religion in Africa*

One of the songs we sang as a house church we learned from the Base Ecclesial Communities of Latin America. Looking back, I think its words were formative on the history of the church.

> Sent by the Lord am I
> my hands are ready now
> to help construct a just and peaceful, loving world
>
> The angels cannot change
> a world of hurt and pain
> into a world of love, justice and peace
> The task is ours to do
> Oh help us to obey
> and carry out your will

The difference a small community can make when it seeks to match medium and message together, when it takes seriously accountability before God to do justice, can be significant.

CONCLUSION: IN THE POWER OF THE SPIRIT

I have written of justice and reconciliation. How does this vision become animated in our lives and communities? The primary way, the Gospels direct us, is through the Holy Spirit. In Luke 4:18-19 (NRSV), we read,

> The Spirit of the Lord is upon me because he has anointed me to bring good news to the poor. He has sent me to proclaim release to the captives and recovery of sight to the blind, to let the oppressed go free, to proclaim the year of the Lord's favor.

Jesus' inaugural sermon begins in the power of the Spirit and leads to the announcement of a reign of justice, a time of jubilee where all have what they need.

If you want peace, work for justice, I argued in this essay. To this I have added pray for the Spirit. God's peace is the end of justice, but indeed is something much more comprehensive. Shalom reaches beyond justice to joy, healing, and redemption.

38(3)(2008): 263-283.

God has come in Jesus to renew the world, to make what is broken whole. God is a God of justice, mercy and reconciliation. Taking this message seriously is at the heart of ministry in a global world.[21]

---

21 For a statement on this, see Harvie M. Conn, *Evangelism: Doing Justice and Preaching Grace* (Grand Rapids, MI: Zondervan, 1982).

.8.

The Aftermath of Ethnic Cleansing: How the Church Can Make a Difference

ONDREJ FRANKA

INTRODUCTION TO THE HISTORY OF BALKANS

The Balkans, and the country of Serbia in particular, have a unique history. Being situated on the crossroads of southeast Europe and the bridge to Asia Minor, Serbia has been a constant prey to any invader. The Turks, Austro-Hungarians and Russians in more recent history have all left their marks on the cultural, social, religious and political life of the Balkan people. Successive ethnic and imperial conquests helped to make the Balkans a byword for ethnic hatreds and political intrigue.[1] Furthermore, in more recent history, the word Balkanization has become synonymous with fragmentation.[2] Many other factors during medieval times and later have contributed to the Balkan turbulent history of wars and national hatreds. This, in turn, influenced the development of a reconciliation theology by the church in Serbia. To understand this is to understand the Serbian perception of God, their culture and Christianity.

The goal of this study is not to discuss Serbian culture but rather to disclose the theology of reconciliation as developed in the aftermath of the civil war and ethnic cleansing in Serbia. According to W. A. Dyrness, reconciliation is an issue

---

1 Patrick Johnstone and Jason Mandryk, *Operation World* (Waynesboro: Paternoster, 2001), 682.
2 Carter C. Irving, *A Strategy for Planting a Large Number of Churches in the Urban Los Angeles Area,* (D.Min. diss., Fuller Theological Seminary, 1993), 23.

to be faced by actual believers in concrete situations.[3] Definitely, as we will see, the Slovak evangelical church in Serbia has made a difference by ministering to the refugees in their great physical need. Moreover, our aim is to trace the theology of reconciliation which corresponds to the present historical reality in Serbia. This in turn shall help us in many ways to contribute to the much needed evangelization of the Balkan people.

Short History of the Balkans

The division of the Roman Empire nearly 1,700 years ago created a major cultural and religious fault-line between the Catholic northwest and the Byzantine southeast. Hence, on this small Balkan Peninsula, where the east meets west, it created a unique culture, many times called the "powder keg" of the world. Historically, the Serbian people were Christianized under the Byzantine Church and its two missionaries Cyril and Method.[4] Being basically of pagan origin, these tribes embraced Christianity, but did not altogether leave their pagan practices. The Orthodox Church, being helpless to eradicate these practices, later embraced them under their auspices. This fact alone had a great impact on the perception of God in that setting. This God has little to do with the God of Scriptures. Whether through the prism of superstition or form of mysticism, this God has been far removed from the ordinary people.

On the other hand the Croatian people were Christianized by the Catholic Church. In this setting the theology that was developed stayed truer to the Scriptures. However, the Church's history of trying to proselytize Serbs and Muslims resulted in distrust and nationalistic hatreds.[5] As a result, each country became very defensive of its own religion and was not prepared to change it.[6]

Next, the Balkans were ruled by the Turks for 500 years. That inevitably left a stamp on the lives of the people. The Byzantine mentality, as it is called by some scholars, left its own marks on the mindset of people. Because of this, for instance, one church leader said that Serbia is a nation which is governed by suspicion of everything.[7] Though most of the Balkan Slavic people initially came from the same

---

3 William A. Dyrness, *Learning about Theology from the Third World,* (Grand Rapids: Zondervan, 1990), 24.

4 Ján Hudec, *Pútnici na Úzkej Ceste,* (Ostrava: A-Alef, 1999), 39.

5 Dragan Novaković, *Verske Zajednice na Razmedju Vekova,* (Beograd: Institut za političke studije, 2003), 280-81. Dr. Novaković is presently Secretary to the Minister of Religion in the Serbian government.

6 Ibid., 281.

7 Jasmina Kocjan, "(Političke) zamke prebrojavanja," *Naša Borba,* 3 (April 1998), 4. Interview with Dr. Alexander Birviš, presently the President of the Baptist Union of Serbia.

Slavic tribe,[8] each one of these national groups was Christianized or proselytized to Islam in different ways and times. Furthermore, as seen through the lens of proselytism, the past Turkish presence produced the strange combination of an unlikely quasi ethnic and religious category: the existence of Slavic Muslims in Bosnia. In the meantime, while the Orthodox Church mainly retreated to monasteries, the people were left to the mercy of the Ottoman invaders.

World War I brought an end to the fragmentation of the small Balkan Slavic nations as the new Monarchy of Yugoslavia emerged. However, many even today are saying that this was the artificial creation and utopian dream of the Serbian royal family of Karadjordjević's.[9] With the monarch being Serbian and thus Orthodox in faith, the great fears of Serbian hegemony started to haunt the Balkans. Thus the Kingdom of Serbs, Croats and Slovenes did not last long. Such ethnic and religious diversity just could not exist in one state. World War II brought an end to Monarchy, but another surrogate tyrant came to the scene—communism. After the War ended in 1945, the country was ruled by the communists. Out of the pains of World War II, the communists managed to rally the nations of Yugoslavia under the false pretense of "Brotherhood and Unity." In the meantime, their goal was to eradicate religion and thus create a new national identity—the Yugoslavian. They almost succeeded in this as communism ruled for almost half a century.

The Role of Religion

While religion was suppressed as an enemy during the communist rule, it nevertheless played an important role in the lives of the people. It secretly continued to nurture nationalism thus preserving the national identity of each ethnic group. Hence the nationalistic passions continued to lie dormant under the disguise of national churches. While the communists tried all along to eradicate religion by creating a new national identity, they were actually fanning the old nationalism and worse. Now religion was tied to nationalism as well. It is not that this is something new—strong links between ethnicity and religion have exacerbated tensions in the Balkans for centuries—but communism provided fertile ground to spawn it and bring about the bloodiest war in modern history by the end of the 20th century.

Thus a new concept of religion evolved which viewed each individual as a corporate part of his or her national identity. In Serbia's case it was the Orthodox Serb; in Croatia it was the Catholic Croat; and in Bosnia it was the Bosnian Muslim.

---

8 Laura Silber and Allan Little, *The Death of Yugoslavia,* (London: Penguin Books, 1995). 229.
9 Ibid., xxv.

In reality it is unthinkable for a Serbian to be anything else but Orthodox and the same idea with Croats and Bosnians. Thus new religious-national entities evolved and definitely left their mark on understanding God and Christianity in general among these people.

The Civil War

In such an environment it was just a question of time before nationalistic conflicts erupted. When communism, which kept these forces in control, was gone at the beginning of 1990, the country exploded in civil war. Ironically, while the rest of Europe was uniting into one country, Yugoslavia was fragmenting into six different republics. True to its meaning, balkanization took place. Instead of democracy, the above mentioned factors brought civil war. In many ways it was a religious war between the Serbian Orthodox, the Croatian Catholic and the Bosnian Muslim people, even though all of these people come from the same national roots of the past. Sadly, the civil war brought into focus national hatreds, discrimination, fascism, genocide and war crimes in the name of religion.

Evangelical Christianity

At this point we need to inject the presence of evangelical Christianity in the Balkans which was started by missionaries planting churches mainly in the late 19th century.[10] In our study we are talking about the Slovak evangelical believers in the Vojvodina region of Serbia. Even though we have not said much about them up to now in this essay, they were determined to follow the true God and to live out true Christianity in the midst of Balkan conflict. In spite of changing systems and the wars, they were able to live out their convictions and thus shape their understanding of the theology of reconciliation according to the situation in which they found themselves. This was true even before and during the civil war. Both communism and religious nationalism (the new enemy on the block in Eastern Europe and Serbia) contributed to the development of a theological model that was unique to this troubled region of the world. This study is an attempt to disclose this theology of reconciliation in Serbia and analyze it.

---

10 Hudec, *Pútnici na Úzkej Ceste*, 177-78.

RECONCILIATION AND SELF-IDENTITY

The identity of each national group in the Balkans is an important factor. As disclosed above, due to many invaders whose goal was always to erase the identities of the people, this was something too precious to give up. As this national identity survived over time, it has been tied to religion and thus, in the minds of its people, represents one and the same thing. As said before, this means that in our context to be Serbian is to be Orthodox and nothing else. The same concept of identity applies to the rest of the Balkan people and their respective religions. Thus any attempt to evangelize and minister to these people is perceived as a threat and a danger to their identity. How can this problem of self-identity be overcome?

National Diversity

The problem of identity in national diversity is as ancient as mankind. Even the Jews and Samaritans, being essentially of same nation, had this problem during the time of Jesus. They developed two different religions, two places of worship, and even two concepts of the Messiah. Hence, in John 4, when Jesus approached the Samaritan woman, she disclosed this problem to him. How did Jesus react? He could have easily made himself the Messiah of the Jews or Samaritans only. Can we imagine what consequences that would have had on the nationalistic level? Actually, there was a temptation to do this when the Samaritans asked him to stay with them, but Jesus stayed with them only two days. In those two days they learned more about the Messiah than had the disciples, who were the Jews and close to Jesus. In their words, Samaritans had learned that Jesus is the Savior of the world and not just their own Messiah (John 4:40-42). Jesus belongs to every ethnic group, every person in this world. Nobody can claim exclusive right to him, whether a church or a nation.

In our situation no national identity can claim God exclusively. No wonder the Balkans yielded such bitter ethnic strife. National identity and religion are thus incompatible and cannot be maintained as taught by the Scriptures. These concepts have to be separated, and God is to be worshipped in Spirit and truth in every place, regardless of the territory, culture and nationality (John 4:19-24). This is what the Slovak evangelical believers were modeling and teaching and preaching, and this truth is now finding its way to the hearts of the people in Serbia.

Personal/Corporate Identity

The national churches have developed the concept of corporate identity for their subjects. No matter what activity or church occasion, people are always treated as a corporate body of worshippers. To them the notion of an individual and personal God is foreign. Moreover, they are seen as a homogeneous body which could not experience God individually but only as a nation. When they heard the message of a personal God and were challenged to have a personal relationship with him, that to them meant changing their national identity. Concretely, if the Slovak Baptist would talk to Serbians about Christ and ask them to experience new life in Christ, they would reason, "You are Slovak, so being Baptist is good for you; I am Serb so Orthodox is good for me." This is "I'm okay, you're okay" conventional wisdom.[11] It is evident that their reasoning is something which should not be touched, even with a ten foot pole. How then should the true Christian personal identity be formulated?

Concept of Personal God

One thing we have noticed when dealing with Balkan refugees is that they have never been treated as individuals, especially as it pertains to their religion. Even when talking to them about a personal God, they are always conscious about their priest and church. They have always been mistreated and abused as a group or just because they belonged to a certain ethnic and religious group, and this has added to their apprehension. When we took time and showed concern for their lives on a personal level, their strong feelings about their corporate self-identity started to melt down and change. They were willing to accept the concept of a personal God, and even considered establishing a personal relationship with him. There was nobody and nothing to stop them from tasting how good the Lord is (1 Pet 2:3). This alone shattered their perception of an exclusive God who acts only through the established institution of their national church and its mediator, the priest.

Of course saying this, a great price had to be paid by those people who embraced Christ. To begin with, they were now perceived by others of their kin as betrayers of their nation and religion. Furthermore, they were ostracized from their families and their national identity. This was always the most sensitive subject to confront, as it had severe repercussions on the potential believer. As we have seen, they could be rejected by their own families, perceived as betrayers of their people and finally be totally marginalized from the community. Many times ministering to the refugees

---

11 Aída Besançon Spencer and William D. Spencer, *The Global God* (Grand Rapids, MI: Baker Books, 1998), 84.

we heard another rhyming slogan, "Do not sell your faith for the supper!"[12] The only antidote for this was unconditional love for those individuals who accepted the personal concept of God. They were loved unconditionally because only personal love leads to corporate love of the body of Christ.

MINISTRY OF JUSTICE TO SUFFERING AND OPPRESSED

Communistic Persecution

Communism in Yugoslavia, which was Marshal Tito's own brand, was more relaxed than in other parts of Eastern Europe. Persecution came in the form of discrimination, especially for the leaders of the evangelical church. This was especially true in the lives of those who studied abroad and came back to minister to their own people. They were always under suspicion of being foreign spies and thus the class enemy.

The leaders of evangelical churches developed a mindset of their own in reaction to this discrimination. They knew more about what not to do than what to do for the Kingdom of God and his church. In this sense the survival theology they developed was restrictive in its character. This was especially true in the field of missions and evangelism. Everything was measured in terms of what you cannot do, and even if something was done, one had to really defend it and apologize for doing it. So once communism and discrimination was over, the true church in Serbia found itself in a vacuum, not knowing what to do with its new freedoms. Forty-five years of being told what they could not do caused the church leaders to believe they could do nothing different so they acted accordingly. Ironically, when the younger leaders who were exposed to western democracies introduced an aggressive type of evangelism and started to minister the gospel publicly in new ways, the older leaders were opposed to it. The restrictive approach to ministry led them to conclude that anything new must be wrong. This irony was also witnessed in many other post-communistic countries like the Soviet Union.

Thus a new theology of freedom from oppression and restriction started to be developed. Christians slowly realized that God is not confined to the four walls of the church as the communists would have us believe, but rather is present in civic centers, cultural centers, and public squares. All became our sanctuaries where God

---

12 Marko Lopušina, "Sekte nam otimaju vernike," *Nedeljni Telegraf,* 7 Septembar 2005, 22–23. Interview with S. Vrbovský, the Bishop of Slovak Lutheran Church in Serbia.

could be freely preached and worshiped. The same thing happened to many other ministries, like radio, film, literature and other ways to proclaim the gospel. The God of the oppressed had become a free God to be preached to every creature in every place. This was in many ways a revolutionary approach to theology, but it was slowly embraced by the church. Instead of taking revenge on the communists, like in some of the Eastern European countries, the ministry of justice started to take place. Now, after almost two decades since the fall of communism, this freedom is a greatly appreciated and rewarding concept of evangelism incorporated by evangelical churches. Nevertheless, yet another ingredient was needed for the Slovak evangelicals to wake up to the call of the ministry of reconciliation, especially to the suffering and oppressed. This is to be discussed next.

Civil War

In 1990, just when the people of Yugoslavia thought that they were free from communistic oppression, a new enemy came in the shape of nationalism. For reasons mentioned above, the country became lost in the smoke of civil war. It was in many ways a war of religious-national identities that clung to ancient territorial enclaves. The people of the former Yugoslavia could not handle the break up of their country if it meant losing the homogeneity of its ethnic groups. Since the former country was a mixture of these groups, the slogan, "all Serbs in one country," (or for that matter replace Serbs with any of the other nationalities) became a vital slogan for survival. This led to the ethnic cleansing repudiated by the international community.[13] Suddenly, every group aspired to have its own country, its own independence and its own ethnically pure territory.[14] People were driven from their homes just on the grounds of their nationality.[15] Actually this was nothing new, but now it was publicized by the powerful international news agencies. Exactly what was ethnic cleansing?

Ethnic Cleansing - The term ethnic cleansing actually denotes an action taken by an ethnic-religious group to root out other groups and, therefore, provide a bigger and ethnically pure, homogeneous territory for its endangered national group. In reality the demographical map of Bosnia, where the cleansing mostly took place, looked different in a very short time. People who for decades lived peacefully and had intermarried now had to run for their lives because they belonged to the wrong ethnic group. Perhaps it "just happened" that they found themselves in the wrong

---

13 Silber and Little, *The Death of Yugoslavia,* 269.
14 Ibid., 271.
15 Ibid., 269.

territory and had to go to where their nationality had settled. In turn each ethnic group had to run and move to its own territory, perhaps in other parts of Bosnia. In no time this caused the demographical map of Bosnia to change drastically. Now everybody felt secure in their own enclave. In the process, many mixed marriages suffered, families fell apart, and ancient homes were lost by appropriation of others or by burning, which sealed the final verdict that those who fled could never return. Others who were not as quick to leave or who refused to leave their ancient homes were captured, went through tremendous oppression and mistreatment, and even faced the possibility of being killed. As Slovaks in Serbia, we can say without bias that the genocide was rampant on all sides. Let us be reminded that all of this was done in the name of nationality and religion.

The Refugees - This civil war produced several million displaced people and hundreds of thousands of refugees who poured over the borders on all sides of the conflict area. Taking their meager possessions or nothing at all, they entered neighboring countries with the hope of finding peace from oppression and suffering. Now the question was, who will take care of these refugees? The temptation of the church was to dismiss them as not its problem and thus ignore it. Who helped these poor and oppressed refugees?

To the surprise of many, it was not the government or the nominal traditional churches but evangelicals who embraced these oppressed refugees. They could not help but see the words of Jesus in Matthew 25:40, "Whatever you did for one of the least of these brothers of mine, you did for me." In the Scriptures it is evident that the ministry of Jesus was always directed toward the poor and suffering (cf. Luke 4:18-19). Consequently, the evangelicals obeyed these words and took the refugees under their wings. Besides providing for their basic needs, they also provided for the refugee spiritually. Through the "Tell and Feed" project the refugees could not only hear the Word about God's loving care but also taste how good God is. To them God and his Son Jesus Christ became real and the way to freedom from oppression and sufferings.

Through this ministry to refugees, the theology of liberation from oppression and justice became a reality in the lives of the suffering ones. The true church of Jesus Christ could now show nothing but love, hospitality and concern for the oppressed, just as the author of Hebrews encourages its readers to act toward the suffering (Hebrews 13:1-3). At first reluctantly, but then with great confidence the refugees started to open up and receive this gift of grace. They realized that Christians were not doing this for some selfish gains, but rather there was no other explanation for their love apart from the grace of God. In the turmoil of nationalism, wars, and refugee crises, our people never experienced this. For centuries these people had been abused, manipulated and harassed by despotic governments. Then the humanitarian and personal ministry to them blew their minds.[16] Their question was, why do you help us? The only possible answer was because of the grace and love of God.

The Poor - Finally, there are those who indirectly suffered from the consequences of the war. It was the poor of the land and even those from the "household of faith." The imposed international embargo, sanctions and economic collapse of Serbia brought many down to the level of poverty. People in the cities were suffering the most, because of the scarcity of food. Here again the evangelicals responded by setting up "soup kitchens" where free meals were served anytime to anyone who was in need. The ladies from the local churches flocked to prepare delicious meals and bake cookies for the poor who now became the object of God's loving care. Besides that, medicine, clothes, shoes and even heating wood and coal were collected and shared with both refugees and the suffering of the land. Many foreign Christians and organizations helped as well. Sometimes we felt helpless or overwhelmed by the great need, but the ministry miraculously went on.

Therefore, a theology of doing justice reconciliation began to take form in the hearts of the believers and suffering alike. They were embraced and surrounded with the love of God as shown by God's people. Christians made sure that their "good deeds" would not be interpreted in any way other than that they were due to the grace of God. This was bound to be different from the humanistic approach of the Red Cross and other similar humanitarian agencies. As the refugees were helped, many turned to embrace Christ as their Redeemer from the slavery of sin, abuse and oppression.

From this concept a new theology of justice and righteousness developed in Serbia. The people had been oppressed, mistreated, and abused long enough to realize that something needed to be changed. Evangelical Christians were convinced that "concern for issues of justice must be transformed into convictions of a new heart that the just God alone can give."[17] Only the Judeo-Christian tradition could give hope.[18] Only God could provide through his people this kind of justice. Thank the Lord that the oppressed readily embraced it. The new slogan in Serbia became, "God did his best when man did his worst." It strongly pointed to the dawn of new

---

16 Pavel Hansman, "Preto, lebo sme kresťania," *Hlas Ľudu*, 25 January 1997, 4.

17 Spencer and Spencer, *The Global God*, 81.

18 Ibid., 82.

freedom in Christ, which is being proclaimed and practiced by the various ministries of the true church in Serbia.

The church should embrace all cultures and nationalities alike. "The Great Commission is to be expressed through the testimonies of individuals with many accents and translations saying that their salvation is bought by the One we affectionately call Jesus."[19] It has been a favorable witness of the Slovak evangelicals in Serbia in the midst of civil strife that their congregations are composed of those from all the different national groups. This is in sharp contrast to national churches which are the bulwarks of nationalism. This attitude and practice of evangelicals should be constantly encouraged as it is biblical. The church is an ambassador of Christ appealing on his behalf for people to be reconciled to God (2 Cor. 5:18-20). As Paul argued in this passage, this ministry of reconciliation is to be an important factor in the missionary life of the church. "Paul here uses the word ambassadors to define what it means to live incarnationally."[20] In a practical way, the church needs to practice the principles of grace if a new culture of peace is to be built in Serbia. In Christ, "His purpose was to create in himself one new man out of the two, thus making peace, and in this one body to reconcile both of them to God through the cross, by which he put to death their hostility" (Eph. 2:15-16). This is the clear mandate of the church in Serbia as well.

THEOLOGY OF RECONCILIATION ITSELF

After the decade of civil war in the nineties, the overall feeling by everybody was that it was enough. But will reconciliation ever really come? What needs to be done so that closure and absolution will take root among the ethnic groups in the Balkans? Let us keep in mind that the inherited Balkan mentality is that of suspicion and mistrust. Even church leaders inherited this attitude of mistrust as seen in their feelings toward other denominational leaders. Actually the communists exploited this to bring disunity among the evangelical denominations. This was overturned successfully by the evangelicals through their united humanitarian ministry during the civil war. The Balkan mentality, which suspects everybody of being an enemy, was dispelled, at least in evangelical circles. The question now is, how can my neighbor become my friend?

---

19 Manuel Ortiz, *One New People: Models for Developing a Multiethnic Church* (Downers Grove, IL: InterVarsity Press, 1996), 13.
20 Paul D. Tripp, *Instruments in the Redeemer's Hands* (Phillipsburg, NJ: Presbyterian & Reformed Publishers, 2002), 104.

The Church's Role in National Reconciliation

At the outset of this section, let me point out that the lives of national groups in the former Yugoslavia and now in Serbia are still controlled by the past. In the long haul, there is a whole history of centuries-old conflict behind every event. Even the civil war, for example, was a result of World War II events. "Suddenly they wanted to repay others for their injured sense of national pride during the post World War II years."[21] Some extreme fractions of these nations fought with the Nazis and killed each other in the name of religion. The blame-shifting game[22] continues, but "the question of responsibility and blame... should be allocated to all parties... each side liberally provoked the other."[23] It is evident that absolution for the past was never done, so the conflict still goes on. Ethnic/nationalistic groups never experienced closure from their oppression, and the church did not significantly help in the past.

Of course the evangelical church has an important role to play in national reconciliation. Its incentive for missions should be rooted in the ultimate reconciliation with God through the gospel of Christ. Its strategy should be to mobilize the church and administer God's justice for the sinners and those sinned against.[24] Only God makes man new, tearing down the walls of enmity no matter where or how deeply they are rooted (cf. Eph 2:14). Any strategy void of this element is doomed to fail.

Gospel Brings Together

From the very beginning of the civil war we noticed that when we preached the gospel in the refugee camps, everybody was there and seemingly felt safe. No problem was raised about coming from different religions or ethnic groups, even if there was enmity between the groups. When people embraced Jesus and heard his claims, their need brought them corporately and individually before God and seemed to disarm the enmity.

One vivid and dramatic example of this was when one young Serb from Mostar came to know the Lord through the ministry of the "Jesus" film. His deep hatred was evident. He wanted revenge because his loved ones had suffered in the hands

---

21 Miroslav Volf, "Exclusion and Embrace: Theological Reflections in the Wake of 'Ethnic Cleansing,' " *Journal of Ecumenical Studies* 29, no.2(Spring 1992): 245.

22 Srdjan Vrcan, "A Christian Confession Possessed by Nationalistic Paroxysm: The Case of Serbian Orthodoxy," *Religion* 25(1995): 368.

23 Paul Mojzes, "The reign of 'ethnos': Who's to blame in Yugoslavia?," 998.

24 Harvie M. Conn, *Evangelism: Doing Justice and Preaching Grace* (Phillipsburg, NJ: Presbyterian & Reformed Publishers, 1982), 45.

of other ethnic groups. However, once saved he became a servant and missionary to all people in Bosnia. God made from this enemy his friend and an ambassador of reconciliation to others. This man's suspicion had been dispelled by the church which displayed the love of God through humanitarian efforts. This man had received the will and power to embrace those whom he had formerly hated. It was evident that this will to embrace came from the divine Holy Spirit of embrace, as Volf calls it, stemming from the gospel. "That will then opens the self-enclosed senses of identity, dispels the fear and breaks down the walls of enmity over the people."[25] The often repeated axiom is thus proven—that the gospel makes friends from all nations and among all religions. There is no need to hide or trick people. The justice and glory of God should be the trademark of the church in reconciling the nations to God and to each other.

Reality of Christ and His Grace

The healing power of reconciliation was exhibited in many cases as the church ministered to the people. God freely offers that healing to everyone who comes to him by faith regardless of his ethnic background or religion. God, through his Son Jesus Christ, provides reconciliation just as he promised through the prophet Malachi, "But for you who revere my name, the sun of righteousness will rise with healing in its wings" (Mal. 4:2). This ancient word became a reality in Serbia.

Slovak evangelical Christians, being a minority themselves in Serbia, have strived to present God who in Jesus Christ embraces all people alike. Even though they have to pay a price for this, they uncompromisingly continue. In the process a lot of threats and other kinds of violence are experienced by the local body of believers. This is especially true in the present time. Many times church planters wake up with threatening graffiti all over their houses, broken windows or Molotov cocktails having been thrown into their churches. Consequently, the "speech of hatred" is being stirred up by the national churches,[26] and some of the country's media.[27] Many times evangelicals are treated like criminals. Recently, an evangelical church in Serbia was not recognized as a church by the new Law but was perceived as a sect. This was viewed as the greatest price. Furthermore, evangelicals are accused of being national betrayers by preaching the gospel to all people alike. They are accused of destroying national spirit and identity. Yet they are convinced that there

---

25 Miroslav Volf, "Living with the Other," *Journal of Ecumenical Studies* 39(2002): 8.
26 Marko Lopušina, "Sekte nam otimaju vernike," *Nedeljni Telegraf,* 7 Septembar 2005, 22–23.
27 Appeal in the letter of the Baptist Union of Serbia to Mr. Rasim Ljajić, minister for human rights and religious freedoms of Serbia and Montenegro, Belgrade, February 24, 2004.

is no other way of living out their faith and grace in the body of Christ, the church. Again, according to Hebrews 13:1-3, they keep loving their own, the strangers and the mistreated alike. Only the life of grace and faith in Jesus Christ can do that. Those for whom Christ died cannot live for themselves anymore but must live for others in love. Their lives do not depend on the endorsement of any nationalistic political system, or religious system for that matter. They live out what they believe, the reality of Christ and his grace in their lives. Consequently, a church which is based on something other than love for God and one another will not last long. Only Christ's love can bring national reconciliation to the Balkan people. What were the results of this reality of God's grace and love in the life of the church?

CONSEQUENCES ON THEOLOGY OF MISSIONS

In Serbia the concept of missions and giving for missions has not been adequately taught and preached in the evangelical church. This is because the communists managed to destroy any missionary activity from within the country. As a child I remember the missionary challenge to help the poor in Cameroon, but soon even that activity was shut down by the government. The church's view of missions became restrictive and static. The church became like a flower pot depending on its nutrients from the outside. "Let somebody else do our job" became the mindset of missions. But what really happened next?

God's Providence

When the conflict in the Balkans began, nobody knew how that would affect the church of Jesus Christ in Serbia. For years Christians have prayed, "Lord, send missionaries to Bosnia and to the other least evangelized parts of the country." Now the Lord was bringing them to us in the shape of refugees. All we needed to do was evangelize them, train them and send them back as missionaries to their own people. This is exactly what has happened. Hundreds of converted refugees have become students in the newly established Bible School and have been sent out as church planters as national missionaries to Bosnia, Montenegro and other least evangelized regions of the Balkans.

It would have been easy to blame others and ultimately God for the difficult situation in the country, but instead evangelical believers have seen the opportunities. Instead of disappointments they have seen God's appointments for service. Just like Esther in her own time had seen the providence of God in establishing her position in the kingdom to be used by him, so the believers in Serbia recognized the providence of God in their historical position. They snatched every opportunity to serve their people. Remembering the exodus of 250,000 Serbs from Krajina in 1995 brings many painful memories to all involved in this conflict, but evangelical Christians have realized that if there were not such tragedies, there would be no refugees and, therefore, no new converts from Bosnia who would consequently become missionaries to their own people. God arranged all of this in his providence.

A young Bosnian girl was particularly moving, when she was asked by TEMA, The European Youth Conference in Utrecht, Netherlands, to give her testimony. She movingly said, "If there were no war in the Balkans, I would never have come to know the Lord personally and thus would not be here at this youth conference." The fact that she was a Christian was a witness to the truth that she was thankful to the Lord even for the war as a means of bringing her to a saving knowledge of Christ. Not one eye was dry when she shared the powerful testimony of her own reconciliation with God and with the enemy. God is able to overcome the worst to bring his best in people. One insightful brother said, "Satan has again miscalculated; instead of destroying the people of the Balkans, they came to know even more the true and living God!" This reminds us of Joseph when he was sold into slavery in Egypt. He later met his brothers again and he instructed them with the words, "You intended to harm me, but God intended it for good to accomplish what is now being done, the saving of many lives" (Gen. 50:20). If that is what it takes for Serbians or Bosnians to know God and serve him, let it be so. The covenant keeping God is always true and faithful to his promises.

Opportunities Not Tragedies

Out of these perilous times a new theology of missions has emerged. It is a church planting ministry. While it is true that for some years no gospel preaching churches were planted in the southern parts of Serbia, Montenegro, and Bosnia, Christians now realized that this is their responsibility and privilege to do. Thus, local churches started commissioning and sending out church planters. Through this great step of faith new life was breathed into our neglected theology of missions. Slowly but surely the people in the Balkans are realizing that this is their debt to pay to their own people (Rom. 1:14ff) and nobody will do this for them. They are in the position to do it best as God calls them to the harvest of souls for the Kingdom.

The God of Impossibilities

Missions, that word which was thought to be impossible, is happening as young couples are called and sent out. Mission agencies are being established and the gospel is being preached by all means to every creature in the Balkans. God's words to Jeremiah, "I am the Lord, the God of all mankind. Is anything too hard for me?" (Jer. 32:27) are ringing true. Jeremiah was in a situation that looked hopeless to the people, but God's word of reconciliation was proclaimed just as it is now among the ethnic groups of the Balkans. Many new agencies are being established for the Lord's ministry, and the people are experiencing God's grace and are being brought to the kingdom. Why is this so? Our God of grace and mercy does the impossible when his people trust him.

CONCLUSION

The theology of reconciliation in the context of the Balkans and particularly Serbia is thriving as it is being shaped every day. A church planting movement has been born out of this. The church which emerged out of communism and civil war is now vigorous and uses every opportunity to evangelize the people of the Balkans. Our turbulent history has brought many problems but also opportunities. God has surely not been removed from all of this, but in his providence through it all, he has been shaping his church to do mission. The ministry of reconciliation has been God's instrument in waking up the church, and it has made the difference. The important thing to realize is that in this context God has spoken clearly and acted in a very concrete way. This essay has only been an introduction to the many facets of the theology of reconciliation coming from the context of the Balkans, particularly Serbia, the beloved home country of this author. May this work be a modest step toward formulating a theology of reconciliation which will guide Slovaks, Serbians and many other Slavic evangelical Christians of the Balkans to even greater adventures of faith in our Almighty God.

.9.

Northern Ireland:
A Time for Healing

WILLIAM A. SHAW

A HISTORICAL PERSPECTIVE

The divisions in Northern Ireland, that northeast part of the island of Ireland "partitioned" off in 1920 and that has remained part of the United Kingdom ever since, are often viewed solely in terms of "religion." It is wrongly assumed to be an ongoing "religious war" being waged between Roman Catholics and Protestants still fighting over sixteenth century issues that have long ceased to be relevant to the rest of the world.

> Although religion has a place in the repertoire of conflict in Northern Ireland, it is apparent that, for the majority of participants, the situation is seen to be primarily concerned with matters of politics and nationalism, not religious issues.[1]

While religion was *one* of the contributory factors and *does* stem from the turmoil that enveloped most of Europe in the 1500s, it is too simplistic and misleading to see the violence that erupted in Northern Ireland in 1969 as merely a continuation of

---

1 R. Jenkins, "Northern Ireland: In What Sense "Religions in Conflict?" in Peter Shirlow and Brendan Murtagh, eds., *Belfast: Segregation, Violence and the City* (London: Pluto Press, 2006), 15.

the Elizabethan Wars in Ireland, the 1641 Rising and Cromwell's bloody campaign of terror and suppression.

The root cause of Northern Ireland's troubled past (and uncertain future) may not in fact be *too much* religion but rather *too little*. As a recent report to the United States Institute of Peace[2] appears to suggest and as Jonathan Swift, the Dublin born Anglican cleric and author, once famously observed, "We have just enough religion to make us hate, but not enough to make us love one another."

The churches, as Liechty and Clegg among others point out, did play their part in fomenting sectarianism that continues to blight relationships between Protestants and Roman Catholics to this day as they regard their church—Catholic, Presbyterian and Anglican—as the one true church and are equally intolerant of the others, aligning themselves with political causes and seeking "victory and dominance over the other parties."[3] This struggle for dominance between these three distinct people groups involved what the historian Ernest Gellner calls "the three classic questions of an agrarian society: Who has the land? Who holds the power? How should God be worshipped? Or more succinctly, 'plough, sword and book.'"[4] The desire to dominate, even "eliminate" the other, whether by sheer military might or ruthless terrorism or through conversion or proselytising, runs like a crimson ribbon throughout Ireland's troubled past and, in particular, the northeast part of the island.

The divisions in Ireland, specifically Northern Ireland, have therefore more to do with a spirit of sectarianism, the act of "dividing, demonising and dominating"[5] than purely with the practice of religion, and it is this all-pervasive and cancerous evil that continues to blight the "land of saints and scholars" to this day. Those divisions remain despite the historic agreement between Rev. Dr. Ian Paisley, Fundamentalist leader of the main Protestant/Unionist party, and Gerry Adams, leader of the main Republican/Nationalist party (and Catholic), in March 2007 to form a power-sharing government. As Bill Meulemans, visiting Professor of Political Science at Queen's University Belfast, observes, "Just because both sides are war-weary doesn't mean

---

2 David Smock, "Faith-Based NGOs and International Peacebuilding," *United States Institute of Peace*, Special Report 76 (Oct 22, 2001): 2.

3 Joseph Liechty and Cecelia Clegg, *Moving Beyond Sectarianism: Religion, Conflict and Reconciliation in Northern Ireland* (Dublin: The Columba Press, 2001), 11.

4 Derek Lundy, *Men that God Made Mad: A Journey Through Truth, Myth and Terror in Northern Ireland* (London: Jonathan Cape, 2006), 57.

5 Liechty and Clegg, *Moving Beyond Sectarianism*, 37.

the issues are resolved. There must be a widespread conclusion that the conflict is settled, and that hasn't happened yet."[6]

It was against this background of sectarian hatred, segregation and violence that one faith-based response came into being.

THE 'TROUBLES' AND THE TRUST

The 174 Trust, a "Christian Community Development" organization, was established in the early 1980s thanks to the efforts, faith and vision of a group of concerned Christians that included members of two churches on the lower Antrim Road in North Belfast. Premises were purchased and became a base for a work dedicated to tackling many of the problems confronting the local community and addressing the real needs of those living in a materially and socially disadvantaged area.

In 1995, after much discussion and consultation, the Trust took the bold step of purchasing the church buildings (including the manse, church halls and extensive grounds) formerly occupied by the local Presbyterian congregation. This not only gave evidence of the Trust's vision for and commitment to the area, but also provided a new, centralized base from which to operate its existing programs and then to expand its community-based work in providing leisure and recreational facilities, as well as employment opportunities and, most importantly, maintaining a presence in what had otherwise become a hostile and alien environment for organizations with an evangelical ethos. This development was, in a sense, "the wheel turning full circle" and the Trust "coming home," back to the buildings that had originally given birth to the organization and now renamed the Duncairn Complex.

The congregation of Duncairn Presbyterian Church, founded in 1862, had a proud tradition of compassionate Christian concern, an interest in the "whole person," and its demise was regretted by many in the local community. Due to demographic shifts the exodus of Protestants and corresponding influx of Catholics over successive generations, coupled with a marked decline in church adherence, meant that by the early 1990s the congregation was no longer a viable entity, and it vacated the buildings that had been its home for some 130 years.

The demographic shift that would ultimately close the church doors (for a few years at least) was not a recent phenomenon. It had been apparent since the late 1940s, although "the Troubles" that erupted in 1969 certainly accelerated the

6 Bill Meulemans, *Hope and Hate: Protestants and Catholics in the New Northern Ireland* (Belfast: Queens University of Belfast, 2008), 18.

process and then cemented it. By the mid 1970s the immediate area had become almost entirely Catholic. This example of what Conn and Ortiz refer to as the "tipping theory" continues across an increasing area of North Belfast, and the same authors' comments on the need to challenge Christians about the underlying racism (sectarianism in the Northern Ireland context) and their calling to "promote justice not segregation"[7] is both helpful and appropriate.

It was, in some ways, a response to this situation that the 174 Trust came into being. Although not a "Presbyterian ministry" per se, it was an attempt to maintain some sort of "evangelical witness" in a community where the people, being Catholic, were of a different Christian tradition, and address the phenomenon Conn and Ortiz refer to as "evangelical absenteeism."[8] It was, at the same time, an expression of a desire on the part of the original trustees to make a positive contribution in an area that was suffering, and not just as a result of the ongoing conflict, which was particularly fierce in that area with almost 25% of the "Troubles" related death toll (variously quoted but something in excess of 3630) occurring within a square mile of the Complex.

The model of community work that was adopted by the Trust from its inception was that of "community care," traditionally the way well-intentioned people, whether Christians or statutory agencies, attempted to help "poor people." As one writer observes,

> Community work which is focused on the model of community care attempts to cultivate social networks and voluntary services for, or to be concerned about, the welfare of residents, particularly older people, persons with disabilities, and in many cases children under the age of five.[9]

For more than fifteen years, this was the Trust's modus operandi and the preferred way of tackling the social and welfare needs apparent in the community. Then, after an intensive period of consultation with management, staff, volunteers, users and other community workers, the Trust embarked on a new direction and method of working summarized in a new Mission Statement, "The 174 Trust is committed to

---

7 Harvie M. Conn and Manuel Ortiz, *Urban Ministry: The Kingdom, the City, and the People of God* (Downers Grove, IL: InterVarsity Press, 2001), 300.

8 Ibid., 379.

9 Keith Popple, *Analysing Community Work: Its Theory and Practice* (Buckingham: Open University Press, 1995), 55.

a process of community development based on building relationships with local people, working together to identify and meet local needs."

The decision to embrace the "community development" model was eventually taken after much soul-searching, prayer and discussion, and sometimes even heated debate. Throughout this process, the comments of someone involved with the Trust in its earlier days, Maurice Kinkead, proved particularly helpful.

> Community development is about a process or a way of working... it is about working *with* people to address their needs, rather than simply doing things *for* people... Community development is about enabling and facilitating people and communities to identify and respond to their own needs, providing support and resources where necessary, but in such a way that does not lead to long-term dependency on our input.[10]

As Conn and Ortiz affirm, when we work *with* people in the local community, it begins a process of restoring their dignity and makes reconciliation with God and their environment, as well as their neighbour, more likely. They also comment in this context, "Not only should we look to the community for creativity, we must be willing to let the community control the process."[11]

It became apparent to those involved, especially members of the management committee, that the "community development" approach was the preferred option, prefixed by the term "Christian," denoting as it does the distinctive ethos of the 174 Trust. This new direction and method of working became increasingly important as the Trust began, perhaps for the first time, to really engage with the local community and they, in turn, began to look to the "Duncairn Complex" as a venue for a variety of community activities. In addition, a growing number of groups and individuals made enquiries about the possibility of starting up new projects or relocating established ones at the former church buildings.

Throughout this process the 174 Trust continued to be a source of healing and hope, accepting people for who they were and helping people where they were. In the same way Jesus did not just preach *at* people but got into relationships with them, accepting them for who they were, as they were, and helping them to move on, the Trust not only provided a base for its own programmes but also for a number of autonomous groups catering to some of the most isolated, vulnerable and

---

10 Maurice Kinkead, *Mission and Community Development Resources for Responding to Social Need* (Belfast: Belfast Churches' Urban Development Committee, 1996), 6, emphasis in original.
11 Conn and Ortiz, *Urban Ministry*, 336-7.

marginalized. Fr. Gerry Reynolds from Clonard Monastery has gone on record in commending the work, "The 174 Trust is a centre of faith and wisdom, of welcome and outreach which brings peace to everyone whose life it touches in the streets of North Belfast and well beyond."

With a rapid increase in the number of "stakeholders," most from the immediate area, the community's perception of the Trust, not to mention that of the former church buildings, underwent a marked transformation. Locals had traditionally viewed the Trust as a distinctly Protestant/Unionist organization and, therefore, "alien," whose aim, they thought, was to proselytize which was something to which they were understandably hostile. Slowly but surely they started exhibiting a growing sense of ownership which hopefully resulted in, among other things, more long-term benefits, a noticeable reduction in vandalism to the property as the local Catholic community began to take an active interest and pride in the preservation and upkeep of the former Presbyterian Church.

The Complex emerged as a focal point for people in the area, playing host to drama/sporting/leisure activities and community meetings on diverse topics from the debate on policing, poverty, racism and housing. This gradual change in perception of the Trust and function of the Complex resulted in the organization's being in an unique position to play a part in addressing the deep-rooted problem of separation, suspicion and sectarianism that continues to divide Protestant and Catholic communities in Northern Ireland in general and North Belfast in particular.

Following an upsurge in violence and civil unrest across this part of the city in the early part of the new millennium, this despite the "Peace Process" being endorsed by the vast majority of the population just a few years earlier, the Trust again reassessed its role and renewed its vision. "Building Peace and Promoting Reconciliation" became its stated aim, taking seriously Jesus' call to be peacemakers in a divided society.

Someone familiar with the organisation's work, and a former Moderator of the Presbyterian Church, Rev. Dr. Ken Newell highlights the important contribution the Trust makes when he comments, "The strategic importance of the 174 Trust is that it represents, in a divided and hurting community, a bridge of true friendship and a river of real hope flowing into the lives of many local people."

Catholic and Protestant communities in North Belfast are often separated by the so-called "Peace Walls" or perhaps more accurately, "fractures of fear" erected over the years and extended in length and height to keep the warring factions apart and provide a degree of security to those living on the "interfaces."

The intricate territorial divisions of North Belfast create some of the most complex geographies of division within the city, a reality that has been reflected in the performance of violence... Unlike most parts of the city, North Belfast has a complex series of ever-changing interfaces and spatial juxtapositions, a process of change that I closely linked to the recent reproduction of violence in that part of the city.[12]

The same authors comment that Belfast, and in particular North Belfast, is in reality an "assemblage of 'villages' within which detachment from other places is crucial in terms of identity formation."[13]

Against this background of almost *total* segregation, suspicion and division, frequently erupting in violence, and where there are still, on average, two "sectarian incidents" being reported to the police *every day,* there are few opportunities for contact, dialogue and reconciliation. Every street and building is "owned" by one side or the other and people feel threatened when they move out of their own neighbourhood. The Duncairn Complex is therefore something truly quite unique in that it is an inclusive, neutral, safe and "shared space" used for all sorts of purposes by people of all ages, both Catholic and Protestant, as well as a growing number from minority ethnic communities.

THE PROBLEM WITH RECONCILIATION

As a direct consequence of having previously adopted a community development model, the 174 Trust subsequently committed itself to the work of reconciliation, believing this is not only to be a way of dealing with Northern Ireland's troubled past but also a visible expression of the coming of the kingdom. Reconciliation is one of the three R's of community development, according to John M. Perkins,[14] the "Father of Christian Community Development" and the Trust's raison d'être.

The term itself is somewhat problematic and the concept more than a little ambiguous, even contentious especially among Christians.

In post genocide Rwanda the word was taboo for many years. In Kosovo the very term 'reconciliation' is so charged within the Albanian community that it is simply not used publicly. In some Latin American and

---

12 Shirlow and Murtagh, *Belfast*, 60-61.
13 Ibid., 17.
14 John M. Perkins, *With Justice for All* (Ventura, CA: Regal Books, 1982), 97ff.

Asian countries reconciliation is often considered a codeword for those who wanted nothing to change or is equated with a "forgive-and-forget" policy.[15]

The same publication points out that reconciliation is both a goal *and* a process and "prevents, once and for all, the use of the past as the seed of a new conflict."[16] As a process, too, it can neither be rushed nor short-circuited, however attractive or desirable this might appear.

John Paul Lederach, one of the world's foremost experts on peacebuilding and reconciliation, emphasises that reconciliation is most definitely *not* a case of "forgive and forget" but rather "remember and change."[17]

Another practitioner, Prof. Ed Garcia, who has spent years encouraging popular participation in peace processes around the world, including Northern Ireland, comments that

> Reconciliation is about building a just peace and constructing a society where people are able to work effectively side-by-side in a common quest, though they may differ or disagree in more ways than one. It is the ability to celebrate diversity, and to respect the dignity of difference in building a world that may be imperfect, but fully human.[18]

In 2004, during a session at the Forum on World Evangelization in Thailand, a group of leaders representing the various Christian traditions pledged themselves to cooperate in forming a global Christian network for reconciliation. A subsequent paper helpfully agreed on a definition:

> Reconciliation is God's initiative, seeking "to reconcile to himself all things" through Christ (Col 1:19). Reconciliation is grounded in God restoring the world to God's intentions, the process of restoring the brokenness between people and God, within people, between people, and with God's created earth. Reconciliation between people is a mutual journey, requiring reciprocal participation. It includes a willingness to

---

15 Gráinne Kelly and Brandon Hamber, *Reconciliation: Rhetoric or Relevant?* (Belfast: Democratic Dialogue, 2005), 7.

16 Ibid., 8.

17 John Paul Lederach, *The Moral Imagination: The Art and Soul of Building Peace* (New York: Oxford University Press, Inc., 2005), 152.

18 Kelly and Hamber, *Reconciliation*, 37.

acknowledge wrongs done, extend forgiveness, and make restorative changes that help build trust so that truth and mercy, justice and peace dwell together.[19]

Lederach develops this concept of reconciliation as a journey, not a march but a stroll involving a series of encounters and detours along the way. He adds, "It is both a place we are trying to reach and a journey we take to get there," a "flight away" as well as a "daring trip back."[20] Reconciliation, he maintains, "is a journey toward a place where Truth, Mercy, Justice and Peace meet."[21] It is a journey too, that we, as followers of Jesus, *must* undertake if we are serious about fulfilling the Great Commission (Matt. 25) because again, as Lederach maintains, this journey of "reconciliation *is* the gospel... [it] is the essence of the gospel. It lies at the heart of God's intention for humanity and with humanity."[22]

Michael Hurley, SJ, is helpful in this respect about what he calls the "spirituality of reconciliation," commenting that "reconciliation for me is primarily about persons, people, parties, groups; only secondarily about issues." He goes on to state categorically that the existence of division and alienation, such as we find in Northern Ireland society, is, when assessed by a spirituality of reconciliation, "unacceptable, intolerable, unChristian, evil." In contrast, he maintains that a spirituality of reconciliation emphasizes forgiveness, involves the will to change things for good and recognizes the sacredness of the other.[23]

PART OF THE PROBLEM – BUT CAN THE CHURCH BE PART OF THE SOLUTION?

In the context of Northern Ireland, which can still boast the highest church attendance figures in Western Europe and the largest percentage of born again Christians, the need for Christians, especially "Evangelicals," to commit to the process of reconciliation is viewed with suspicion. It is seen by many as being not just a distraction but actually antithetical to Jesus' call at the climax of the first

---

19 "Reconciliation as the Mission of God: Christian Witness in a World of Destructive Conflicts" (Paper produced by World Vision International Peacebuilding and Reconciliation, 2005), available at www.reconciliationnetwork.com, accessed 7/25/08.

20 John Paul Lederach, *The Journey Toward Reconciliation* (Scottdale, PA: Herald Press, 1999), 23.

21 Ibid., 159.

22 Ibid.

23 Michael Hurley, SJ, *Reconciliation in Religion and Society* (Antrim: Institute of Irish Studies, 1994), 2-3.

gospel account. In reply, Liechty and Clegg would counter that reconciliation should be understood as a "desirable goal" for *all* Christians and one that "will not necessarily diminish difference but will always allow difference to live in harmony and mutual respect..."[24]

John Dunlop, another former Moderator of the Presbyterian Church in Ireland, in his critique of his own denomination but with reference to the wider context within Northern Ireland, came to the conclusion, "Our society is scarred by a divided church. Since the seventeenth century religion has become the key marker in Irish identity."[25]

Given that indictment, contested by some but generally self evident, can the Church, even if it were willing, legitimately exercise a ministry of reconciliation or, because of its role in fomenting division and providing a sub text (*proof* text even) that reinforced sectarianism, has it forfeited the right?

The Catholic theologian Robert J. Schreiter has written extensively on the spirituality and theology of 'reconciliation' and comments pertinently, "Because the church mirrors society, it may find that the lines dividing society run right through the center of the church."[26]

Without wishing to overstate the case, there are certain similarities with the situation that formerly pertained in South Africa. Like the Church in that country, the Church in Northern Ireland (almost universally, with only a few notable exceptions) was guilty, since the formation of the state in 1921 until violence engulfed it in 1969 and even afterwards, of what the Kairos Document (1985) called "Church Theology." The absence of proper biblical exegesis and application allowed our own form of apartheid to take root and, unchallenged, become a way of life in every strata of society, even giving it a legitimacy that prevented this particular sin from being acknowledged, confessed and then repented of. In this way, sectarianism was provided with a cloak of decency by our own "Church Theology" thus ensuring it prospered, perverting and polluting relationships in Northern Ireland both inside and outside of the church. To quote Schreiter again, "The church must stand for truth in its entirety and with all its uncomfortableness if it is to witness to the gospel of Jesus Christ."[27]

---

24 Liechty and Clegg, *Moving Beyond Sectarianism*, 2-3.

25 John Dunlop, *A Precarious Belonging: Presbyterians and the Conflict in Ireland* (Belfast: The Blackstaff Press, 1995), 20.

26 Robert J. Schreiter, *Reconciliation: Mission and Ministry in a Changing Social Order* (Maryknoll, NY: Orbis Books, 1992), 67.

27 Ibid.

As a Christian organisation, with links and access to all the mainstream Protestant denominations and to a lesser extent perhaps the Catholic Church, the 174 Trust, largely through the efforts of its Director, have sought to remind the churches and the Christians who make up the congregations that reconciliation is not an optional extra to the gospel mandate, a fringe activity or hobby that may or, more often, may not be indulged. It is rather, the heart of the gospel and the very reason God is at work in our world (and the countries and communities that make up our world). "As followers of Christ, we are called to align ourselves with this mission and methodology, to embody God's reconciling love and make it present in the world."[28]

As Northern Ireland enters a new era with, for the first time, a power-sharing government representing all sections of society, it is incumbent upon the church—all traditions and denominations—to exercise a prophetic role in not just preaching but also modelling reconciliation.

Throughout the Old Testament God sent preachers, prophets (Heb.1: 1, 2), whose theme was often justice, mercy and truth as they reminded their hearers of Yahweh's demands that the poor be treated with equity and the marginalized to be brought in from the cold, all to no avail. The defining moment in God's mission of reconciliation came when God gave Himself and the Word became flesh (John 1:14), and it is in Jesus surely that we see God's reconciling love most clearly.

Of course any consideration of *why* Jesus became incarnate and *what* He came to accomplish and *how* He went about it calls into question our understanding of that great biblical theme of atonement. Lederach argues that we rob it of some of its richness and depth of meaning if we restrict it to merely seeing it as a sacrifice that satisfies the sinners' debt before a holy God—such a narrow definition also tends to diminish God's mission in the world.

> In the Pauline vision, atonement does simply mean a sacrifice that satisfies an individual debt. There is a greater emphasis on atonement as a personal, social, and political *process* of reconciliation and healing. Holiness is not driven by a concern for boundaries that protect purity. Instead, holiness is carried out through people who embody the reconciling love of God and take up residence in real-life problems and relationships, with all the ambiguities they bring.[29]

---

28 Lederach, *The Journey Toward Reconciliation*, 160.
29 Ibid., 162, emphasis in original.

The resultant reconciliation that takes place when the "dividing wall of hostility" (Eph. 2:13) is demolished is "simultaneously a personal, social and political process" and not "merely an individualistic event." It has to do with groups of people and communities.[30]

God calls the Church to be actively involved in this work, for Christ's followers to give themselves to this ministry of reconciliation (2 Cor. 5:18-20) by being peacemakers and bridge-builders between divided, disillusioned individuals and communities.

Churches must adopt Christ's methodology (as well as his motivation) and move out of their self-imposed ghettos of sectarian isolation and move *towards* one another, giving expression to the Lord's vision for his Church (John 17:21). As we do so we will find ourselves in new relationships with one another, creating an entirely new narrative, one that will be fit for purpose in this post-modern (post-Christian?) era, not just in Northern Ireland but in Western Europe and beyond.

---

30 Ibid., 164.

Section 3:

Church Planting

.10.

The Ends of the Earth
Have Come to New York:
A Church Multiplication Movement
in the NY Metro Area

JOHN A. ALGERA

There is no place in the U.S. that more personifies the effects of globalization than New York City and its metropolitan area. From its beginnings New York was the door through which the immigrant masses flooded into this country, a function it still fulfills. Churches were established by each national group according to the creeds and practices of the churches in their home countries. Now that our shores have been opened to multitudes never before dreamed of, is this still occurring? These new groups are bringing non-Judeo-Christian religions with them, and that alone poses questions. But even for those who are Christian, can we meet their needs? Do they need something else, something new? How do we welcome them into that portion of the kingdom that is present in the New York metro area?

Increasingly denominations are recognizing the lack of their established churches to bring these new brothers and sisters into fellowship. Often their answer to this dilemma is to turn to church planting—establishing new ministries specifically designed to be culturally relevant to the new groups while at the same time remaining true to their individual denominational creeds and commitments. But is this enough?

I firmly believe that we need more than a spattering of churches planted by our existing churches or denominations. What we need is a church planting movement—church plants organically reproducing so that the number of church plants will grow exponentially. Only in this way will we even begin to make headway as we learn new ways to love and serve.

This essay will begin by reviewing what Scripture tells us about church planting. We will then look at an exciting ecumenical church planting endeavor designed to saturate the New York metro area with Christian contextual models of doing church planting. We will conclude with reviewing one denomination—the Christian Reformed Church in North America (CRC), an ethnically Dutch denomination—in more detail as it moves from its own ethnic heritage branching out to enfold many new people groups into its fellowship.

CHURCH MULTIPLICATION IN ACTS AND THE EPISTLES

Jesus' Great Commission of Matthew 28 is often used as the "ought" of doing mission or evangelism. However, neither Jesus' disciples nor the early Christian churches functioned out of an "ought" mentality but rather out of the excitement of living a new life with Christ, having been filled with the Holy Spirit. They had literally discovered a new way to live that was even called "the Way" (Acts 19:9ff). The church was not an established institution as we think of it but was the people of God, the followers of Christ in the midst of the world. Wolfgang Simpson makes a compelling case for a return to house churches in *Houses that Change the World*. The church not only has a message but "is a message."

> The nature of church is not reflected in a constant series of religious meetings led by professional clergy in holy places specially reserved to experience Jesus. Rather, it is the prophetic way followers of Christ live their everyday life in spiritual extended families, as a vivid answer to the questions that society asks, and in the place where it counts most—in their homes.[1]

This is clearly seen in the picture of the New Testament church of Jerusalem in Acts 2:42-47,

---

1 Wolfgang Simpson, *Houses that Change the World* (Emmelsbull, Germany: C & P Publishing, 1999), xv.

They devoted themselves to the apostles' teaching and to the fellowship, to the breaking of bread and to prayer. Everyone was filled with awe, and many wonders and miraculous signs were done by the apostles. All the believers were together and had everything in common. Selling their possessions and goods, they gave to anyone as he had need. Every day they continued to meet together in the temple courts. They broke bread in their homes and ate together with glad and sincere hearts, praising God and enjoying the favor of all the people. And the Lord added to their number daily those who were being saved.

We see that the life of the body of Christ was happening in homes all over Jerusalem. This was church multiplication at its best. The profound result is that there was continued growth both spiritually and numerically. We are also told that as a result of the Pentecostal outpouring of the Holy Spirit in which people from every nation on earth were gathered in Jerusalem, over 3,000 believed. In this first century globalization we can only imagine how many new believers from other nations returned to their own cities, towns and villages and began doing exactly what was happening in Jerusalem.

In Acts 8, the persecution of the church led to a scattering of believers through-out Judea and Samaria. This led to the multiplying of new groups of believers beyond Jerusalem as they "preached the word wherever they went" (Acts 8:4). On a recent visit to pray for and encourage the churches of Sierra Leone, West Africa, I experienced a similar pattern after their horrific civil war. Before the war the Christian Reformed Church had about sixteen "preaching/prayer stations" in the north, mostly among the Koronka people. After the war this number had nearly doubled as a result of the scattering. New churches were the natural result of the movement of Christians.

We see from Acts 9 that such groups were established in the north in Damascus where Saul was headed when he experienced his dramatic encounter with Jesus. About all we are told is that "in Damascus there was a disciple named Ananias," (9:10), and later that "Saul spent several days with the disciples in Damascus" (9:19b). This group of disciples was the church of Damascus. We also see that there were saints in Lydda—30 miles from Jerusalem—and Joppa, and Cornelius became the well known convert of Caesarea. There was a progressive spreading of Christians into the fabric of the Mediterranean world as the natural extension of a real lived-out, life-changing faith. In Acts 11 we are told, "Now those who had been scattered by the persecution in connection with Stephen traveled as far as Phoenicia, Cyprus and Antioch" (11:19). The message was now going beyond the Jewish community to the Gentiles as well. In Antioch the message included Greeks as Christians, "telling them the good news about the Lord Jesus. The Lord's hand was with them and a great number of people believed and turned to the Lord" (11:20-21). Paul was currently living in Tarsus where there was probably another gathering of Christians. For a year Barnabas and Saul met with the church in Antioch and taught "great numbers of people" (11:25). Since they did not have a church building, and since the church—*ekklesia*—was considered the people, we can speculate that this teaching occurred throughout the city of Antioch in many different homes.

It is important to observe that even before Paul and Barnabas went out on their first missionary journey we already could see gatherings of believers multiplying, from the one group of 120 in the upper room of Jerusalem to many groups all over the Mediterranean world and probably as far as Babylon, Cyrene in North Africa, Corinth, and Rome. Just in the first ten chapters of Acts we know for sure that Christians were in at least Jerusalem, Damascus, Samaria, Cyprus, Antioch, Tarsus, and Lydda.

The commissioning of Paul and Barnabas by the church of Antioch was not the result of a humanly devised strategic initiative or long-range plan to reach the world for Christ. Rather, it was the prophetic word that the Holy Spirit gave during a time of fasting and worship. "While they were worshiping the Lord and fasting, the Holy Spirit said, 'Set apart for me Barnabas and Saul for the work to which I have called them'" (Acts 13:2). After another season of fasting and prayer, they laid their hands on them and sent them off. The work of prayer and direction and power of the Holy Spirit are vital to church planting.

Throughout the book of Acts we see not just churches being planted but churches *multiplying* as new believers came to Christ. This is a vital principal of healthy church life that has often been lost today. People are baptized as they respond to the gospel and are made into disciples by being taught to obey everything Jesus commanded them. After the Apostle Paul did initial teaching he would leave a more seasoned leader in charge, as with Titus in Crete. "The reason I left you in Crete was that you might straighten out what was left unfinished and appoint elders in every town, as I directed you" (Titus 1:5). These elders would give leadership to the new group of believers along with the other apostles, prophets, evangelists, pastors and teachers who "prepare God's people for works of service, so that the body of Christ may be built up until we all reach unity in the faith and in the knowledge of the Son of

God and become mature, attaining to the whole measure of the fullness of Christ" (Eph. 4:11-13). This focus of evangelism and discipleship was at the forefront of the mission of the church and led to continual multiplication of new groups of believers. All of these "church plants" were really households of faith meeting in people's homes. This pattern continued and is evidenced by all of the references in Acts and the Epistles to households.

> The meeting places of the Pauline groups, and probably of most other early Christian groups, were private houses. In four places in the Pauline letters specific congregations are designated by the phrase *hē kat' oikon* (+ possessive pronoun) *ekklēsia,* which we may tentatively translate "the assembly at N.'s households"... The number of such household assemblies in each city will have varied from place to place and from time to time, but we may assume that there were ordinarily several in each place. In Corinth, for example, Paul gives special prominence to the household of Stephanas, as we have seen (1 Cor. 1:16; 16:15f.). Acts mentions, besides Aquila and Prisca, who soon moved on, Titius Justius as a host (Acts 18:7), and the conversion of the "whole household of Crispus" (18:8).[2]

The apostle Paul also recognized the strategic importance of the cities and of cultural, political, economic, education and trade trends for the extension of the gospel. Meeks makes a compelling case for this in his classic work, *The First Urban Christians,* cited above. In surveying the places where Paul went on his three missionary journeys, Meeks summarizes,

> In size they range from rather small towns like Philippi, to sprawling cities like Ephesus and Corinth, but they are all cities in terms of government, culture and the perception of their inhabitants. Two, Philippi and Corinth, are Roman colonies, but of very different types, the one primarily an agricultural center, the other a center for crafts and commerce. If we were to be convinced that the Pisidian cities Antioch, Iconium and Lystra were places Paul meant by "Galatia," these would be added to our list of colonies. The dominant language is Greek in all except the two colonies in Greece, Philippi and Corinth, and even in those there was

---

2 Wayne A. Meeks, *The First Urban Christians* (New Haven: Yale University Press, 1983), 75- 76.

a substantial population for whom Greek was the normal language. All except Philippi are centers of trade and even in Philippi there are reasons to think that there were alongside the Italian farmers a good many foreigners who made their living by trade. Every one is well located for access by sea or land or both; even the cities of northern Galatia are connected by good Roman roads and the rest of Asia Minor.[3]

Tim Keller, speaking at the Mission America Coalition National Leadership Forum in New York City, demonstrated that because of globalization our world today, especially the New York metro area, is more like the world of the Apostle Paul than ever before in history. After noting that Christians have, for centuries, returned to the book of Acts to re-learn ministry practice, Dr. Keller outlined four features of ministry strategy in Acts that are crucial for our own world and time. "New Testament ministry," he says, was "church-multiplying, gospel-centered, context-sensitive, city-focused."[4]

This conference provided a great momentum to church planting in the Northeast by clarifying a church multiplication vision that many churches and denominations were already carrying out. Just three years after 9/11, and after ten years of a prayer movement led by Concerts of Prayer Greater New York, this momentum led to the formation of a Church Multiplication Alliance comprising eighteen different Christian denominations in the Metropolitan New York area. What we had been doing individually we are now doing together as brothers and sisters in Christ.

CHURCH MULTIPLICATION ALLIANCE

In February 2004 the first meeting of the Church Multiplication Alliance was held in New York with ten different denominations represented. Dr. Tim Keller presented a paper entitled "A Vision for New York City." This paper offered a compelling challenge to those present that New York City and the New York metro area presented a historic opportunity to affect the world with its "social, family, and cultural capital." Keller passionately argued that this would require a great increase in new believers who are discipled, and that this would require a great increase in the number of gospel-centered churches in New York. One of the initial goals discussed was 1,000 new churches in the next ten years.

---

3 Ibid., 49.
4 Timothy Keller, "Advancing the Gospel into the 21st Century," a series of morning talks on Acts 13-19 at the Mission America Coalition National Leadership Forum in New York City, October 2003.

As mentioned above, currently there are eighteen different denominations committed to this Alliance and the church multiplication efforts in New York City. The purpose of the Alliance is to provide shared vision, partnership, mission and goals in church planting in the New York metro area. The initial goals gathered from each group were to plant 128 churches in 2005, 294 by 2008 and 693 by 2014. This multi-denominational alliance was truly a John 17 movement of the Holy Spirit. All of this was providentially timed to invite Billy Graham to New York in June 2005 for what was then deemed his last crusade. The most recent brochure states the current purpose, "Vision New York believes the Gospel can renew the city and individuals through a movement of city-serving churches. We aspire to see God renew Greater New York through a church planting movement supported by prayer."[5] The ministry board continues to focus on sharing planter-recruiting strategies, models for planting, places of planting and best practices as we multiply churches throughout the New York metro area. We are focusing on three types of churches that include City Center (south of 110th Street, Brooklyn, and Jersey City along the river); Outer Borough and International Ethnic; and Metro New York (Long Island, New York, Connecticut, New Jersey within a 50-mile radius of Times Square).

We are also seeing many churches successfully using multi-site models to multiply rather than beginning new churches. Redeemer Presbyterian Church has been doing this through four worship services at four different locations and different times every Sunday in Manhattan with the same sermon preached at all of them. A church called The Journey in southern Manhattan recently began a satellite site in a Jersey City theater near the Holland Tunnel. On the first Sunday over 150 attended. The Cathedral International of Perth Amboy, pastored by Bishop Donald Hilliard, Jr. is now "One Church in Three Locations." Its ministry includes Cathedral Assembly by the Shore in Asbury Park, and the Cathedral Assembly in the Fields in Plainfield, New Jersey.

In addition to the denominations represented in Vision New York there are many other Christian denominations and non-denominational churches that are planting and multiplying new churches in the New York metro area.

---

5 Vision New York brochure.

CASE STUDY: THE CRC IS CHALLENGED

As one of the denominations included in Vision New York, the CRC has planted thirteen churches, rebirthed two churches, and brought three other ethnic churches into affiliation, all within the New York metro area since 1990. Some of these new churches have indeed reproduced themselves, contributing to the overall church planting movement in and around New York City. This is their story.

For the last 28 years I have served in various pastoral positions at Madison Avenue CRC in Paterson, New Jersey. This church was "planted" in 1910 as a daughter church of what was the Third CRC of Paterson. As the Dutch immigrant population of the city was growing, new CRC churches were started to gather them in. This was the mode of "church multiplication" for the CRC in the Northeast for its first 100 years, 1856-1956. Generally new CRC churches were started when there were enough Christian Reformed people in a given area to organize and support a pastor. These churches were usually more congregationally focused than community focused.

In 1955 we see a radical change from this pattern when Manhattan CRC was started by Rev. Eugene Callender, the first African American minister ordained in the CRC. The Back to God Hour first hired Rev. Callender to follow up on African American listener contacts in Harlem. Then Christian Reformed Home Missions hired him to do evangelism and discipleship with a view to planting a new church.

A similar work began in the late 1950s in Jamaica, Queens, with new Chinese immigrants pastored by Rev. Paul Szto. Queens CRC was organized in 1960. During the 1970s the Eastern Home Mission Board was one of the first "Classical Home Missions Committees" to hire a fulltime "Home Missionary." The role of this position was to help the CRC churches of the Northeast carry out the Great Commission. The leadership of this position and of Christian Reformed Home Missions led to the beginning of several new churches on the east coast. However, this was still along the same pattern of gathering together people who were already Christian Reformed. Church planting was more of a gathering of the saints—CRC ones at that—than a calling of the sinners. As a student at Calvin Theological Seminary in the 1970s I did not have even one class on church planting or multiplication! Although we studied the mission of the church and the *missio Dei*, doing that by planting new churches was hardly even thought of. According to the Heidelberg Catechism, the marks of a true church were the proper administration of the sacraments and of discipline. Some were beginning to realize that the mission of the church might also be one of its marks, but seeing that mission as the multiplication of churches was overlooked.

Since that time, there has been a great awakening in the CRC and in the body of Christ in general as to the biblical foundations of church planting as a mark of the early church. Christian Reformed Home Missions has given tremendous leadership over the last twenty years in teaching, training, assessing, equipping parent churches, casting vision, and helping to finance church plants. Calvin Theological Seminary now offers a Master of Arts in Church Planting and has a student-run "church planting club." As much as we believe that a biblical church must include worship, discipleship, fellowship, ministry and mission, so too we are now seeing that a biblical church must multiply.

During the early 1980s a friend of mine who pastored a Free Methodist church in Clifton, New Jersey, embraced the vision of church multiplication as a means to global evangelism. He saw that within the New York metro area new immigrant groups held great potential to reach the world with the gospel. Pastor Dwight Gregory planted one of the first Japanese churches in Ft. Lee, New Jersey, targeting Japanese families who were here in the U.S. on business. Most of these businessmen were relatively low on the corporate ladder, and as they moved up they would return to Japan. Reaching Japan with the gospel through Ft. Lee, New Jersey, was a new strategy for me and many others. We no longer needed to choose between "home" and "foreign" missions but, due to globalization, we could do them both together. Our World Mission and Home Mission missionaries needed to talk to each other locally and globally. This is what has been called the new *Glocal* mission, including both global and local. This is exactly the condition of the world at the time of the growth of the New Testament church in the Roman Empire. For all of the years that the CRC had been in the New York metro area, we had never realized the strategic location in which God had placed us.

THE CRC RESPONDS

The first Christian Reformed church to grasp the biblical principles and *"glocal"* opportunities of mission was *El Buen Pastor* (The Good Shepherd) in Prospect Park, New Jersey. Some visitors to this, the only Spanish-speaking CRC in the metro area, were coming from Union City and Jersey City along the Hudson River, ten miles distant. Edwin R. Arevalo, an elder at *El Buen Pastor,* started conducting Bible studies and doing evangelism in Jersey City. In 1990 he began leading a worshipping group of mostly newer Latin American immigrants in the building of Summit Avenue Baptist Church in downtown Jersey City, near Journal Square. Church planting and multiplication was so foreign to the CRC North Jersey community at this time that this effort was actually looked on with suspicion and skepticism as a splinter group. Nevertheless *Jersey City Misión* grew and flourished under the leadership of Pastor Arevalo. He was ordained as an "evangelist" in the CRC and launched an evangelist training program (*Adalente*) to equip new Spanish-speaking leaders to be ordained as evangelists for the purpose of multiplying more churches that would reach the growing Latino immigrant populations in the New York metro area. He continued to pastor his church and, after training another evangelist, birthed a new church in Bayonne, New Jersey, and another one later on in a village in Honduras from where many of his members had come. Pastor Arevalo went home to be with the Lord in 2001 after a long battle with cancer but his vision continued on.

In 1992 the CRC of the New York metro area began an intentional urban church planting movement. After years of suburban retreat, the local classical ministry arm of the CRC, the Eastern Home Mission Board, adopted a vision and strategy for urban ministry. The urban populations of Bergen, Passaic, Union, Essex, and Hudson counties had swelled with new immigrants during the 1970s and 1980s, providing opportunities to reach all the nations with the gospel. "The ends of the earth have come to New Jersey," was our cry. However, as noted above, the CRC had been retreating from the urban areas. CRC churches had closed or moved away from Hoboken, Englewood, Passaic, Lodi, and Paterson, all in New Jersey. Eastern Christian School Association, heavily supported by the CRC, had also closed schools in Paterson, Passaic, and Prospect Park, New Jersey. The new strategy called for an end to this retreat from the city. It recommended evaluating the remaining urban churches with a view to stabilizing, expanding, discontinuing or relocating. It also recognized that the two churches in transitioning communities, Unity CRC (Prospect Park) and First CRC (Haledon) must adapt their ministries or they, too, would die. Second, the strategy recommended the planting of six new urban congregations before the year 2000. In a slide and video presentation prepared for Classis Hudson and Hackensack the conclusion states,

> Now is the time to reverse this retreat; now is the time to plant new
> urban churches... Now is the time as the nations are coming to the city...
> to plant self-supporting churches that will continue to multiply new

churches.... The time has come for Classes Hudson and Hackensack to adopt this strategy and to implement it.[6]

The two Classes adopted the proposed vision, strategy and goals. This was also a time when Christian Reformed Home Missions was pushing church multiplication as an evangelism strategy. Many times it was repeated at board meetings and in publications that the average established church added only one new convert a year for every 100 members while a new church plant tended to add ten new converts for every 100 members. This difference arose from the missional emphasis of the church.

In a recent church redevelopment project in which our congregation participated, consultants Ken Priddy and Patrick Bragg, Jr., described the lifecycle of the church in terms of incline, recline and decline. Incline is the point of beginning where every new church plant starts and is future oriented, vision driven, and community focused. Recline can be described as present oriented, program driven, and congregation focused. Decline is described as past oriented, structure driven, and core focused. They document that 80 percent of the established churches in the United States are at some stage of decline leading to nearly 9,000 churches a year closing in the U.S.[7]

These realities were being experienced by the CRC through a series of mergers and closures of many of its churches in the metro area. Christian Reformed Home Missions was busy trying to provide consultation to form healthy churches as well as support for church planting.

As we have seen, the CRC church multiplication effort in northern New Jersey began with the natural birth of congregation from *El Buen Pastor* as *Jersey City Misión* in 1990. The next plant from this adopted strategy came in 1993 with a new Latino plant designed to reach the growing immigrant population in the Passaic/Clifton area. This church, called "*Gozo, Paz, Amor*" (Joy, Peace, Love) moved through several locations with little growth and finally needed to discontinue. The next church plant came out of one of the larger suburban churches that was conflicted over worship style and ministry focus. Rev. Howard Vugteveen led a group out of Faith Community CRC to form a Willow Creek-style seeker church called "New Life Ministries." In 1996 Pastors Trevor and Linda Rubingh moved east to plant what was envisioned as a "multi-racial English-speaking congregation" in Jersey City. The

---

6 "A Strategy for Urban Ministry in the 1990's," produced by the Urban Committee of the Eastern Home Mission Board.

7 Dr. Kenneth E. Priddy with J. Patrick, *Project 6:15: A Two-Year Commitment to Church Redevelopment* (Richmond, VA: United Front Ministries, 2003), 6.

location was strategic because of the racial diversity of Jersey City and in locating it near *Jersey City Misión*. A year later Trevor met a Christian Reformed pastor from the Philippines who was planting a church in Jersey City. Rev. Albert Sideco, a recent Filipino immigrant to the United States, was simply living out the New Testament model of church multiplication by evangelizing and discipling people who spoke his language in Jersey City. This led to a closer relationship and the birth of Filipino CRC. Today there are over 30,000 Filipinos in Jersey City, and this congregation that began in 1998 is a thriving community of believers that includes many other nationalities. These three Jersey City congregations all ended up using the Summit Avenue Baptist Church building, and in 2000, *Jersey City Misión* purchased the building from the Baptist church. We have discovered that there is great value in clustering churches together to build synergy and momentum in ministry as well as to provide encouragement for one another.

A growing number of Korean immigrants to northern New Jersey led to planting the first Korean CRC church in the area in 1997 under the leadership of Rev. Sung Ho Chung. After worshipping in the afternoon in several different CRC churches, they were finally able to purchase the building of a CRC church in Clifton that was closing after years of decline. Since this time there has been a growing number of Korean churches developed through new plants and affiliations. Two New York City affiliations in 2002 were with Rev. Chang-Guk Byun of East West Church in Flushing, Queens, and Rev. Hong–Suk Kim of New Life community in Staten Island. In 2003 Rev. Kook-Sung Kim moved from Boynton Beach, Florida, to northern New Jersey in response to the Lord's call to plant a church there. He believed he could reach the westward migration of Koreans in Bergen County by using the facilities of Cedar Hill CRC in Wyckoff. However, after several years of struggling he strategically moved his location east to reach more recent Korean immigrants in the Englewood/Palisades Park area along the Hudson River. In 2004, Rev. In Chul Choeh affiliated his emerging congregation in Livingston, New Jersey, with the CRC. In 2005 the first second generation Asian-American congregation was planted under the leadership of Rev. Jae Park. Rev. Park had come to the CRC from a large Korean church outside of Philadelphia after over ten years of ministry to the English-speaking youth there. He was passionately disturbed about the number of Korean young people leaving the Korean-speaking churches. This "silent exodus" was the focus of Grace Community Chapel's being strategically planted in New Brunswick. This church is attracting second generation Asian students from both Rutgers and Princeton Universities as well as graduates and young adults who are now established in their careers. Although it is primarily Korean, it also includes Japanese and Chinese members. This has been one of the fastest-growing church plants we have had and launched a satellite site in Cherry Hill after two years. This past year we have also launched another Korean-speaking church plant in Edison, New Jersey, pastored by Rev. Eunboem Kim. Many of the Korean church plants and affiliations have come from the natural immigration patterns of Korean pastors into the New York metro area.

There has also been a continued response to the growing Latino population in the New York metro area. *Jersey City Misión* daughtered a Spanish-speaking congregation in the neighboring town of Bayonne in 1998. *El Regalo de Dios* (The Gift of God) began under the leadership of Roberto Calix, an immigrant from Honduras, who had completed his studies in the Evangelist Training Program and was ordained as an evangelist in the CRC. After seven years this church was unable to be self-sufficient and returned back to the mother church. Pastor Ricardo Orellana of the *El Buen Pastor* church became a church planting leader in advocating for the Hispanic community and envisioning the planting of new churches. He continued to find and disciple new leaders and prepare them in ministry. Although *"Gozo, Paz, Amor* CRC" in Passaic/Clifton had closed, there was still an evident need for a new church in this area. Marco Avila had been discipled by Pastor Edwin Arevalo of *Jersey City Misión*. Having graduated from Reformed Bible College (now Kuyper College) and Calvin Theological Seminary, he returned to New Jersey in 2000 to plant a new Spanish-speaking congregation in Passaic. *Nuevo Horizons* has grown well and is currently one of the strongest Latino CRC churches in the area and has officially "organized." In 2003 another new Latino church, *Gracia de Queens*, was planted in Jackson Heights, Queens, by a recent Peruvian immigrant, Arturo Olguin. As a pastor with the gift of evangelism, Arturo naturally witnessed and led people to Christ and began discipling them. This was followed by Madison Avenue CRC's daughtering a Latino congregation in 2004. Paterson is a city that has nearly 75,000 Latino residents, and the neighborhood around Madison Avenue is over 55% Latino. A multi-racial congregation of mostly African-Americans and Anglos, the church had worked for five years on a Spanish-language ministry and worship service as one united church. In doing an extensive evaluation of this effort in 2002, it was determined that there was little ownership of the ministry by the Spanish-speaking members of Madison Avenue. A new strategy was developed to actually daughter off the church while it continued to use the same facilities. For a limited time, the mother church would provide finances, facilities and infrastructure to help the plant grow, as well as seek a full-time evangelist to lead the congregation. This church is now known as *Jesús te Llama* (Jesus Calls Me) and is led by a recent immigrant from Chile, Guillermo Godoy, who was ordained as an evangelist. Every one of these ethnic church plants happened as a result of globalization and gifted pastors and leaders from around the world immigrating to the United States.

In addition to these church plants we have also experienced two "church rebirths." In the years before 1995, Flanders Valley CRC in Flanders, New Jersey, had been struggling to survive. In an intentional process the church made a decision to die and rise again. A core group with a vision of a new evangelistic outreaching church committed itself to being part of a new work of the Spirit. Pastor Paul Ingeneri was called to give leadership to this core group and in 1997 they were reborn as Crossroads Community Church. This was one of the first "rebirths" in the CRC and has proved to be an effective model of ending years of decline and lack of mission and attachment to tradition and beginning a restoration of the mission of the church. A similar process occurred in 2000 with First CRC in Haledon, New Jersey. This was the oldest CRC church on the east coast with over 100 years of history. It had declined to barely fifty people who were unable to find a pastor. The church voted to "rebirth" and forty people signed a covenant to be part of it. Those who did not want to sign the covenant were graciously assisted in finding another church to which they could commit their lives. Rev. Andy Sytsma was called as pastor and for six months discipled the core group in basic spiritual formation. To keep the group from falling back into the past, he strategically kept them from worshipping in the sanctuary for six months while they formed their new vision, mission, and strategy. Bridgeway Community Church had its first worship service on Palm Sunday, 2001, and has now grown to be a healthy multi-racial congregation of about 200.

As a result of our partnership with the Church Multiplication Alliance and Redeemer Church Planting Center in 2007 we began two new plants in Manhattan. Rev. Steve Wolma and Rev. Ben Spalink planted City Fellowship Church targeting urban professionals around Ground Zero. This area of lower Manhattan is one of the most influential places in the world and one of the most unchurched in the United States. Uptown in East Harlem, Rev. Johnny Acevedo, a native New Yorker is planting a "Spanglish" church targeting second generation Latinos.

As mentioned before, many other denominations are attempting to reach the new multitudes entering the New York metro area through establishing new church plants designed around the needs and worship styles of each new group. This rendition of the CRC's entering this globalized milieu with new mission eyes is only meant to be an example—not a perfect example, but an example nonetheless—of how God is beginning an organic church movement in this most globalized area of the U.S.

CONCLUSION

In conclusion, Jesus said, "I will build my church, and the gates of Hades will not overcome it" (Matt. 16:18). We have been seeing the fulfillment of Jesus' promise in the New York metro area with new churches being born as the nations of the world move to New York. We are in a time of human history that is strategic for reaching the most influential city in the world with the gospel. Those moving to New York today are more open to the gospel and spiritual things than the longer established European immigrants of a generation ago. These new immigrants will also become the power brokers of New York in the next twenty years. We have an opportunity as never before to bring about personal renewal as well as cultural renewal that can influence New York and thereby the world. To God be the glory.

.11.

Repentance and Bonding Dynamics Within Cross-Cultural Church Planting Teams

KYUBOEM LEE

With globalization's rise come new opportunities and new challenges for the Church and her mission. As the great urban centers that the Church seeks to reach grow more multiethnic, more multinational, and more interconnected with the other great urban centers of the world, the potential to reach the nations with the gospel dramatically increases. The challenge for the Church increases in equal measure, however. When it is said that a local church can reach a number of unreached people groups with a travel of only a few miles (if that) in the same city, instead of having to travel halfway around the world, it begs the question, "Great, but how?"

The answer to that question is multifaceted and too broad to cover in this essay (much of this book seeks to provide other perspectives to that answer), but for the sake of focusing our discussion I will try to offer only a small slice here. For the sake of focus, too, we will assume a few things and leave the theoretical support of those assumptions to other pages.

One assumption we will make is that church planting is the strategy of choice. There is a great need for many kinds of new wineskins in order for there to be adequate responses to the multiplying of new realities in the mission field, that is, our cities. Older churches have a much harder time responding quickly. Therefore, new churches that will approach ministry with new strategies will need to be deployed and planted in our cities to meet the new challenges of globalization.

The second assumption that we will make is that these church planting efforts will best be led by a team. The church planting team is like the seed of a church—within it is a micro-community of faith that is covenanted together to care for each other and to be on mission together. Without this community, missionary work becomes nearly impossible to sustain over the long haul. And without this community, the gospel is not truly incarnated, for the gospel operates visibly and tangibly in relationships. It also follows on the biblical precedents of Jesus' sending out his disciples in pairs on their short-term mission trips, and of Paul and his co-laboring companions traveling together on their missionary journeys.

Our third assumption is that these church planting efforts will be cross-cultural in nature because the new urban realities make crossing cultures an imperative for gospel mission, resulting in multiethnic communities of faith. Our increasingly multiethnic society makes multiethnic churches not only possible but necessary. And true peace among the nations living together in our cities can only be mediated by multiethnic churches that have found reconciliation through the power of Christ. This is also the eschatological vision that all history is marching towards: "the New Jerusalem, a place of multicultural cohabitation."[1] Moreover, to continue the imagery of the church planting team as the seed, the seed itself should carry the multiethnicity in it and be made up of ethnically diverse disciples, reconciled to God and to each other, serving together.

Building on these assumptions, the purpose of this essay will be to outline the human personal factors involved in the formation of cross-cultural urban church planting teams. Other factors include providential factors (church planting is not only a human work—indeed, though essential to the work, the human factor is nevertheless secondary—instead, it is God's work, first and foremost, from beginning to end), contextual factors, ecclesial factors, educational/institutional factors, and denominational factors.[2] We cannot give adequate treatment of them all here; for the sake of focusing our discussion, we will concentrate on the personal factors of church planting team development in this essay, specifically, the dynamics that involve bonding and repentance.

Before we delve into our discussion proper, a quick note. Much of what follows has been forged out of reflection on my personal experiences while church planting

---

1 Vinoth Ramachandra, *Faiths in Conflict?: Christian Integrity in a Multicultural World* (Downers Grove, IL: InterVarsity Press, 1999), 130.

2 I have engaged in a more in-depth discussion of these factors in my doctoral dissertation, *A Manual for Developing a Healthy Multiethnic Leadership Team for Urban Church Planting* (D.Min. diss., Westminster Theological Seminary, 2006), chapters 5 and 6.

in the Germantown neighborhood of Philadelphia, and therefore aspects of my thoughts may not fit into a given ministry setting exactly the way I have expressed them. These are not intended to be hard and fast rules. There is a lot of freedom in the actual application. Also, I must state at the outset that much of what follows owes its genesis to my own past failures in ministry partnerships. Hopefully, you can learn from my mistakes and be forewarned of what not to do and where not to step. I do not speak as a stellar model to follow or an expert in the field—far from it. Instead, I offer these thoughts as a small part of an ongoing conversation that will prayerfully help us all grow as more Christ-like practitioners of the gospel ministry.

BONDING WITH THE MISSION COMMUNITY

Much of a church planting team's development has to do with the bonding process. Bonding takes place at several levels—not the least of which is the bonding that needs to happen with the target community. The potential members of a team have a responsibility to actively engage the mission context. Some mission agencies require that new arrivals in foreign mission fields only make contact with the nationals initially, intentionally excluding themselves from contacts with other expatriates, and keeping themselves largely within contexts that require the usage of the national language.[3] While urban mission usually means traversing less cultural distance (M-2) than foreign mission (M-3) because new language acquisition may not be necessary and because home culture is still easily accessible, it is nevertheless a cross-cultural journey if the leadership candidate is not indigenous, and the leader must deal with culture shock. In fact, "M-2 cultural moves produce as much culture shock as M-3 moves" and will need just as much preparation.[4]

Roembke's recommendation for M-3 missionaries dealing with culture shock is a deliberate immersion into the mission culture on arrival, starting as quickly as possible the process of forging friendships with the nationals and learning to enjoy activities with the nationals. While this evokes fear and is a hard road to travel initially, the missionary and the work will benefit tremendously in the long run; after all, the missionary is there to serve the nationals, not themselves.

---

3 Lianne Roembke, *Building Credible Multicultural Teams* (Pasadena: William Carey Library, 2000), 67.

4 Ibid., 76. Ralph D. Winter's categories for evangelism includes M-1, evangelism within the same culture; M-2, evangelism to a sister language/culture; and M-3, evangelism to a completely foreign language/culture. See footnote in Roembke, *Building Credible Multicultural* Teams, 76.

The same principle applies to urban missionaries. Many find it extremely difficult to live out incarnation when they cannot let go of former support structures. In fact, the M-2 transition could be a more difficult challenge than M-3 because many missionaries are still in close physical proximity to family, friends, and other support structures that they had relied on before moving in. It poses no great difficulty or expense to hop into a car and drive half an hour to search out the familiar friendships in the more comfortable settings of the suburbs, for example. This can result in a "social commute" and a mission compound mentality that can go undercover without being identified and challenged. It is wasteful and counterproductive to spend much time, effort and resources to construct living situations that house workers from similar cultural backgrounds together. Instead of an incarnational ministry (in which the Christians act as salt that permeates into the nitty-gritty's of the community), this creates a "ghetto within a ghetto"—an inward, isolated group that serves its own needs and not the world's.

However, an effective leader will seek to embrace the mission context as his/her own, and work hard to bond with it, cutting out old support networks as necessary from daily life and replacing them with local resources, and persevere through the initial discomfort of settling into a new culture. David Robinson sees as crucial to mission the process of renting the right place in which to live and the process of finding local help with the repairs on the residence and local resources for groceries and other necessities for livelihood.[5] In such ways, the missionary must do all he/she can to forge interdependent relationships with the community. This, of course, does not mean that one is required to disown families and cut off all contact with old friends; however, it does mean that you intentionally and deliberately focus your affections onto the mission field and work to find your main source of day-to-day companionship and community there. Otherwise, bonding will not take place.

Related matters are decisions concerning lifestyle. For instance, how incarnational are you willing to be with your recreation? In other words, is there a readiness for taking on as one's own leisure activities that will include the community? Are you fostering a genuine enjoyment of the community, instead of only seeing it as a "client" of your service?

When Mark Gornik first moved into the Sandtown neighborhood of Baltimore to plant a church, he spent a lot of time on the neighborhood basketball courts, building relationships through down times spent with the community. The initial group went off on many trips together, played together, and relaxed together. My

---

5 David Robinson, "Bangkok Church Planting: How to Get Started," *Urban Mission* (June 1997): 51.

wife and I chose to join the neighborhood YMCA not only for the sake of convenience but also to spend our leisure time in the community. This is not only so that the leader will gain networking contacts and evangelize (although certainly these opportunities will arise in leisure times and ought to be pursued for the sake of the kingdom). More importantly, it helps the leader in the immersion process. Compartmentalization is the evil that we fight against—whenever the community and the personal areas of life are compartmentalized from one another incarnation gets stunted or it simply doesn't take.

Again, this doesn't mean that every aspect of life must be conducted within the community or that there are no personal or family times. A regular rhythm of Sabbath-taking is crucial—for obedience's sake and for the sake of ministry longevity. But must Sabbath mean taking a break from the mission context as well? "Escapes" that become routine rather than occasional means that an emotional distance grows between the leader and the context. The leader must be aware of this pull away from the community that exists simply because he/she is coming in from the outside, and take the necessary precautions to nurture and develop incarnation, and not hurt it or kill it off through lifestyle choices.

A critical element of incarnational ministry is relocation. Because an M-2 move might not entail a great travel in physical distance, it becomes possible to commute into the community every day while living in locations outside the mission context, but not without great detriment to the bonding process and to the credibility of the ministry. In my opinion, to proclaim the incarnation of Christ while maintaining physical and social distance from the community hollows out the message, especially if one is living in a wealthy, comfortable area and working in a poor, struggling neighborhood. But relocation opens up many doors that remain closed to commuters—it means that the community's problems become your problems and its joys become your joys. If the schools in the community are in trouble, then it will also affect your children's education. When your children form friendships with children of your neighbors, you have a personal stake in serving the neighborhood children and working for more godly values among them. By thus taking on the issues of the mission context as your own, you can become a bona fide member of the community, and thus qualified as a leader in the community.

Relocation is a necessity even for those from the same cultural background, in my opinion. When I have spoken with African-American Christians on the subject of incarnational ministry, I have often heard them say, "I come from a neighborhood like that; I lived the life of that neighborhood. I don't need to live there for me to identify with the people and them with me." However, once you "made it out" of a poor neighborhood, your life's trajectory is set, and it is not in the direction of the community. Your affections and vision for life are not centered around the life of the mission community anymore but on the other life that you are seeking to further in another community. Increasingly, there will be a separation between the concerns of the community and your personal concerns, and your credibility as a servant of the community will be eroded.

So, as a leadership candidate prays and moves towards the mission work, it would do well for all involved in the decision to ask, "Is bonding with the mission context taking place?" "Has the candidate truly counted the cost in terms of relationships and work needed for bonding?" "What are the plans for immersion into the new context, and what are the plans for dealing with culture shock?" and "What are the steps being taken for relocation, if it has not yet taken place?"

REPENTANCE

Probably the single most important character trait of a cross-cultural leader is repentance. When entering into a cross-cultural ministry context, it is paramount that the Christian worker does so as a student who humbly learns from the community. Many have entered as a teacher or expert—some even entering as judges—with disastrous results. Triumphalism among Christian missionaries has caused much harm to the missionary enterprise in the past, and continues to wreak havoc to the witness.

In cross-cultural situations, racism is an ever-present danger that can corrupt the witness and undermine the credibility of the gospel. The danger is ever-present because ethnocentrism is a natural part of the fallen condition of humanity. The Reformed doctrine of radical depravity of the human heart should alert us to this situation. Therefore we should start by assuming that we walk into a cross-cultural situation with a sinful propensity for setting up superior-inferior relationships based on ethnicity and class. It is naïve—and in cross-cultural ministry situations, dangerous—to believe that one has "arrived" in this area, even if there have been many years of exposure to the context.

I am a Korean by ethnicity and lived in Kenya from the age of ten until eighteen, but I would be deceiving myself if I claimed that this cured me of racism against those of African descent. Years later, when I served with an African-American church, I would have to come to terms with my naïveté in assuming that, back in

Africa, I had worked through all the issues that I needed to concerning race. As I write, I know I still have a long road ahead of me in this matter. To believe otherwise is dangerous. To believe that one is free of ethnic or racial prejudices is to be blind to one's own innate racism. The only way to effectively counteract this danger is a commitment to a lifelong pilgrimage of repentance.

Mark Gornik's journey in incarnational ministry prominently involved the "strategy" of repentance. Recasting John Perkins's strategy of Christian community development, summarized by the "three R's" (relocation, reconciliation and redistribution), Gornik and his colleague Allan Tibbels added a fourth "R" that precedes the others—repentance. It was a move that they deemed highly necessary because they were raised in white suburbia, and were moving into a black inner-city neighborhood. Unless repentance permeates the process of incarnational leadership, triumphalism poisons the whole enterprise.

This repentance involves not only a confession of individual sins, but also the confession of corporate sins and how the individual benefits from it, knowingly or unknowingly. Moreover, repentance involves embracing a new way of living over against the status quo that perpetuates the corporate sin—discipleship after the pattern of the Lord who took on downward social mobility and "moved into the neighborhood" with us (John 1:14 The Message). Gornik writes:

> Repentance means owning sin as an offense against God but also moving forward to a new way of obedience, a turning in a different direction... Allan and I took the pain, brokenness, and racial oppression of Sandtown [the Baltimore neighborhood that Gornik served in] to be our responsibility, the history of Baltimore to be our common history and therefore a call to *metanoia* [repentance]... African-American neighborhoods that should be flourishing before God lay torn, and we were part of the break... We might not have been there when Sandtown was constructed, but we were living off the world of myths and privileges on which Sandtown was created, and therefore subject to its judgment. We knew we were complicit in the racism and systemic injustice that led to the brokenness of the neighborhood... If we really grasped our faith, we had no choice but to repent.[6]

---

6 Mark R. Gornik, *To Live in Peace: Biblical Faith and the Changing Inner City* (Grand Rapids, MI: Wm. B. Eerdmans Publishing Co., 2002), 169-170.

Repentance is also necessary when seeking to minister across class lines. We have focused mainly on the dynamics in crossing ethnic and cultural lines, but repentance should also be the motivation for the "privileged" seeking to serve the "underprivileged" of the same ethnicity, because triumphalism is still a great danger. Consider the following scenario.

An African-American church is made up of middle-class members who commute into the church's impoverished neighborhood for church functions and occasionally hold events that reach out to the poor residents, whether it be clothing giveaways or Thanksgiving turkey dinner baskets. In and of themselves, there is nothing wrong with these events. But is there a relationship of interdependence between the church and the community, or is the help always going down a one-way street? If the latter is the case, these efforts end up being paternalistic. The relationship has become one between a superior and an inferior, one between the haves and the have-nots. The two groups are not on equal terms—interdependent neighbors who give and receive help from each other—but on unequal terms—superiors who have the upper hand that condescend to hand out the occasional help to their inferiors. Those receiving the help are thus robbed of their dignity. There is a reason why those who receive such help do not join in the life of the church.

This scenario is one that has been repeated throughout the history of the church—one need only turn to James 2:1-7 for proof—and the church today is by no means free of this. It is important for minority churches that have historically experienced oppression to have a special sensitivity to this dynamic—if they don't, who will? Historically oppressed churches have not gained an automatic immunity from the charge of perpetuating oppression in other ways. Classism is a sin that persists, and it must be identified, owned, and repented of within the church. It is no less harmful than racism.

Unless humility, teachability and intentional positioning of oneself as a student who learns from the community and who seeks to foster interdependent relationships with the community are there, incarnational ministry will be shipwrecked.

HEALTHY RELATIONSHIPS WITHIN THE TEAM

Not only is there a necessity for bonding with the mission context, there must also be bonding within the team. In my case, this bonding has primarily been with the core-group of our church plant. Paul always traveled with his partners in ministry, and these colleagues provided him with the friendships that he could count on through thick and thin, not only with the ministry labor. Although Paul was the dominant figure of his group of traveling missionaries, he never placed himself "over" them; instead, he came "alongside" them, relating to them as his partners rather than as a teacher with his followers.[7] That provides the model for us today: no leader is in a position of being the only head over the other leaders in the church—that position is already occupied by Christ. Instead, he/she is a part of a community of servant leaders with whom he/she shares a common life and a common work.

Of course, this does not negate the need for differentiation in the roles nor of the need for special offices within the church (pastors/elders and deacons)—indeed, to uphold these offices is to submit to the design of the biblical paradigm of church.[8] However, just as Paul observes that the sinful flesh perverts the law of God, so the sinful flesh that glories in power perverts the good and godly nature of church offices. We must be careful not to allow struggles for personal power and control to dominate the team dynamics. Quibbling over relative statuses and positions is a waste of energy and time that a mission team cannot afford. Besides, the beginning stage of a church will set precedents that will impact the life of the church for many, many years to come. The precedents set at this time ought to be one of mutual submission under the one headship of Christ, and not that of rivalries or divisions.

The scenario that I have seen in too many church leadership structures is this: the pastor is the one with all the responsibilities and decision-making power, while the elders or the board abdicate their leadership responsibilities. The pastor is the professional who has been hired to do the work of the ministry, while the other Christians can go about their living without being burdened with matters of the kingdom. The pastor can then either become the star of the ministry (thus creating many pitfalls of pride and abuse of power) or alone and isolated (leaving the pastor struggling to do the "thankless" work of the ministry by himself, divorced from his community of faith, looking for spiritual sustenance from other quarters).

---

7 Robert Banks, *Reenvisioning Theological Education* (Grand Rapids, MI: Wm. B. Eerdmans Publishing Co., 1999), 116.

8 When thinking of the church planting team, not all in the team need to be a pastor or an ordained office-holder or a full-time worker. Certainly, there are many successful models of church planting partnerships between two or more full-time pastors and their spouses. However, one ought not to feel tied down to a certain model. The key here is flexibility and adaptability, according to the situation and the context, as well as the individuals that God has called together for the work. "Lay leaders" are invaluable partners and in many instances act as fully bona fide team members in the church planting effort.

Much of this has to do with a consumer mentality that pervades the modern church life.[9] Instead of a missionary community of faith that we commit ourselves to, many Christians come to a church in order to get their personal needs met. So there are baby boomer churches that are marketed to baby boomer Christians raising their families in the suburbs and Generation X churches for young artists that seek to tap into this niche market. Churches supply the demands of the consumer Christians. C. John Miller critiques this approach to church life:

> The local church was intended by Jesus to be a gathering of people full of faith—strong in their confidence in him—not a gathering of religious folk who desperately need reassurance. Perhaps seeking personal comfort is not wrong in itself. But it is desperately wrong when it becomes the primary reason for the existence of the local church. When that happens, the local church is not living fellowship at all, but a retreat center where anxious people draw resources that enable them merely to *cope* with the pains of life. The church then becomes a religious cushion.[10]

As a result, I have listened to many pastors and their spouses who seek to serve their congregations but at the same time hold a deep-seated suspicion of them. They will solve the people's problems, but they won't ever depend on them for theirs. And no wonder—many congregants and elders will scrutinize and criticize, without serving alongside the pastors. And the atmosphere of mistrust, envy, bitterness and un-grace grows in the church. Thus many pastors feel very much alone in their struggles to serve, with no one from their churches that are coming alongside them in the struggle, and must seek out other pastors for emotional and spiritual support. The inner struggle goes on behind the façade that spiritual leaders take great pains and spend enormous efforts to put up. This disclosure comes from many Presbyterian pastors, whose form of church government is theoretically all about teamwork among a plurality of elders or presbyters. This atmosphere of disunity and isolation of leaders is one of the biggest internal problems facing church leadership today, hemorrhaging the life out of the church.

I believe that a different structure of ministry is needed; one that more closely resembles that of Paul and his colleagues—and it is a missional structure. Paul and company came together for a common mission of bringing the gospel to unbelievers,

---

9 Harvie M. Conn and Manuel Ortiz, *Urban Ministry: The Kingdom, the City and the People of God* (Downers Grove: InterVarsity Press, 2001), 463.

10 Calvin Miller, *Leadership* (Colorado Springs: NavPress, 1986), 20 as quoted in Ibid., 455-456.

a wide-open, outward orientation directed towards the world filled with "outsiders." In contrast, many churches today stay together to maintain what they have inside the small realm of the church, for inward concerns, to attract people who are already believers and "insiders." Paul and company shared all things in common as they lived together and worked together; many Christians lead their private, separate lives that hardly intersect apart from church business meetings and worship services. Paul and company saw each other as colleagues and co-laborers, no matter that Paul was the most recognizable and authoritative figure, and therefore were flexible in the methods they used to carry out the work. Many churches have a rigid, hierarchical view of the positions, treat full-time staff workers differently than they do a regular member—one is in the professional class, the other is not—and moreover place the senior pastor on the pedestal. But Paul and company was not Paul with a group of underlings that supported him and his work. Paul and company was a group that was on mission together, each a servant of the gospel in his/her own right. Paul treats his coworkers as such in his epistles.

What is needed is a renewed sense of community and mission among the leadership and by extension the local church as a whole—a new Reformation in ecclesiology, if you will. A church planting endeavor creates wonderful opportunities for forming such a leadership structure and atmosphere. There can be an invigorating creative energy that will experiment with new methods and arrangements, a clean slate without the burden of obsolete or irrelevant traditions (while guarding the traditions that *are* valuable to the mission context), and a willingness to adapt for the sake of reaching the mission context—to become all things to all men in order that some may be saved (1 Cor. 9:19-23). The best setting for encouraging church renewal is in the midst of doing mission.

But what about decision-making? Will a sense of collegiality not bring about confusion and chaos? If disagreements should arise about decisions, is it not more expedient to have a hierarchical approach—in which a single leader takes charge and leads at the front?

There are no easy answers to this, but I believe some more foundational matters need to be addressed first. A critical element to a team approach is a basic agreement and ownership by all involved on the direction or philosophy of ministry—on the vision of where the ministry is going. Without this basic commonality, teamwork will be but a dream and the group will stay mired in conflict unless there is a change of personnel or a submission of one party to another for the sake of mission.

To ensure that this basic agreement is there, the initial selection process is very important. Initially, every candidate ought to be very frank and up-front about the direction he/she is headed in, about any fears and reservations, and about potential pitfalls and obstacles. There must be a candid assessment of all that has been expressed. Is this a team that really can work together? Does this team truly have a common goal? Does this person belong on this team, or will he/she be better off somewhere else, doing something else, with some other people? Very often, these direction issues do not surface until some steps down the road; therefore it is important to hold these discussions regularly, especially in the beginning. It is also difficult to communicate these personal goals and visions in a meeting that lasts only an hour or two—several prayer retreats may be necessary. What I have found is that the process of envisioning is just as important as (if not more important than) that the visions match up. The process is how relationships get built up, how people truly get to know each other, and build trust and rapport.

When we speak of vision, let us also remember that vision isn't just about ministry philosophy. Vision must include vision for relationships and for community. Therefore, the team must intentionally and continually speak about personal relationships within the team. This is an area that church planters may not give enough attention to and this can hurt them later on. Our church planting efforts encountered the most problems precisely in this area, and Roembke speaks from her long experience when she alerts would-be cross-cultural team members of the great need to tend to this area.[11] As much as possible, the team will initially need to work at communicating the expectations they bring to the common life of the team. The team will need to resolve to address as quickly as possible what they see as red flags in each other—a series of unaddressed red flags over a period of time results in complications to the relationships and can jeopardize the mission.

For instance, red flags that may come up are spouses that do not feel a sense of calling to the ministry or are experiencing growing doubts about the ministry; team members that do not feel they can participate in the decisions important to the group because of exceptional circumstances (such as relocation posing difficulties to the family); personal decisions that will end up affecting the ministry but are made individualistically and independently of the team; and unresolved personal conflicts. When these difficulties come up, the team must honestly ask, "Is this something we all can live with, or is it better for us not to be yoked together for this venture?"

---

11 See Introduction to Roembke, *Credible Multicultural Teams*, 1-12.

If it becomes clear that there ought to be a parting of ways, the team must work hard to communicate that it supports the person and loves the person, and that a parting of ways in no way speaks less of the person who will not set off together. In fact, owning up to the incompatibility and walking away at the outset speaks volumes about the person's maturity and integrity. But accepting and loving a person does not equal having to partner on a common mission endeavor. It would be much better for all concerned and for the work if the decision to part ways comes at the outset rather than in the middle of the journey, when unresolved disagreements can boil over into outright conflicts that have the potential to destroy the work altogether.

When all on the team are agreed about the direction in which it is traveling, decision-making as a team ought to become easier. Assurance that the team is going in the same direction takes the tension out of a decision-making process, and an easy-going collegiality becomes possible.

Another ingredient for a healthy team dynamic is mutual accountability. Collegiality does not mean individualism. Biblical love does not say, "Live and let live." Rather, biblical love means a much more intimate submission to one another. Good leadership presupposes good follower-ship. "[No] one will be a good leader unless he has first been a good follower."[12] This principle does not cease to be true once a person has been put into a position of leadership. He/she continues to be accountable, not only to a usually distant and uninvolved presbytery or denominational office, but also, and especially, to the group that is closest to him/her on a daily basis. Therefore, a teammate should be given the right to ask about matters that might in other circles be considered private or invasive. A senior pastor or team leader should not take offense when an elder questions him on matters of spiritual accountability. This cannot be something that can be demanded as a matter of law, nor should this right be abused or carried out without sensitivity or care, but there ought to be a level of mutual trust, confidence and grace among the team. There ought to be a regular time of confessing our faults to one another and offering Christ's forgiveness to one another, as well as regularly reporting on each one's tasks and interceding for each one's work. By thus actively fostering vulnerability and confession within this group, the group members learn to trust one another and depend on each other, and models the grace that is found in the church of Jesus Christ to those to whom they minister. If there is no sign of growth in this area, or if there are signs of mistrust and competition growing among the team, the team

---

12 Günter Krallmann, *Mentoring for Mission: A Handbook on Leadership Principles Exemplified by Jesus Christ* (Waynesboro, GA: Authentic Media, 2002), 111.

should take a step back and reexamine the basics of their relationship to the Lord and the calling he has given them.

Another ingredient that significantly contributes to like-mindedness is the growth in friendships and a sense of community within the team. Do the teammates spend their down times together? Are they finding common interests and coming up with new things everyone can enjoy doing together? There must be intentionality in this area, otherwise after meetings and services people will go their separate ways and find their emotional support in other places. This does not mean that one is not allowed to have other friends or that one must have best friends within the team—it does mean that one gives up old community in order to gain a new community of the kingdom.

The pursuit of friendship, of course, "is more difficult than we imagine."[13] Friendships do not occur simply because we group together a bunch of people, even when everyone is likeminded, pursuing the same mission in the same way. Nor do friendships occur simply because a group chooses to live together, as in a community housing situation. It is true that one will more likely get closer to others in community housing situations, but I have seen instances when such closeness resulted not in love and mutual care but in hostility and conflict. Friendships take work to develop—and that means intentionality. Friendships also take commitment to one another over a long period of time—and that means covenantal relationships. Friendships also mean there will be offenses and abrasions due to personality differences as well as disappointments due to unmet expectations—and that means there needs to be grace and readiness to forgive. In a church planting situation, being pressed to address many needs and to perform many tasks, it is easy to slip into a business mode in which people see each other solely as coworkers and not as friends committed to one another in the Lord. This is true especially when the leadership team is made up of personalities that tend toward introversion and maintaining a distance. The relational distances need to be overcome and the team must work hard at fostering interdependence. After all, it is in this core group that the new community of the kingdom must be modeled to the rest of the church and to the community at large. As Jesus prayed for his believers, "[May] all of them be one, Father, just as you are in me and I am in you. May they also be in us so that the world may believe that you sent me" (John 17:21).

At various points of the team's development, the team must ask themselves: Are we depending on one another for all things? Are we sharing our struggles with one

---

13 Conn and Ortiz, *Urban Ministry,* 441.

another? Are we finding deep friendships within the church body? Are we growing in our love for each other? Because simply asking these questions can lead to in-grownness, the team will also do well to ask: Is our love for each other attractive to the community? Is our love for each other inviting others to also partake of it? Is our love for each other equipping each one to go outward in mission? The area of friendships among the team is crucial, since (as is widely known) conflict among missionaries is the number one cause of missionary work breaking down. Working hard at caring for each other, loving one another, overcoming our independence and insularity, and sharing all things in common is key to the ministry's longevity. (We are so far talking about covenanting, of course. The team covenants to walk together on the same road of life, following a common calling from the Lord. The team covenants to submit to one another, care for one another physically, spiritually, and emotionally. The team covenants to love one another and enjoy each other. The leadership team forms a bond that is ratified by their promise to the Lord and to each other.)[14]

A very important area that is related and that every team must give attention to, of course, is conflict resolution. One cannot overemphasize the importance of this area. No matter how well each knew each other prior to embarking on mission together, and no matter how much of close relationship each enjoyed beforehand, you can be sure that once the mission gets underway, conflicts will arise. The team will need to commit ahead of time to the biblical means and motivations of conflict resolution. Each member will need to resolve ahead of time in his/her heart and with one another how they will conduct themselves when differences, disagreements, hurt feelings, and offenses arise in the relationships. The team needs to outline the biblical teachings and will need to keep each other accountable in obedience. In this way, the team can work at prevention rather than only after relationships have long been eroding and the situation has reached a crisis.[15]

Lastly, we return to the style of decision-making. If the other ingredients are in place, this area should not be as difficult as it could be. Roembke recommends

---

14 A great resource for growth in relationships is Tim Lane and Paul Tripp, *Relationships: A Mess Worth Making* (Greensboro: New Growth Press, 2006)—a book that I would encourage the team to read and work through together. Such studies together are invaluable since they help to build a common biblical foundation for the partnership and combat the various worldly and fleshly expectations that we bring to the communal life of the team.

15 For the area of conflict resolution, too, laying a common biblical foundation early on will be crucial for the team's common life. For this, I recommend the team take time for studying and working through Ken Sande, *The Peacemaker*, 3d ed. (Grand Rapids, MI: Baker, 2004) and a companion volume, Alfred Poirier, *The Peacemaking Pastor* (Grand Rapids, MI: Baker, 2006).

a dialectical process of decision-making by consensus for multicultural mission teams.[16] A person expresses his/her viewpoint (thesis), which is then countered by an opposing opinion (antithesis), which gives way to a (sometimes heated) discussion, finally resulting in a decision that everyone can own because everyone has invested into the process of coming to this decision—a consensus (synthesis). This is helpful, but it can in some settings go against Roembke's other recommendation: "The host culture should play the most significant role in forming the leadership style of the team."[17] How much of Roembke's preference is shaped by the German context that she works in, where freethinking and dialectical reasoning is highly valued? Perhaps a mixture of decision-making styles is appropriate, depending on the nature of decisions that need to be made, with an appreciation for different cultural backgrounds and their preferences. Individual leaders, while keeping the leadership team informed, should make the minor, day-to-day decisions that fall within their realm of responsibility. More important decisions that require the action of the leadership group can be made in the dialectical fashion that Roembke proposes, working towards forming a consensus rather than a majority rule; while the big decisions that significantly affect the life of the church can be made by the whole membership—though the leadership team ought to take the lead in directing the process.

POWER

The power factor has to do with the leadership's ability to give up its power for the sake of raising up new leadership. In many cross-cultural ministry contexts, the incarnational leader is the one with the most power. He/she usually comes from an affluent background into a neighborhood struggling with poverty; he/she is the one with the most education; he/she is the member of an ethnicity or social class that holds the upper hand in the larger society. The most "natural" tendency is to hoard the power and decision-making abilities and limit these to the circle of the transplants, often because it will seem the most efficient way of getting things done. However, such short-term gains will be a grave detriment to the long-term ministry. It will end up perpetuating the marginalization of those they have come to serve, even aiding and abetting injustice, rather than serving the good of the neighborhood.

---

16 Roembke, *Credible Multicultural Teams,* 165.
17 Ibid., 153.

John McKnight reminds us of the social service industry that ends up perpetuating the dependency of those it is supposed to help.[18] By filling the ranks of decision-makers with the members of the dominant culture and by leaving the "client" population out, many social service agencies with good intentions of helping the poor have kept the powerless marginalized. Professionalized services have, instead of helping the community, kept the communities crippled, because they have ignored the strength found within the communities themselves. Churches and Christian ministries have ended up doing the same thing. So well-meaning transplants and outsiders hold on to the control rather than passing it on to those who are affected the most.

Therefore, it is incumbent to ask: What plans do we have for giving away power to the indigenous population? I put the question in this way because some would question the very legitimacy of members of the dominant culture leading a ministry in the marginalized neighborhoods. Viv Grigg's answer from his years of serving in the Two-Thirds World slums is that "it is rare to find a natural leader in a slum community who can develop a church beyond seventy people."[19] His recommended strategy is to provide "two levels of leadership... an educated catalyst, with a broad perspective and managerial skills, leads a score of squatter leaders who function as pastors. That catalyst may be a foreigner or may be one of the converted, educated rich who chooses to renounce all."[20]

In other words, although an outsider group that relocates may (and often ought to) start off the work because of initial scarcity of local leadership, there must be in place a plan of transitioning the control over to an indigenous leadership over a period of time. That means leadership development. A significant effort of transplants should be directed towards the work of educating, discipling, and supporting new leadership raised up from the soil of the mission context. Their work is to work themselves out of their jobs.

This kind of work requires a long-term commitment. A neighborhood like mine does not offer up a population of bright, willing and capable youngsters who can readily be groomed for leadership in the kingdom. Much of the work must be done at the foundational level, because here, much of the social infrastructure (such as family, schools, employment) has collapsed. In particular, many men are incarcer-

---

18 John McKnight, *The Careless Society: Community and Its Counterfeits* (New York: BasicBooks, 1995).

19 Viv Grigg, "Sorry! The Frontier Moved," in Harvie M. Conn, ed., *Planting and Growing Urban Churches: From Dream to Reality* (Grand Rapids, MI: Baker Books, 1997), 155.

20 Ibid., 158.

ated or are involved in illicit activities, and therefore there is a scarcity of good role models for the young people. Plenty of other role models abound, however. When I survey the neighborhood youth, they follow a depressingly similar and familiar path. For the boys, sell drugs on the streets, establish a street credibility, and get incarcerated, or get killed at an early age. For the girls, get pregnant while still a teenager, then collect welfare checks and child support in order to survive. There is no ready-made class of indigenous leaders waiting for the transplanted missionaries. This means that, if a church is serious about indigenous leadership development, much of the work must be done with the children and the youth who are not yet claimed by the "streets." Then, through a long-term, committed discipleship, painstakingly and prayerfully train them up to be the next generation of leaders for the church. It is a path fraught with much heartache and hardships, but also one with great rewards for the kingdom.

Through the Lord's providence, there may be local leaders who are mature and capable who join the team. Or the initial missionary team may include local leaders. In fact, this may perhaps be the most ideal arrangement of all—and therefore rarely the case. The only caveat is that a team ought not to rush to include any local leader into its ranks, just because he/she is indigenous. The local leader ought to go through all of the steps in the process I have outlined above, and seek to become one of the team, contributing his/her own unique gifts into the mix. The others ought to examine their own willingness to submit to the indigenous leadership. This will mean a long, hard and prayerful self-examination in regards to their ethnic prejudices and their classism. The team itself is on a journey, a microcosm of the struggles it will face as it seeks to be a kingdom witness to the community. In order to be effective, credible, and model a kingdom life of reconciliation, there must be a visible model of mutual submission—those from the dominant culture submitting to the lead of those from the minority and vice versa. Power is not something to be grasped after but shared. In this way, the leadership team incarnates the Trinitarian community in which one does not seek honor for oneself but honors the other (John 5:20-23; Phil. 2:5-11)—a picture of the life in the kingdom, an embodiment of the reconciled and flourishing relationships in all dimensions within the shalom of God. Unless this vision guides it, a ministry seeking to be incarnational carries the danger of fostering dependency and superior-inferior relationships marked by paternalism, and it can quickly lose credibility among a population that has historically experienced oppression.

There is much else to discuss, of course, including the "big areas" that a team will need to constantly be in conversation about—decisions about personal finances, decisions concerning the rearing of children, and marriages. These are usually thought of as private matters that others have no right to interfere; however, in cross-cultural situations, these are the very areas that communicate the gospel the loudest or hinder the work the most, and therefore become matters of accountability for the whole mission team. One's nuclear family and the adopted family of faith are not divided, but merged. This then becomes a concrete way of seeking the peace of the city—the main item of this strategy is "Marry and have sons and daughters; find wives for your sons and give your daughters in marriage, so that they too may have sons and daughters. Increase in number there; do not decrease" (Jer. 29:6). This has a direct application for the development of a church planting team.

CONCLUSION

It has been my hope to draw attention to the oft-overlooked areas of bonding within the mission context, bonding within the team, repentance as a strategy of mission, and facilitating the transfer of power, so that this in turn will facilitate a better-informed conversation and preparation for future church planting efforts in our increasingly globalizing cities. I conclude with a prayer: may the Lord of mission raise up many incarnational teams that will cross cultural boundaries for the sake of sharing the gospel and planting churches in our cities. May the Church respond to his call and reach the nations now living in our cities!

.12.

Hybrid Church Planting
Among North African Muslim
Immigrants Living in France

JOHN S. LEONARD

This essay is a story of a team of international missionaries and North African Muslim immigrants living in France, who had converted to Christianity. The story begins in the late 1980s and continues to the present. During that time we were involved in a movement, albeit small, where a significant number of North Africans came to Christ and were discipled through a hybrid church planting model called Oasis.

Some, after reading this essay, will conclude that we started a para-church organization, but our description of this ministry as "hybrid church planting" is based on the theological conviction that churches are the best means for planting other churches and if this work is going to spread across France, it will only be because of the local church. Also, if the local church is going to reach immigrant communities around them, they must use those same principles that are used in church planting. We want churches to plant churches even if that means planting them within their own walls. Hybrid church planting is using existing churches to reach out to new immigrant communities and incorporating them into those churches thereby creating entire new communities of believers.

This essay is a reflection on our experience in light of what Scripture teaches about how Christ is building his church. Although the context is very specific, there are principles that should carry over into most church planting situations. This essay will not address the theological issues that one normally may expect to consider when working with Muslims (for example, the doctrine of the Trinity, the divinity of Christ, etc.), but it will address the social context that makes this particular work a fascinating study that challenges conventional wisdom. I hope it will cause you to think in new ways about church planting among the growing immigrant groups that are filling up the global cities of every country on earth and who are the key to planting churches in every people group.

IMMIGRANTS: THE BRIDGE OVER WHICH THE GOSPEL PASSES

The world and its cultures are in an upheaval. Technology has connected more people in more places than ever before. While the developed nations have built a web of connectedness to exploit new markets for themselves, the people of the underdeveloped nations are using these same networks of connectedness to migrate for economic, political, and cultural advantage. Although migration has always been a part of the human story, in the twenty-first century the magnitude of the migration in terms of the number of people moving and the places from which they are coming and to which they are going has never been as great or the process as easy. Everywhere one experiences the impact of this shuffling of humanity. Even people in remote villages, in little known parts of the world, can name a friend or a relative who has migrated to a major urban area and whose family has benefited from the products, information and funds that are sent back home.

Technology has made it possible for immigrants to bring "home" with them wherever they travel. Many immigrants know more about what is happening back home than they know about the city in which they are living. The new connectedness allows immigrants to maintain their language and culture and relationship with home even though they are thousands of miles away. Cities, because of immigration, have become microcosms of the world, where scores of cultures are stacked on top of each other producing a vibrant energy of sights, sounds, smells and tastes.

All this change frightens most people. Underdeveloped nations feel that their culture, customs and values are being swept away in a tsunami of globalization. The developed nations are afraid that all of these immigrants from so many places will weaken their culture, customs and values, putting their own nation in peril. While some underdeveloped nations are calling for boycotts, developed nations are building walls to keep immigrants out. As Christians, we need to see a world of opportunity lying before us to finish the commission given to us by our Lord to take the gospel to all nations. Instead of speaking about building walls, the church should be trying to build bridges, bridges over which the gospel will pass from the global megalopolises to every village on earth. The key people in this process, just like in the book of Acts, are immigrants: those like Philip, Paul, Barnabas, Lydia, Priscilla and Aquila, and Apollos, who lived and were at home in at least two cultures. These bi-cultural people were the bridges over which the gospel passed from one group to another. The model in the book of Acts was not the sending out of missionaries but lay people taking the gospel home. They may have been pilgrims in Jerusalem who heard the gospel and took it home to Rome or Alexandria or to the East. Even Paul and Barnabas traveled first to Barnabas' home island of Cyprus on their first missionary journey. What could be more powerful than the people who have known the new believers all their lives being able to see the transformation that the gospel had made in them? These early Christians were not like today's missionaries. They had learned how to live cross-culturally before they had become believers. Crossing cultures for many of the first Christians was as easy as going home because that is, in fact, what many of them did in the book of Acts. Those fleeing persecution in Jerusalem shared the gospel as they traveled towards home. The 21st century, like the first century, will be changed by large numbers of Christians migrating not just around the Mediterranean Sea but across the entire globe. Most will not need financial support nor will they need cross-cultural training. They are already adept in the language and culture as they return home with the gospel. They may even be the means by which Europe and North America are re-evangelized.

The North African immigrants that make up ten percent of France's population frighten her. Many believe that because North Africans are Muslims they either cannot or will not assimilate into French society. The riots by some North African youth that occurred in France in the fall of 2006 have only raised the difficulties that the nation has, both economically and socially, in assimilating this community into the life of the nation. While many are predicting apocalyptic problems ahead, there is a small movement of believers working in the shadows, and God is blessing their efforts. So while some are forecasting the Islamatization of France in the wake of a religious revival among some in the North African community, Christians are seeing other North Africans turn to Christ.

One reason for this new wave of North African Muslims converting to Christianity was the impact of Christian refugees who fled Algeria in the wake of the Civil War (1990 –1994) between fundamentalist Muslims and more moderate or secular Muslims. It was their testimony, even in the face of persecution, that gave many North Africans the strength to stand firm before persecution and opposition in

France. The Muslim extremists' violent and bloody record in Algeria turned many North Africans away from their cause. Muslim evangelism is counter-intuitive, what appears to be the worst time is the best time to reach out to Muslims. Now the movement seems to be going back the other way. There is a growing burden by North African believers in France to reach out to their brothers and sisters at home. Groups from France regularly visit the Maghreb[1] for evangelism and discipleship. Leaders from North Africa are invited to special events in France and both the French and North Africans are collaborating on projects from theological education to evangelism and worship music. Migration across the Mediterranean has brought about growth of the church in both France and North Africa. This cross-fertilization of the gospel is an example of what can happen on a global scale.

CHURCH PLANTING

One of the biggest mistakes made in church planting, particularly among Muslims, is believing that the best way to reach this communal people is through one-on-one evangelism and then, after a number of converts are in place, shift over to group meetings. Many who work with Muslims have experienced that those who come to know Christ through a private one-on-one relationship with an expatriate are not very open to becoming part of a group. The result is that much work among Muslims is one-on-one with little or no chance of getting people together in groups. No matter what the obstacles or the difficulties, you must give Christianity a communal face. You must plant the church.

In our work, we did not have any converts but we started the hybrid church plant with our mission team and French lay people. You cannot wait until you have the converts to begin a plant; you must start the group first. The reason for this is two-fold. First, when we had no converts, it was an act of faith to start a church plant. Starting the group was a public commitment and statement of faith that "we believed God would give us converts." Two solid believers moved to our city within the first year that we began our church plant, and God honored our commitment. Part of the problem in reaching Muslims is the cultural differences between us. Western Christians are very individualistic. Without knowing it many Westerners working with Muslim people in an individualistic way are raising the barriers and difficulties of their coming to Christ because the Muslim never sees a community to which he can belong. Along with that, they have never seen another

1 Arabic for western, and usually refers to the countries of Morocco, Algeria and Tunisia.

Muslim who has converted to Christianity, and many believe that it is not possible for a Muslim to do so. Seeing Muslims who have converted to Christianity and hearing their story shows the Muslim that it is possible for Muslims to convert, and they also have an opportunity to see and hear what it means to be a Muslim convert to Christianity. The most powerful work among Muslims that I have ever seen is in the Oasis group where ex-Muslims are speaking to interested Muslims, sharing their testimonies and how they became Christians. Can it be frightening for Muslims to attend a public Christian meeting? Absolutely! But once they taste the joy and blessedness of such a gathering, seldom is the one-on-one approach enough. They long for the fellowship and the camaraderie of a group. Our usual experience was that a Muslim interested in the gospel would come to our meeting for about a year to a year and a half and then would make a profession of faith. Most of them would speak about the group's witness corporally and the testimonies of individual Muslims as having the greatest impact on their decision to place their faith in Christ. A community is a non-negotiable for Muslim culture and from a biblical understanding of the gospel.

Jesus does not tell us to win individual converts. When Jesus commands us in Matthew 28:19-20 to baptize disciples and teach them, he is calling us to build communities of converts. The Christian life requires a community; it is called the church. The Reformers were right when they declared that outside the church there is no salvation. Paul and Barnabas planted churches wherever they went. Anyone working on the mission field with Muslims who is not trying to give Christianity a communal face is failing to see the importance of community in the Muslim culture and in Biblical teaching. If your ministry is only winning individuals to Christ, you are failing to unleash the most powerful spiritual tool for the transformation of a society and a culture, the church.

This approach does not downplay relational or friendship evangelism. A community makes relationships more important because there are multiple relationships in which a person is involved rather than merely one friendship with a foreign missionary. In a hybrid church plant, the Muslim is in deep relationship with several Christians, and from these relationships the Muslim has a multi-sided view of the Christian faith. The only person on which this approach may be difficult is the foreign missionary who feels that he or she must be the central and key person in an outreach ministry. In the communal approach the missionary is just one among many. The missionary's job is to do indirect evangelism by helping to put together interested Muslims with Muslim converts. Why? It is much more important that

Muslim converts see that there are Muslims interested in the gospel, and God can use them to lead other Muslims to Christ. The missionary's most important job is to work "behind the scenes" where he or she trains young converts and gives them opportunities to lead, teach, witness and serve. This process of training begins the moment the Muslim converts. We want every believer to consider teaching, testifying, witnessing and serving to be a regular part of the normal Christian life.

MORE THAN A HOMOGENEOUS CHURCH

Conventional wisdom says that the way to reach immigrant communities is through homogeneous churches. The fact that immigrants do congregate and form new communities that recreate their home shows the importance and power of homogeneous groups. But this is only one approach. It does not fit every situation and can fall short both theologically and culturally.

Theologically, the church is called to be a new humanity that transcends and challenges every culture's way of seeing and categorizing the world. Our churches must not become places that reinforce ethnocentric sin. In Galatians 2:28, Paul describes the church as a new society that crosses ethnic divides between Jew and Greek, transcends the gender barriers between male and female, and breaks down class distinctions between slave and free. It is not sufficient for the church to speak of its unity and catholicity as eschatological realities that will exist in the next age or as spiritual truths that are only seen with the eye of faith. The church must become now what her Lord redeemed her to be.

Culturally, we have learned that identity is not fixed and can be created by outsiders or insiders: molded, transformed and changed. We have also learned that no group is homogeneous. Each culture is made up of competing subcultures. This is particularly true of immigrant communities where there are very different attitudes towards assimilation and each generation has very different needs and desires. While marketers continue to identify and create a more horizontal segmentation of society, and our twenty-first century lifestyles encourage this new form of tribalization, the church must be a vertical institution that seeks to cut across as many of humanity's segments as possible. The church's role is to help us to both accept and challenge our identities, teaching us to hold our identities like a dance partner, sometimes close and sometimes at a distance, and sometimes choosing a different partner.

The French North African population connotes an identity that was created by outsiders and that has been embraced by the second and third generation North

Africans in France. However, there are deep divisions that keep it from being a unified community. There are national divisions—Moroccan, Algerian and Tunisian. There are ethnic and linguistic differences—Arabic and Berber (there are several groups of Berbers both culturally and linguistically). There are religious differences—although most North Africans would identify themselves as Muslim, you have folk Islam which is animistic, secular Muslims, political Muslims and orthodox Muslims. There are North Africans who hold on strongly to their culture and seek little interaction with the larger society and others who want very little to do with their home culture. A North African church is insufficient. There are at least thirteen important variables which produce an unmanageable number of possible sub-groups.

Another problem with the concept of planting homogeneous churches is the context in which you are working. Not all nations have the same values when it comes to assimilation. France, for example, does not have the same understanding of assimilation as we do in America. In America it is normal for immigrants to have a hyphenated identity (for example Italian-American, Irish-American, etc.) for ten generations, but France does not recognize such distinctions. In France one can only be French or *un etranger*. Immigrants are given one generation to assimilate. The French are very concerned about exclusion, and any attempt to separate a group from the larger society, either by the group itself or by outsiders, is unacceptable. Therefore, Arab churches in France would be looked upon as strange by the larger society. Most of the resistance to ethnic churches comes from inside the French church itself. The French church has a difficult time understanding why it is necessary to divide the church along cultural lines for theological or social reasons.

The church needs to develop other models that use the forces that make homogeneous groups so powerful but do not leave the church in a balkanized state. A better way would be to provide for specificity in evangelism but catholicity for communion. Some would say that this is exactly what para-church organizations do, but the goal of hybrid church planting is to equip the church to reach out to immigrant communities and incorporate them into the church, as a ministry of the church from beginning to end.

HYBRID CHURCH PLANTING

Most Christians who are active and growing in their faith are involved in several church experiences. Some involve the entire church family, other experiences involve age, life stage or gender specific groups. These groups are so important to church life that youth groups, women's programs, men's groups, young marrieds, and seniors have become a requirement for churches to provide for their people.

Hybrid church planting works on the same principle as these other groups, only it is culture that is the specific around which the group is centered. Like everyone else in the church, the immigrant has experiences that can involve both the entire church and the ethnic specific group. If churches are small and it is difficult to gather enough people so that each church can have its own culturally specific group, then churches can cooperate with one another across geographical and denominational lines. Such a group can provide for the culturally specific needs of the individual and at the same time this group is never seen as the church.

Oasis was to be one of several church experiences that most North African Muslims needed. The difference between French culture, the dominant culture of the church, and Arab culture, along with their Islamic background, is so great that it is difficult for North Africans to feel at home in the church. North Africans also have a difficult time bringing their family and friends to the church. Oasis puts a North African face on Christianity. Its purpose is to celebrate faith in Christ and one's North African background. Oasis is a party, North African style. Everything about it was to recreate home and for many converts it became their only home because they had no other place where they could be themselves. In the French church North Africans felt they had to be French, and there was no one that under-stood the problems they were facing. In their community and family they had no one with whom they could share what they were experiencing and thinking. One North African stated, "It felt as if I were schizophrenic, living two lives." Many found Oasis to be the place where they were whole, where they could be fully Christian and fully North African.

It is at Oasis where new converts can cry with older believers over struggles the new convert is having and know that they are not alone. It is at Oasis where they can ask questions about whether they should keep Ramadan, or when do they tell their family they have converted, or where will they find a Christian wife or husband that is acceptable to their parents? It is at Oasis where Muslim converts feel most safe to bring their Muslim friends to hear the gospel. Oasis has a powerful impact on Muslims because they can see and hear from people just like them.

Creating groups like Oasis is important theologically and socially for immigrants. If the only expression of Christianity one has is foreign, it is easy to believe that God does not accept them and their culture, and that to be Christian one must become like the majority culture. For Muslims who converted to Christianity this has meant changing their names, dress and losing all connections with family and friends. It unconsciously says to North Africans, who feel racism and prejudice in France, that God does not love them as an Arab; to be acceptable to God they need to become French. Oasis, by wrapping itself in the sights, smells, sounds and tastes of North African culture says to North Africans that God loves them as North Africans and that they can love God as North Africans.

For many North African converts, Oasis is a place of healing. There are converts to Christianity who are running from their North African identity; they have come to believe the negative remarks and racism of the larger culture. Embracing Christianity is a way of escaping their roots, but one needs a better reason to be Christian than simply running from one's culture. Oasis can bring reconciliation so that God's salvation can bring healing to the soul. A North African young lady shared, "I used to be ashamed of my mother and would not want to be seen with her because she was so traditional. She always wore a *djelaba* and a head scarf. But coming to Oasis has made me proud of my background. Now when I walk down the street with my mother, I hold her hand."

By being involved in both the church and Oasis, North Africans are benefiting from both the structure and stability of the church as an institution, while at the same time enjoying all the closeness of a family in Oasis. By not creating a church it allows North Africans to do much more than they would be able to do if they were only involved in the church. Oasis, because it is a fellowship, does not have to have a doctrinal statement. This approach gives very theologically different churches the opportunity to work together for evangelizing and discipling North Africans. It also allows North Africans the opportunity to lead, teach, testify and serve. In most church settings immigrants have little to no responsibility in leadership roles, but in these culturally specific groups they are given a great deal of responsibility and can develop their gifts.

By being part of the larger church a group that has no history of Christian institutions can be a family first and not worry about the legal, administrative and financial issues of operating an institution. This allows the group to enjoy a "honeymoon experience" without struggling with so many questions that must be dealt with if one is starting a church. At the same time the church or churches that oversee this work must allow the group a great deal of autonomy, while providing encouragement and spiritual support. This will help develop a healthy group that will produce leaders for the future. What this may mean is that at some point the group may want to become an independent church. The church or churches that have been supporting the group should not consider this a betrayal but an opportunity to grow the kingdom. Good relationships must be maintained so the church is multiplying and not dividing.

By not planting an independent ethnic church, this approach allows the group to collaborate with churches because the group is not in competition with the church but works in a symbiotic relationship. Our group was able to begin and thrive because many of the churches within an hour's drive of our town knew of our work and supported our group. We would tell the churches about our work and they would send us converts from Islam and interested Muslims. We would help the church disciple them and send them back to the church trained for leadership. Most pastors were very happy for the help because they had more than they could do themselves and knew that the Muslim converts they had in their church needed specialized help. Not only did we have pastors call us when they had a Muslim who was very interested in knowing about the gospel, we even had one pastor drive 45 minutes so that a North African could attend our meeting.

GREATER FLEXIBILITY

In a church you must be careful how you do things the first time because it can become a tradition. A hybrid approach to church planting is much more dynamic and flexible, which is important when you are dealing with groups where conversions are few. This approach allows you to work along the assimilation spectrum because it is made up of bi-cultural people who can move toward the immigrant culture or the host culture. Groups like this can be created and disbanded relatively quickly as needs change.

Once a church or a group of churches catches the vision for having culturally specific groups, the only thing that limits the number of groups you can have is the number of immigrant communities that are geographically close to the church.

The group can vary in its purpose from offering evangelistic to discipleship programs. We had two different kinds of meetings: one for discipleship and leadership training, the other for evangelistic outreach.

AN EASILY REPRODUCIBLE MODEL

So effective was Oasis that we believed it needed to be reproduced in as many places as possible. This meant that the ministry could not be built around paid staff and buildings but volunteers and borrowed facilities. Borrowing facilities was the easiest.

If you begin a church, it is expected that you will need a building, but because Oasis is a fellowship, no building is needed. The complementary relationship with the local church gives it access to as many buildings as it needs. By refusing to tie ministry to a building we hoped that we could demonstrate that ministry did not require this expense and maintenance. There are too many ministries that are tied to facilities and seem to always be waiting or raising funds so the ministry can begin. Time and resources in ministry are short; we should not waste either. By not developing a model that requires a facility we were hoping to show others how easy it is to have a community of converts and seekers of Christ from Islam.

Volunteers are more difficult to find and train, but this is the key to rapid multiplication. If one feels that paid workers are necessary, then it is important to choose these workers from volunteers and see who has the calling and gifting to do the work and hire these people. Although we had a large team of missionaries working with us, we had both lay French and Muslim volunteers that did as much work as those of us who were full time. One very pleasant surprise was that some lay volunteers were much more effective than paid missionaries because they were either converts from Islam, evangelists, or both.

REACH A NATION, NOT JUST INDIVIDUALS

This essay has laid out a rationale for utilizing hybrid church planting as a means to expand God's kingdom among North Africans in France. We looked at one-on-one evangelism and found that it limited the number of contacts each missionary could have as well as the number of Christian contacts with which each non-Christian North African could dialogue. In my experience with Muslims this is a failed approach. My wife and I have been deeply involved in this way with many Muslims who are no more interested in Christ today than the first day we met them. Hybrid church planting allows the unbeliever to have many more relationships with Christians. Missionaries who do this kind of work must see themselves as more than friends trying to relationally lead people to Christ. They need to be trainers, equipping both Muslim converts and national volunteers to start, lead and develop hybrid church plants.

Another approach is to work impersonally with many people. These methods include literature distribution, open air preaching, and door to door. The hybrid church plant approach combines the deep personal work with methods that allow the missionary to minister widely to many individuals at the same time. Each person in the group has a number of friends with whom they are involved, and the exposure to a Christian community may be what the Lord uses to bring them to himself.

There is another difference with a hybrid church plant. A friendship should be just that—a friendship. We should not try to manipulate people to Christ with our kindness. We are called to be friendly and kind to all without using coercion as a means of conversion. But there is no ambiguity about the reason and the purpose of the hybrid church plant. It is a meeting to introduce Muslims to Christ and learn more about Christianity. Those who come may come through the invitation of a friend, but they know what the purpose is, and if they are not interested in Christianity, they will soon quit coming. As word spreads that there is a group of Christians from an Islamic background, Muslims who are interested in Christianity will find the group and want to attend.

The creating of a group helped introduce us to Muslims who had a deep interest in Christianity. This changed the whole nature of our work. Before, we were either arguing with Muslims in the marketplace about the Trinity, or the nature of Christ, or we were hanging out with Muslim friends hoping that we would have opportunities to share our faith, but rarely did that happen. When the group began, interested Muslims started showing up and the conversations were very deep and very spiritual. These new guests became our friends and many became our brothers and sisters in Christ.

Since we left France, the movement has continued to grow and to be one of the most powerful methods of evangelizing and discipling Muslims. The Oasis model of working with immigrants that uses the specificity of culture but continues to connect the immigrants to the larger church will only become more important in the twenty-first century as more of the world migrates. The Church must show the nations the way forward.

.13.

Church Planting in South America's Urban Centers

MANUEL SOSA

A CASE FOR HOUSE CHURCHES

Today, in this twenty first century after Christ, many churches are finally "emerging," others are becoming "simple," others choose to be "cellular" as an alternative to the traditional church, and some are finding that being "organic" is a healthier way of doing church today. There is certainly a stir in the Church presently to do things differently, to make a deeper impact in this world, to see how God might be leading his Church to mobilize itself for reaching the lost more effectively. While all this is going on in our mainline Christian denominations, Frank Viola and George Barna, in their latest book, are simply calling many of these efforts and those that precede them as nothing more than "Pagan Christianity."[1] Among all the latest raves and in-vogue methods of evangelism, Christ's Great Commission is the equalizer for all the Great Commission Christian (GCC) groups that are ministering across the globe. The majority of us working in South America would merely affirm that church planting, either in the first world or the two-thirds world, is "the single most effective evangelistic methodology under heaven."[2]

---

1 Frank Viola and George Barna, *Pagan Christianity?: Exploring the Roots of Our Church Practices* (Wheaton, IL: Barna Books, a Division of Tyndale House Publishers, 2008).
2 C. Peter Wagner, *Church Planting for a Greater Harvest: A Comprehensive Guide* (Ventura, CA: Regal Books, 1990), 11.

Evangelism Through Church Planting

New church plants simply afford this world more availability in more locations and more opportunities for people to hear the gospel! New church starts' tentacles are able to access unreached communities and people groups if done correctly and contextually. A church planting model is always just that, a model and not a method to be implemented without prayer and consideration for each local situation. "Rather I want us but to take the New Testament principles and values seriously... and only then to create a house-church movement in our time, local soil, specific culture—even tribe. This is much more a process of incarnation than contextualization, of God becoming flesh again in your context, rather than making cheap photocopies of existing models somewhere else."[3] If any church planting model would ever become an exact principle from which to function, we would not have to continually work at improving our effectiveness at reaching the world. God is the only One that can convince you of how you and your church should be reaching the lost around you. This essay lays out only one example of what is working in many places and what I have experienced in my personal church planting efforts. "Effective church planting requires using tools that work in the context of the environment. And today no two environments are the same."[4] This is a fact that holds true in any remote part or metropolitan area of the world as well as in the U.S. That is why there is no such thing as an infallible church planting method but rather models from which to learn and attempt to implement in our context led by God's own Holy Spirit.

Not all agree with this assessment of evangelism as we can see when Rick Dugan, in his blog, "st george the dragonslayer," writes, "Rather it, (disciple-making), seeks to see churches planted *by* making disciples rather than planting churches *in order to* make disciples."[5] Guy Muse states, "Our focus must be on getting back to multiplying healthy reproducing disciples. Trying to get churches to multiply who are filled with non-reproducing, so called 'disciples' (like me), is futile. Until we get back to the basics of being disciples and multiplying ourselves in others, there is little chance of ever seeing a CPM (church planting movement) in our midst."[6]

---

3 Wolfgang Simpson, *Houses that Change the World: The Return of the House Churches* (Emmelsbull, Germany: C&P Publishing, 1999), 81.

4 Ed Stetzer, *Planting Missional Churches: Planting a Church That's Biblically Sound and Reaching People in Culture* (Nashville: Broadman & Holman Publishers, 2006), xii.

5 Rick Dugan, "disciple-multiplying strategies vs. church planting strategies," http://honest2blog.word-press.com/2007/05/17/disciple-multiplying-strategies-vs-church-planting-strategies, accessed 5/17/07, emphasis in the original.

6 Guy Muse, http://groups.yahoo.com/search?query=churchplantingforum, accessed 4/18/08, in a reply to a contributor.

This appraisal was posted on an internet church planting forum, in which many of us missionaries participate here in South America. Guy has been involved in planting new churches for the last ten years in Guayaquil, Ecuador, and has been one of the leaders in the Baptist church planting movement in South America. But at this point discipleship making is also being looked at more closely by his group rather than exclusively planting churches. These two seem to put forth the same question in church planting and/or discipleship making as the proverbial, "Which came first, the chicken or the egg?" In this case, the question being asked is, what comes first, a church from which to make disciples or disciples so a church can evolve from them? It cannot be an either/or question but one in which the two foci go hand in hand with each other. Church planting must focus on making disciples and a disciple-making model ought to always result in stronger and new churches. A church, in spite of being new or established, should consistently be spiritually strengthening its adherents and not only be concerned about swelling its membership rolls or simply notching yet another new church start.

If church planting is not the single most effective evangelistic methodology under heaven, it is one of the most used ones, especially in the last ten years. "Today, church planting is the default mode for evangelism... It's the cutting edge."[7] More specifically, one form of small group plants, *house churches*, is permeating the church planting mentality worldwide. "There is currently a global shift going on in the church... the Spirit of God is birthing the global house church movement. This phenomenon is sweeping across many parts of our planet... and is gaining momentum in North America."[8] While this is a true enough statement, we must also recognize that, "The sad reality is that many of our established evangelical churches seem determined to reach only people who look like themselves—if they are committed to reach anyone at all."[9] Therefore, the model that is put forth in this essay is two fold—a church planting evangelistic emphasis and its accomplishment through a house church movement. I concur wholeheartedly with Robert Fitts when he says, "The fastest way to evangelize a city is to start new churches,"[10] and without doubt the house church model should be the one most used to accomplish the task of evangelizing any city.

---

7 Tim Stafford, "Go and Plant Churches of All Peoples," *Christianity Today*, 51(9)(9/07):1.

8 Rad Zdero, *The Global House Church Movement* (Pasadena: William Carey Library, 2004), 1.

9 Albert Mohler, "Church Planting Movements and the Great Commission," http://www.albertmohler.com/bog_read.php?id=1016, accessed 09/28/07.

10 Robert Fitts, *The Church in the House: A Return to Simplicity* (Salem, OR: Preparing the Way Publishers, 2001), 84.

As is most obvious today and in all of the history of Christianity, what a church is and how it should function is without doubt a cornucopia of ideas that can easily be labeled as good, bad and usually ineffective. But in most Protestant Evangelical groups the one common denominator that continually tries to unify some of our efforts is the unyielding belief that the biblical command, the already mentioned Great Commission from Matthew 28:19-20, must be carried out. Working together, at least in these areas of the world where workers are even fewer than normal, is a priority and not an option. Great Commission Christians are joining forces more than ever to accomplish new things through innovative ways because our God is "not willing that any should perish, but that all should come to repentance" (2 Peter 3:9, KJV). That is why we need to keep in mind that "it has been shown repeatedly that one of the fastest ways for any church to grow is to plant new churches."[11]

Hopefully more and more evangelical groups will see the things that each have in common with each other instead of only targeting their differences. This will help to accelerate the proliferation of the gospel in the southern continent of the Americas where many have been deceived for centuries to believe a religion and a gospel that is not fully biblical. "While researchers have identified more than two billion individuals in the world who claim Christianity as their religion... calling oneself a Christian doesn't mean it's so."[12] The Catholic News Service cites one of the surveys of the Chilean polling firm Latinobarometro that demonstrates "that 71 percent of South Americans consider themselves Catholic"[13] thus considering themselves Christian, since the Catholic Church falls under the umbrella of Christian denominations. The lifestyle and lack of Christian witness displayed in their daily activity would lead anyone to question their relationship with the one true God and creator of the universe.

House Church Movements

"What is happening around the world right now through house-church movements is spectacular"[14] and it is spreading. As Ed Stetzer observes, "A seismic shift is beginning to rumble in the North American church, especially in church planting."[15]

---

11 Tony Dale and Felicity Dale, *Simply Church* (Austin, TX: Karis Publishing, 2002), 97.

12 Inernational Mission Board, *Something New Under the Sun: New Directions at the International Mission Board* (Richmond, VA: International Mission Board, 1999), 29.

13 Barbara J. Fraser, "In Latin America, Catholics down, Church's credibility up, poll says," http://www.catholicnews.com/data/stories/cns/0503707.htm, accessed 7/25/08.

14 Larry Kreider and Floyd McClung, *Starting a House Church: A New Model for Living Out Your Faith* (Ventura, CA: Regal Books from Gospel Light, 2007), 6.

15 Stetzer, *Planting Missional Churches*, 16.

While this might be a new trend in the U.S., this same model has also been shaking up many organizations and individuals around the world and probably not any one more than the International Mission Board of the Southern Baptist Convention for over the last ten years now. "In January 1997, the leadership of the Foreign Mission Board, (now the International Mission Board, 'IMB'), adopted a bold new vision. Rather than simply shaping our administrative structure to fit our existing personnel deployment, we would look instead to the whole world."[16] "What was new was an emphasis on church planting that resulted in movements or the contagious exponential expansion of churches."[17] This was called New Directions when first instituted and later changed to SD21 or Strategic Directions for the 21st Century.[18] With this new strategy, the IMB has focused on reaching unreached people groups throughout the globe by starting church planting movements within these groups and in areas where missionary personnel were already deployed.[19] While the IMB is not the only missions organization instituting new missiological approaches in its ministries, it is the one with which I am most familiar, since I work for them. More will be explained about these changes and their effect on a particular area in the second part of this essay.

So the problem to consider in this essay is, how do we make a bigger impact on lostness in South America and, in particular, in its cities and mega-cities? Of course it is not about solely presenting a problem here but also a plausible solution which comes from personal experience in this specific region of the world. Why particularly the cities and mega-cities can be queried at this point. The Food and Agriculture Organization of the United Nations (FAO) gives some vital and revealing statistics for us to ponder. "By 2020, the total population of Latin America is projected to increase from 480 million to 612 million. This will be 28% higher than the current population level (i.e., in 2000)."[20] The same document also discloses that "the pace of urbanization in Latin America is faster than in any region of the

---

16 IMB, *Something New Under the Sun*, 44.

17 Keith E. Eitel, "Vision Assessment: The International Mission Board of the Southern Baptist Convention, 2003," http://www.baptiststandard.com/postnuke/pdf/visionassessment.pdf.

18 Jerry Rankin, *To the Ends of the Earth: Churches Fulfilling the Great Commission* (Nashville: Broadman & Holman Publishers, 2006), 3-4.

19 David Garrison, *Church Planting Movements: How God is Redeeming a Lost World* (Midlothian, VA: WIGTake Resources, 2004).

20 Sandra J. Velarde, under the supervision and coordination of Adrian Whiteman and the collaboration of Sandra Ines Rivero and Shayman Saadat, "Socio-economic trends and outlook in Latin America: Implications for the forestry sector to 2020, Latin American Forestry Sector Outlook Study Working Paper" (Food and Agriculture Organization of the United Nations, 2004), section 2.2., http://www.fao.org/DOCREP/006J2459E/j2459e06.htm.

world... In Argentina, Chile, Venezuela, Brazil and Uruguay, the urban population [will have] reached 80-90% of the total [population] by 2000."[21] Excluding Surinam and Guyana it is projected that most South American countries will have over 70% of their populations living in urban centers by 2020. Paraguay is the lone exception but still will be at almost 70% by the same date.[22]

Jack Dennison asks a profound question in his book, *City Reaching,* "Can a whole city be transformed by the presence and power of God?"[23] And for our consideration the following question is posed, can whole countries or a whole continent be transformed by the presence and power of God? Most assuredly the reader of this question who professes to being a Christian will give an affirmative answer. William Carey's "Deathless Sermon," first preached in 1792 and based on Isaiah 54:2-3, apparently had two points as historians can best account for. They were first, expect great things from God and, second, attempt great things for God. We need to focus dramatically more on the attempting part of Carey's sermon for no doubt most of us expect great things from God. The desolate cities referenced in Isaiah 54:3, are no longer uninhabited but continue to expand without precedence and in need of a redemptive word. As we expect great things from God, he, too, is expecting that we attempt great things for him as we try to reach these burgeoning cities and now also mega-cities. We have to confess that the Church, in any part of the world, has not kept up with the growing population in which it finds itself nor have our attempts of the past been sufficient to say that the cities have been transformed by the presence and power of God.

Ecuador's evangelical rate is 12% reported by Fred Morris of Faith Partners in a 2005 document,[24] while Chile and Argentina have evangelical rates of 15.9% and 11% respectively according to the latest Joshua Project statistics.[25] I cite these countries because I have served in the first two and am presently in the third. These are countrywide statistics and in most surveys the urban areas show a much lower evangelization rate. From these figures we cannot but be overwhelmed by the implication of how many people die without the gift of eternal life daily, for only

---

21 Ibid., section 2.4.

22 Ibid., section 2.3, (UN statistics 1998).

23 Jack Dennison, *City Reaching: On the Road to Community Transformation* (Pasadena, CA: William Carey Library, 1999), xiii.

24 Fred Morris, "Faith Partners of the Americas Initiates New Project of Solidarity with Indigenous Christians in Ecuador, http://www.faithpartnersofamericas.org/EcuadorProject.htm, accessed 7/25/08.

25 Joshua Project, "Unreached Peoples of the World," www.joshuaproject.net, accessed 7/25/08.

"this is eternal life, that they may know You, the only true God, and Jesus Christ whom you have sent" (John 17:3, NKJV).

What is being expressed in this essay unequivocally affirms what many are today recognizing as a reality, that "the most rapidly growing church planting and evangelistic movements today utilize house-sized churches and cell groups. These efforts are outstripping more traditional approaches to evangelism, church growth, and church planting."[26] Traditional church, as we know and accept it today, plus any other biblically based model of evangelism will always continue to have a part in sharing the gospel, but we need to keep on seeking ways of improving and increasing our outreach efforts. "New expressions of church are continually needed to accommodate believers who do not fit into the current church structures."[27] There is no better way of doing it than the oft forgotten way of the original church in the first century because, *What has been will be again, what has been done will be done again; there is nothing new under the sun,*" (Eccl. 1:9, emphasis added). So we must accept that, not unlike the first century when the first believers were meeting in homes and causing *"trouble all over the world"* (Acts 17:6), this retro church planting movement is doing the same today! "The early church did very well without buildings and without many full-time leaders for the first few centuries."[28] Have the spiritual needs of Christians changed or has the church conformed to the status quo in these last few centuries?

Why did house churches work then and why are they working again in this post-modern society of which we are all a part? One basic reason it functioned at that time was due to the fact that the early Christians had no other place to meet. They were displaced Jews who were no longer welcome in their synagogues because of their new faith and for allowing a growing number of non-Jews, called gentiles, to join them in their worship practices. There was a need that was easily met by opening the doors of the one thing any family cherishes most, its home. By doing so the new groups of converts into "the Way" displayed the level of belief they had in their new found faith and the trust they were willing to extend to their family, friends and neighbors. "The house church is a way of living the Christian life communally in ordinary homes through supernatural power."[29]

House churches are functioning today in many parts of the world differently than they are in the U.S. Although the house church movement is in its beginning

---

26 Zdero, *The Global House Church Movement*, 1.

27 Kreider and McClung, *Starting a House Church, 9-10.*

28 Dale and Dale, *Simply Church*, 31.

29 Simson, *Houses that Change the World*, 80.

stages in the U.S., "most of the North American church has not caught a vision for church planting and New Testament reproduction—at least not yet."[30] Due to church members being "disappointed at the meager results that have come out of long-term efforts to bring new vision and life into mainline churches, many are calling for nothing less than the reinvention of the congregation."[31] George Barna seems to believe that is why many born-again Christians are exiting the established church and bases his whole book, *Revolution,* on this premise.[32] These disappointed churchgoers want to see changes in what they know as church and are open to that which is being experienced by others who are exemplifying a vigorous and daily living out of their faith. Ralph Neighbour, Jr., shares with us his own pilgrimage and heart in seeking relevancy to this faith as he says, "I had left the traditional church 20 years earlier, seeking to find a more effective and biblical model for church life."[33] It is believed that people seek out different ways of expressing their faith because they are disgruntled with the church, but we are seeing more and more people just wanting to have a meaningful relationship with God, and they are missing out on this in the established church model to which many have gone for years.

In the two-thirds world house churches are achieving great goals never before seen in evangelism and/or church planting efforts. The reasons are diverse but are mostly different from those being embraced in North America. First, as we all know, it is the first and probably the only model used by the church in the first century. There is no doubt or controversy about where the early church met. "Greet Priscilla and Aquila... Greet also the church that meets at their house" (Rom. 16:3,5). "And so does the church that meets at their house" (1Cor. 16:19). "To Nympha and the church in her house" (Col. 4:15). "To Philemon, our dear friend... and to the church that meets in your home" (Philemon 1-2). "The church" which is mentioned in each of these passages is not many but one church that met in different locations during the early period in homes.

Stewardship

In metropolitan areas all across the world buying land comes at a premium price. Construction of buildings has also become almost impossible to achieve due to the

---

30 Stetzer, *Planting Missional Churches,* 14.

31 Robert Banks and Julie Banks, *The Church Comes Home* (Peabody, MA: Hendrickson Publishers, Inc., Peabody, 1998), 1.

32 Geroge Barna, *Revolution* (Wheaton, IL: BarnaBooks, a division of Tyndale House Publishers, 2005).

33 Ralph W. Neighbour, Jr., *Where Do We Go From Here?: A Guidebook for the Cell Group Church,* rev. ed. (Houston, TX: Touch Publications, Houston, 2000), 13.

high cost of materials and labor. It doesn't matter that countries might be poor; land in urban settings is always accompanied by a very elevated cost. Therefore, house churches, although biblically correct but long ignored, are again becoming a viable option. Every house is a possible church! What an incredible statement and truth that is so accessible to all but has been relegated to a lowly option in opening new works for centuries. The lack of finances has kept many churches from opening traditional new works that in the past always required either buying property, constructing buildings, or renting space in which the new group could meet. Money is not a reason to be viewed as an excuse for not opening a new work when all one has to do is look around and realize that every home, every building, every office, every dorm room, and even every park can house "the church." We must never forget that "the Church is a people—not a building, an organization, a business, or an institution."[34] A house is a sensible solution for the church as the dilemma of finances is removed when meeting in a family setting and ownership of a building and its maintenance is no longer a deterrent for reaching out.

Inviting a friend, relative, fellow student or coworker to a home, especially one's own, is far less threatening than asking them to go to church with you. The simple invitation "to go to church," strikes fear into the hearts of those that have had bad experiences in churches, have never gone to one or simply do not want to go to a church with which they feel no affinity. Being able to meet in a small group, being part of that group and having participation in the discussion of the group is another of the reasons why house churches continue to impact all factions of society. It doesn't matter if people are rich, poor or in between, they all have homes where they live and that can become a place where a church could meet. While it is true that many places around the world can meet only in houses or in small groups due to political or societal pressures we would hope that the church at large that has the freedom to worship in buildings will not resort to being a persecuted church before it will rediscover the origin of its biblical roots of being church. In those early church days "if you had asked another for directions to a church in any important city of the first-century world, you would have been directed to somebody's private home!"[35]

House church groups have almost no expenses, but the group decides how to expedite whatever expenditures they might incur. There is no building to gobble up

---

34 Fitts, *The Church in the House*, 12.
35 Del Birkey, *The House Church: A Model for Renewing the Church* (Scottdale, PA: Herald Press, 1998), 40.

the monies of the group, and the leaders are volunteers instead of paid clergy staff. "Didn't the church thrive in its first couple of centuries without putting all of that money into structures that would only be used for a few hours per week? Come to think of it, the churches under communist persecution seem to be proving the same point!"[36] Many references say that 85% of any church budget is consumed internally and that only the remaining 15% is used to reach out to a world to which the church is supposed to be ministering. *Christianity Today's* periodical called, *Your Church Magazine*, gives the following statistics from a church survey done by them. They discovered that the average size church in the U.S. spends its money in the following fashion:

- 43 percent for staff compensation
- 20 percent for facilities (rent, mortgages, utilities, upkeep)
- 16 percent for missions
- 9 percent for programs
- 6 percent for administration and supplies
- 3 percent for denominational fees
- 3 percent other[37]

It is easy to see why so many committed Christians are having a reaction to their church's spending 85% or so of the budget on themselves. In house churches the numbers can easily be inverted to represent 85% or even more for reaching out to the community needs. That makes better sense and stewardship of the offerings to the church. Times have changed and people's mentalities are a lot more open and critical of how churches have done ministry in the past and how they should be doing it today.

Reproducible

As is obvious, the reasons for house churches are "legion." Every proponent of this model will list some of the ones already noted here plus other reasons that will fit their current situation. But the one reason that is universal and that most would advocate is the fact that house churches are reproducible. In order to start a house church all that is needed is a leader that serves as facilitator for the sessions

---

36 Dale and Dale, *Simply Church*, 31.
37 Phyllis Ten-Elshof, "Church Budgets: You Are What You Spend" in *Your Church Magazine* by *Christianity Today* (Jan/Feb 2000), http://www.christianitytoday.com/yc/2000/001/10.70.html, accessed 7/25/08.

and someone willing to open the doors of their living or work space for believers and seekers to congregate. "Because house churches are simple, inexpensive, and adaptable, movements by default made use of them, freeing themselves up from building and program maintenance to concentrate on the weightier matters of evangelism and discipleship... The most rapid church planting movements today deliberately multiply and plant house churches... "[38] This reproducibility factor of the house church is the key reason it is being accepted universally and put into practice. Any place can be a church and homes are the dwellings we have most in this world, so why not put them to use the way the first church did? The building will never be the church. In fact Wade Akins, who wrote *Pioneer Evangelism* which has been published now in many languages, always says in his conferences, "Buildings should never have signs that read First Baptist Church or any other name. Rather the sign should say the First Baptist Church Meets in this Building."[39] Many people continue to call the building "church" and forget that "church" is people.

House church planting has its own three R's that make it an effective and easy tool for evangelism—Reproducible, Receptive and Reachable. House churches are *reproducible* so that anyone anywhere can start one. They are *receptive* in accepting anyone that comes to join them irregardless of race, color, economic status, society level or creed. House churches usually reach out to likeminded friends and family thus making it easier for them to assimilate. Finally, they should be *reachable*. A good city goal is to have a church for every person in that city within a ten-minute walking distance of their home, no matter where they live.

The case for house churches is being experienced and written about by many in our different Christian denominations. My personal pilgrimage has not come from reading about it or being convinced at the many training sessions I have attended. It comes from prayerfully agonizing over how best to reach the city in which I found myself between 1999 and the turn of the century. It did not come by my having heard the term house church but by my seeing it done by someone who merely wanted to impact her community, and this helped open my eyes to the possibility of replicating what she was doing. It comes from having lived all its joys and sorrows and from being convinced that at a certain time and in a certain place it was of God.

---

38 Zdero, *The Global House Church Movement*, 77.

39 Thomas Wade Akins, *Pioneer Evangelism* (Rio de Janeiro, Brasil: Junta de Missões Nacionais, Convenção Brasileira, 1995).

A HOUSE CHURCH CASE

Guayaquil, Ecuador, in 1999, had forty-two Baptist churches that had been started after almost fifty years of missionary presence in that city. The city at that time was approaching two and a half million inhabitants in the greater urban area and continuing to grow. Although it is not as commonly known as Quito, the capitol of Ecuador, Guayaquil is the largest city in the country and also its economic base.

I was asked in that year by the regional leadership of our organization, the IMB, to be the Strategy Coordinator for Guayaquil. My job was to develop a strategy for reaching that city in ways that had not been done before. With New Directions as the focus of the IMB, we were challenged to start works in new and more effective ways than before. We would no longer have the funds that past generations had used to purchase properties and build buildings. One of our leaders plainly told me, "Manuel, you will need to open new works with only paper, pencil and the Bible, which is the only way they will be reproducible." At the rate of less than one church per year established by our Baptist work in its efforts in Guayaquil before New Directions, it was evident that something different would have to be attempted, a different strategy that would try to keep pace with the growing population of the city and the declining ratio of churches to people. Our team at that point was to consist of Guy and Linda Muse, Barbara Rivers, Ed and Elenir Ridge plus my wife Berta and me.

The Need for Prayer

My first concern was that before any strategy could be developed we would have to spend a lot of time in prayer. We did not want to develop a strategy that was ours and then ask God to bless it but rather we wanted the strategy to come to us through our close relationship with him. Being in a right relationship with God will always give you a vision of what he wants you to be engaged in as you seek to enlarge his kingdom here on earth.

The following are excerpts from the first e-mail I sent to my team after being appointed Strategy Coordinator. The letter was written on July 11, 1999.

> Before us we have a great task, to win this city for Jesus Christ—a huge task, but for God nothing is impossible. And I know that God has brought you and me to this city at this time to fulfill that task... Prayer will be the priority from which we work. All that we might attempt or accomplish without prayer will be ours and not his. We must all pray

more!... I believe that prayer will lead us to our goals and objectives with a united, positive and single spirit. Our main goal is to "LEAD OUT IN THE PLANTING OF NEW WORKS." All that we are about do and plan must focus on this one goal. All activities that we get involved in must have this as an end result... I am excited about what I feel God has in store for us and Guayaquil.

That was the beginning of an incredible experience that still continues in that city! Prayer thus became a priority. We would meet every Tuesday without any agenda but to seek through prayer that God would enlighten us as a team before we ever decided on how and what to do in reaching our goal of attempting great things for him. Those were special times as fasting was also added to our prayer days. Tony and Felicity Dale would also agree with our praying strategy. "How do you get started? Pray and keep praying."[40] "House-church ministry *must* be birthed in prayer... Starting a house church cannot be just a good idea; it must be a *God idea*."[41] Nationals even asked one of our team members if we were now getting paid to pray since they perceived we were spending too much time in this activity. Not a bad thing to be accused of, is it?

A New Vision—A Team Approach

None of us in the team had any church planting experience prior to this time. All our knowledge of church planting was what had been done in the past—scout out a new area, purchase property, build a temple. It was as if the voice from the movie "Field of Dreams" kept saying, "If you build it (a building), they will come." One church start in each four-year term was considered a very successful ministry of planting new works. During that time the church planter could get it off the ground before he would go home on furlough. Next term would hopefully bring about the same process if the church planter were granted enough funds. It all depended on the money! This was the model being used, almost exclusively by our organization, for over 100 years across the world and the model we had in our minds when launching out in this endeavor.

My wife and I had returned to Guayaquil in 1997 from furlough, and I had changed my prior job description from theological education to church planter just before New Directions was instituted. By this time we had been in that city fifteen years, all our missionary career. I, too, had that one church every four years mentality

---

40 Dale and Dale, *Simply Church*, 105.
41 Kreider and McClung, *Starting a House Church, 98.*

at this point. Upon arriving back on the field that year the Lord immediately began to impress on me a different set of numbers. Instead of one church every four years, why not dream of four new works every single year? I knew that it would personally be almost impossible to do that so I began to share my vision with the local pastors. One was opposed to new works because his church had opened one twenty years before and it had failed within a year, so he did not want his church to get involved in this effort. I responded by paraphrasing Alfred Lord Tennyson and said, "I would rather plant a new church and fail than never to have attempted it at all."

Even before I was appointed Strategy Coordinator of Guayaquil, Fanny Mena, a lady who helped around our house, had asked Berta to pray about doing something for the children in her neighborhood. One Sunday while on her way to church, as was her custom for years, a neighbor stopped her and asked, "Fanny, you go to church every week. Why don't you do something here from what you learn there?" That gripped her and convicted her to reach out to her own community. Berta agreed after much deliberation since Fanny lived in a dangerous neighborhood that was on a dirt road where many gangs and drug dealers made it their territory. The house Fanny had was made of bamboo poles split open to form the walls and tied together around her dirt floor and zinc sheets on beams to make a roof.

All I knew during those first few months was that first Berta was going every Saturday and then every Sunday. We were in the middle of our six-month period of praying when Fanny and my wife asked me to go and preach at the first anniversary of their group. I agreed to go, not knowing that on that particular Sunday my world view for planting churches would forever be challenged and changed. I prepared a simple sermon or lesson since I knew that the attendees would be mostly children.

I arrived to find the street in front of Fanny's house closed off because they had over 100 children and parents there. This in itself was truly amazing, but that was not what impressed me the most that afternoon. This cleaning lady, a single high school dropout mother of a teenage boy, had assembled not just my wife but three other young persons and a married couple to help her every week. These volunteers were from three different churches but were working together at this ministry. They paid their way every week at least once a week but usually two or three times for planning and preparing for the Sunday meeting. They were not paid by anyone and usually helped out to buy refreshment and materials for the children. The glow I saw in their eyes as they scurried around trying to keep that unruly group of children from getting too loud was one that to this day I can see in my mind. Eureka, here it was! A team approach to opening new works—all of them lay persons who continued to work in their church but now had a different ministry to work in.

The following Tuesday at our team meeting I could not contain my excitement. My question to the rest of the team was, "Why can't we duplicate what Fanny has done?" I was sure that God had many others in our churches that would be willing to team up, without any financial help, to be blessed as I saw this team being blessed by what they were doing. I wanted us to go out immediately and share the joy that could be had by being involved in this ministry. Our prayer time began to get results soon after that. The team also captured my vision and soon each one had ideas to put forth to try and develop a church planting emphasis using this approach.

Training for the Harvest

God had indeed put us all together at that special time. The idea began to take shape as everyone contributed to enlarging our vision. Soon it was decided to call the emphasis, "La Iglesia en tu Casa," or "Church in Your House" based on Luke 10:1-12. We would develop a program to train church planters and we would get trained right along with them as none of us were church planters. We would teach the tools for the task and go along with the planters as they did the work. We came up with the slogan, "We don't teach people to open new works, we open new works while training people." A practical approach for training church planters!

We felt impressed to interpret Luke 10 in the following manner. In verse 1, Jesus sent the disciples out where he himself was about to go. Jesus had a strategy, he knew where he was going to go and sent the planters before him in groups of two. We too must have a strategy for our work. Verse 2 tells us we are to pray for laborers to be sent to the harvest. Then in verse 3, Jesus says, "Go your way... I sent you out as lambs among wolves." After praying we might discover that the laborer is us. He warns us that it will not be easy! Prepare yourself for the task. Verse 4 continues by warning us not to take our baggage with us or to waste time talking. We decided that in order for the church plant to be reproducible we would not use computers, transparencies or any kind of electronic equipment to which the church planters had no access. We would leave our baggage behind and only use what was at hand. In verse 5 we learned we were to bring peace to the homes we enter. If we find a "man of peace" there, like in verse 6, our peace will rest there. A man of peace is one God has already prepared to receive us, probably without even knowing about it. In verses 7 and 8 we again find Jesus contextualizing the experience by having us eat what they have, not things from the outside but what is available. All these components together makes church planting reproducible. We agreed that in our training we would use pencil, paper, copies and cassette tapes. Copiers can be found in any neighborhood in that city and cheap copies can be made. Also, every family, almost without exception, has a sound system. Verse 10 commands us to heal the sick both physically and spiritually. The last two verses confirm to us that our calling is to obedience even if we are rejected.

God laid it on our hearts not to teach another course like so many before then. We would require anyone who felt led to come and learn to make a commitment with God that they would open a new work within six weeks of the first class or they could not remain in the class. The reasons for this were to get a true commitment, to weed out diploma seekers, and to discern that they trusted God that this is what he wanted of them. They would have faith enough to depend on God to open the doors for a place to open a new work. In fact we told them we would not give any diplomas or certificates. Their new work would end up being a Ph.D. in opening churches. We took our goals from the Luke 10 passage and decided to train seventy church planters, send them out two by two, hopefully opening thirty-five new works in the first year of the emphasis. We wanted to almost double the existing Baptist churches in Guayaquil in one year, in a city where it had taken almost fifty years to start forty-two churches. We believed God had given us the vision and also believed he would give us that number. These were the new works we were proposing to open at that time. From day one they would function as a church and not a mission or a cell relating to a mother church. Our training would be geared in that direction.

The Churches Began

The first step was to present our vision to the pastors of our Baptist congregations in the hope that they would allow us in their churches to share with their parishioners. We had big question and answer meetings twice without anyone accepting our offer. They were more indifferent to the idea than opposed to it at this time. At our third meeting one pastor finally agreed to allow us to present our vision on a hot steamy Sunday night at his church. This had to be the poorest church in Guayaquil, if not in the whole country of Ecuador, but this church decided to open our first church planting training center. In July 2000 we started with eighteen students who, in the course of four months, opened a total of twelve new works. The pastor also participated in the training and opened a new work in his home that was only a couple of blocks from his church. He said with excitement, "My neighbors are willing to come to my home but in twenty years they have never accepted my invitation to come to church."

The enthusiasm in us began to grow as we saw God at work transforming idle lay persons into vibrant church planters. This first church was a catalyst for us, too, because we knew that if this financially strapped and little-educated group could open new works, anyone could. We even had two ladies who were illiterate attend class and memorize the materials. They would take tracts and ask people to read the tracts for them. At the end they would give an invitation to accept the Lord. They started two new works outside of Guayaquil. This gave us another slogan, our www. for church planting, "It doesn't take the *w*ise or the *w*ealthy to open new works, it takes the willing."

A second church opened its doors to the training and again we saw things that we had never dreamed off. A couple, who were both lawyers and worked for the municipality, asked and were given permission to open a new work once a week with other lawyers at city hall. We continued to pray and felt led to open up the training in our local Baptist seminary but now inviting like-minded GCC participants. We even announced it on the radio and gave an invitation to come and hear our vision. People came and forty of them committed themselves to trusting God to lead them to open a new work in six weeks or less. This group had men and women from different denominations willing to go wherever God would open the doors for a new work. At the end of the training session this group had opened twenty-two new works. An Alliance and Missionary Church from sixty miles away paid to send two young men each week to the training with the understanding that they were supposed to go back and teach others in their church what they learned. This group ended up opening up six new works in rural areas and buying a church van to transport the church planters to the fields.

As the first year of "La Iglesia en tu Casa" drew to a close, we did not meet our goal of seventy church planters and thirty-five new works. We exceeded it! We ended up training a total of one hundred people and opening up sixty-two new works in and around Guayaquil. The second year's statistics were almost identical. After two and a half years it was certain that over 100 new works were meeting weekly with an average of ten per group of new Christians gathering in homes, offices and even outdoors.

Not every church that opened stayed open and that would keep us praying even more. We never felt it was a failure if one did not continue meeting because the vision had been captured and new people had heard the gospel maybe for the first time in their lives through these house churches.

As Berta and I prepared to leave Guayaquil in November 2002 to take on an administrative position in Chile, we attempted to gather together for the first time as many of the new Christians that were meeting in the homes as possible. A new and wealthy believer allowed us to use her house and patio. We bused almost 300 people to her house to celebrate a joint service. That day several of the house leaders baptized their new believers in the pool and I, too, had the privilege of baptizing over twenty that day. A total of thirty-five were immersed in that pool. What an awesome experience of joy and sadness we experienced that afternoon—joy at seeing what Jesus was doing and sadness at moving on to a new ministry in a different place.

Our leaving did not hinder the work at all. They continued to attempt great things for the Lord in Guayaquil. One of the first church planters started a church planting church in his home and is now a missionary for the Ecuador Baptist Convention. Also, along with the training centers, there is a Theological Education by Extension Center for those wanting more training and the once all missionary team is now made up of two IMB missionaries and ten nationals. Churches continue to be planted and the testimonies are entirely too many to even begin to share in this small space.

CONCLUSION

Remember Fanny Mena and the work she did with children and their families? Well in July 2009 they will celebrate ten years as a church. They continue to meet in the street with ministries to women, children, and youth. Friends of her ministry efforts have helped her install some ceiling fans, a concrete floor and now most of her walls are of blocks. They presently want to buy a property that is across the street from where she lives and her church now has legal status before the government of Ecuador.

God is faithful! Do I believe in house churches? Without a doubt, because God allowed us to experience all of the above, and now we are in Buenos Aires, Argentina, seeking his guidance. Will we use house churches here? We will only seek his will for, "it is not a particular model that motivates us, but what the Spirit of God does in people's lives when they discover the New Testament principles of doing Church in small communities."[42] If doing house churches here is what he desires for us, we know that new works will begin and will function in this city with their own gaucho flavoring to them.

---

42 Kreider and McClung, *Starting a House Church*, 6-7.

Section 4:

Leadership Development

.14.

Perspectives on Emerging
Church Leadership

TIMOTHY Z. WITMER

Over the course of time there have been many "waves" that have washed over the church, claiming to be the answer for the church as it has sought to reach its respective generation. For example, over the course of the past generation the waves of the church growth movement and the metachurch movement have appeared. Each movement always has its gurus, imperatives, model venues, and ideal leadership profile. The most recent wave is the emerging church movement. The particular concern of this essay is the concept of leadership found in the emerging church movement.

How are these movements to be evaluated? A very helpful approach to epistemology has been developed by John Frame and Vern Poythress which has become known as multi-perspectivalism, or more simply, perspectivalism.[1] They advocate that there are three perspectives at work which are the normative, the situational and the existential perspectives.

> So I distinguish three perspectives of knowledge. In the "normative perspective," we ask the question, "what do God's norms direct us to believe?' In the "situational perspective," we ask "what are the facts?"

---

[1] Space does not permit an exhaustive explanation of perspectivalism but the reader should see John Frame's own brief summary, *A Primer on Perspectivalism* at http:www.frame-poythress.org/frame_articles/ PrimerOnPerspectivalism.htm. For Vern Poythress see *Symphonic Theology* (Grand Rapids, MI: Academie Books, 1987).

In the existential perspective we ask, "what belief is most satisfying to a believing heart?"[2]

The normative perspective is revealed in God's Word. The situational perspective "will analyze what we know about the world, to suggest a biblical understanding."[3] This addresses the matter of knowledge in its context. The existential perspective acknowledges that the individual person doing the knowing is also an important factor. This is nothing less than knowledge of ourselves. These three perspectives merely reflect the point that we don't know things in a vacuum. There is no such thing as a "brute fact."[4] It is important to note at the outset that this way of looking at reality does not relativize truth.

> So perspectivalism is not relativistic, as some have charged. Rather, it presupposes absolutism. To say that our own views are finite is to contrast them with the absolute, infinite viewpoint of God Himself. And we are able to consult God, and through his word and in prayer, in some measure access his infinite perspective.[5]

This approach is not only helpful to theologians wrestling with epistemology but also to practitioners who are seeking to evaluate models of ministry. For example, understanding the concept of *leadership* in the church should take into account all three perspectives.

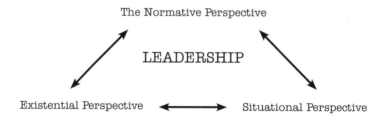

The Normative Perspective

LEADERSHIP

Existential Perspective ⟷ Situational Perspective

---

2 Frame, *A Primer on Perspectivalism*, 7.

3 John Frame, *The Doctrine of the Knowledge of God* (Phillipsburg, NJ: Presbyterian & Reformed Publishers, 1987), 75.

4 This is an expression coined by Cornelius Van Til indicating that there is no such thing as a fact that is a reality in itself, uninterpreted by God.

5 Frame, *A Primer on Perspectivalism*, 2.

The normative perspective examines what the Bible says about leadership. The existential perspective looks at the dynamics of the individuals involved in leadership.

The situational perspective focuses on the cultural context in which leadership is practiced.

It is important to note that the normative perspective takes precedence over the other perspectives. The word of God is the "unnormed norm" or the "norming norm." The very fact that the normative perspective in the diagram is not on the same plane as the others indicates that the normative perspective as revealed in his Word is an expression of his Lordship over all.

PERSPECTIVES ON LEADERSHIP IN THE EMERGING CHURCH

Perspectivalism is valuable as an analytical tool. How might it be of help in addressing various approaches to leadership? Let's take a look at the subject of leadership in the emerging church movement. What impact has this movement had on the nature and function of leadership within the church? Before proceeding to the details of this analysis, a broad summary of the emerging church movement should be considered as it is found in *Emerging Churches: Creating Christian Community in Postmodern Cultures* by proponents Eddie Gibbs and Ryan Bolger.

> Emerging churches (1) identify with the life of Jesus, (2) transform the secular realm, and (3) live highly communal lives. Because of these three activities, they (4) welcome the stranger, (5) serve with generosity, (6) participate as producers, (7) create as created beings, (8) lead as a body, and (9) take part in spiritual activities.[6]

The thought is that churches with these characteristics will be more effective in reaching postmoderns. Inasmuch as this chapter is addressing the issue of leadership, the focus will be on "(8) lead as a body." What does this mean? What are the implications? How can the multiperspectival approach be of help in analyzing this important aspect of the emerging church movement? The focus in this analysis will be primarily

---

6 Eddie Gibbs and Ryan Bolger, *Emerging Churches: Creating Christian Community in Postmodern Cultures* (Grand Rapids, MI: Baker, 2005), 45.

on the normative and situational perspectives, though the existential perspective will be considered when the implications for leadership training are addressed.

THE EMERGING CHURCH ON LEADERSHIP: THE FLATTENING OF CHURCH STRUCTURE

Emerging movement leader Scot McKnight has clearly proclaimed that "the emerging movement is an attempt to fashion a new ecclesiology [doctrine of the church]."[7] Upon what is that new ecclesiology to be based? At the heart of the emerging movement's view of leadership is that the "hierarchical" approach to leadership is severely flawed and is a vestige of the church's capitulation to modernism.

> What organizational structures did modernity hand to today's church leaders and members? During the twentieth century, the church, already hierarchical and rationalized, became even more so as it mimicked Henry Ford's hierarchical, assembly-line construction to maximize productivity, resulting in dehumanization and disempowerment. As the twentieth century progressed, characteristics of McDonaldized society reigned inside the newest forms of church as well.[8]

The driving concern of the emerging movement is the concept of authority or power of those in leadership. This criticism of "modern" leadership flows from the modern view of God who is "a willful God who commands all reality through his awesome power."[9] The following conclusion emerges.

> Modern churches resemble this modern God. Their leadership is based on power, control, and submission to authority. For the church to resemble the kingdom of God, current notions of church power must be drastically altered.[10]

Ultimately, in view of this, "all previous power structures are made relative."[11] "Hierarchy" seems to be the bad word. Lest there be any doubt about this, "Emerging

---

7 Scot McKnight, "Five Streams of the Emerging Church," *Christianity Today* (February, 2007): 37.
8 Gibbs and Bolger, *Emerging* Churches, 20-21.
9 Ibid., 192.
10 Ibid.
11 Ibid.

church leaders are opposed to *any* hierarchical understanding of leadership out of the conviction that it inevitably stifles people and creativity."[12] In asserting the need for the new model of network development Gibbs places the network over against the hierarchy:

> Rather than developing and replicating an organizational machine by way of an expanded bureaucratic hierarchy, network expansion is more akin to the growth of an organism. In this regard leaders have been likened to gardeners who plant, prune, fertilize, cultivate and harvest. The leader does not *control* but *cultivates*.[13]

What does this look like?

> Emerging churches, in their attempts to resemble the kingdom, avoid all types of *control* in their leadership formation. Leadership has shifted to a more facilitative role as emerging churches have experimented with the idea of leaderless groups.[14]

This effort to flatten leadership structure has led to an egalitarianism that threatens to quench the distinctiveness of other gifts that call for an "up front" expression as well. One example of this is in the matter of those who teach in the church. Has God given teaching gifts to some?[15] How does it encourage that individual if *everyone* is a teacher? If everyone is a mouth, where are the other gifts? Notwithstanding this, emerging leaders Gibbs and Bolger press for this model.

> Many people need encouragement to overcome their reluctance to speak in public. Emerging churches require small venues to create a level of affirmation for such people.[16]

Then they make a connection with ecclesiastical models that reflect this perspective.

---

12 Ibid.,194, emphasis added.

13 Eddie Gibbs, *Leadership Next* (Downers Grove, IL: InterVarsity Press, 2005), 63, emphasis in original.

14 Ibid., emphasis added.

15 See Ephesians 4:11; Romans 12:1.

16 Gibbs and Bolger, *Emerging* Churches, 171.

> There is nothing new in an emphasis on participative worship. It has been the position held by the Quakers (Society of Friends) and the Plymouth Brethren. In their meetings, any individual moved by the Spirit is free to speak.[17]

He immediately identifies the shortcomings of such an approach.

> However, with the passage of time and the emergence of certain individuals who have biblical knowledge and discernment or, in some cases, who like to hear the sound of their own voices, the same individuals speak at each meeting. This predictable routine can be avoided when everyone is involved in the planning of worship experience.[18]

Does the effort to have everyone teach flatten the distinctiveness of those who are called and gifted to teach? Might it be that those who have biblical knowledge and discernment are those whom God has called to minister the Word in that context?

For the purpose of this study, has the emerging church also flattened those whom the Lord has called, gifted, and authorized to serve as leaders in his church?[19] It is fascinating to note that, in the discussion of the emerging movement, the expression "emerging *leaders*" is used without pause. How do these individuals become *recognized* as leaders. Who *authorized* them to speak for the movement? Is it because they are the ones who have the most influence? As the saying goes, "if everyone is the leader, then no one is the leader." Unfortunately, in the effort to address "disempowerment," the very source of power and authority is at risk of being disempowered.

In all fairness, the concept of authority is not completely disenfranchised by leaders in the emerging church movement:

> Even in postmodernity, there can be no leadership without an appropriate exercise of authority. Such authority does not arise from a leader's position or title but originates in the trust built up on the basis of character, competence, respect, and consistency. Authority is based on the twin pillars of

---

17 Ibid.
18 Ibid., 171-172.
19 See Romans 12:8.

responsibility and influence, and leaders are not simply those who impose their own wills but are individuals from whom opinion is sought.[20]

While it cannot be argued that such a description fits into the biblical picture of the *exercise* of leadership, it falls short in its description of how this leadership might *arise,* that is, what is the source of that authority. The normative perspective of the Word of God makes it clear that the authority that comes to the leader comes together with the calling and gifting of the Lord of the church. The authority of the leader does not "originate" or "arise" with the people but with the Lord. It is on that basis, and that basis alone, that the leader can act with confidence.

THE NORMATIVE PERSPECTIVE: LEADERSHIP IN THE CHURCH

The Need for Authoritative Leadership

The attempt of the emerging church movement to reverse the "disempowerment" of the people of God through deconstructing the modernistic hierarchy found in the church may just be throwing out the baby with the proverbial bathwater. There is a great danger of doing disservice to the biblical view of authority and its ongoing exercise through the ages. Granted, the concept of authority is one which is increasingly alien to postmodern culture. However, the New Testament speaks clearly of its existence and exercise in the world. The word "authority" (*exousia*) is rich in the biblical lexicography. At its most fundamental level *exousia* is the "right to do something or the right over something."[21]

If the concept of authoritative leadership does not exist, why then does the Bible use the terminology of "submission?" If there is no authoritative leadership, the call for submission becomes moot. It is clear that both dynamics are at work and for a very clear purpose. At the root of the word *hupotasso,* often translated "submit" in the New Testament, is the word for "order." Perhaps the following illustration will be helpful. Back in the day, children would assemble on the local athletic field with the intention of playing a softball game. What is the first thing they would have to do? They agree on captains who would then choose teams, set up the batting order, etc. Or, have you ever been appointed to a committee? What is the first thing that

---

20 Gibbs, *Leadership Next,* 66.

21 Gerhard Kittel, ed., *Theological Dictionary of the New Testament,* Vol. 2 (Grand Rapids, MI: Wm. B. Eerdmans Publishing Co., 1964) , 562.

has to be settled? The group has to identify the person who will be the chairperson. These simple illustrations remind us that without leadership even on the most basic level, there is disorder. God has simply exercised his prerogative as creator to appoint the "team captains." They are 1) the civil government in society, 2) the father in the home, and 3) the elders in the church. This is for the sake of order, not so that they can "give orders." As Rushdoony has said, "The alternative to submission is exploitation, not freedom, because there is no true freedom in anarchy."

It is clear, therefore, that all human authority is derived. "Then Jesus came to them and said, 'All authority in heaven and on earth has been given to me'" (Matthew 28:18). Ultimately, all authority is the Lord's.

> All authority in the church belongs to Christ. From his place of authority at God's right hand, Christ gives the keys of his kingdom; he validates in heaven what is done in his name on earth.[22]

The Bible is clear that only God's authority is underived. Any and every human authority is delegated from the Lord above. Paul writes,

> Everyone must submit himself to the governing authorities, for there is no authority [*exousia*] except that which God has established. The authorities that exist have been established by God (Romans 13:1).

Pilate claimed to have authority to crucify Jesus. Jesus reminded him that, "You would have no power (*exousian*) over me if it were not given to you from above" (John 19:11).

The authority of the elder is from above as well. Paul reminded the Ephesian elders that the "Holy Spirit has made you overseers" (Ephesians 20:28). This note is sounded in Peter's words as well.

Peter could not have warned the Asian elders against "lording it over those allotted to your charge" (1 Peter 5:3) if they had no authority. As shepherds of the church, elders have been given the authority to lead and protect the local church.23

---

22 Edmund P. Clowney, *The Church,* (Downers Grove, IL: InterVarsity Press, 1995), 202.
23 Alexander Strauch, *Biblical Eldership* (Littleton, CO: Lewis and Roth, 1995), 97.

All authority comes from the Lord and is exercised in his behalf. Ultimately, it is his authority.

Since that is the case, the exercise of this authority is to be directed by God's Word, the unnormed norm. In the elders' "right over" the flock and "right to act" they are under the authority and direction of the Good Shepherd Himself. Elders are responsible to look to him for wisdom and direction in caring for the flock. This wisdom and direction is to be found in God's Word through the illumination of the Holy Spirit.

> Church authority, grounded in the Word of Christ, is also limited to
> it. Christian obedience to church rule is obedience in the Lord, for His
> Word governs the church, not the other way around.[24]

Therefore, the exercise of authority in the church must always be grounded in the Scriptures and, conversely, loses its legitimacy when it calls those under its care to ignore, contradict, or contravene the truth found therein. But exactly how is this authoritative leadership to be exercised in the church?

The Exercise of Authoritative Leadership in the Church

Through the ages there have been many debates over the details of the structure of what authoritative leadership in the church should look like. This is displayed in the various examples of polity or government that exist in the church. While a detailed overview of these variations is beyond the purview of this essay, the case must be made that elders, as God's shepherds, have *exousia,* "the right to act" on behalf of the Good Shepherd. This is not in contradiction of the concept of the "priesthood of all believers" or what is often referred to as the general office (rights and privileges) of every believer. It is not contradictory to this but complementary.

It is clear that elders were called to lead in the church. In the first missionary journey of Paul and Barnabas it is reported that they "appointed elders for them in each church and, with prayer and fasting, committed them to the Lord, in whom they had put their trust" (Acts 14:23). This clearly implies particular elders for particular churches. When Paul was on his way to Jerusalem, he "sent to Ephesus for the elders of the church" (Acts 20:17). In Paul's letter to Titus he instructs him to "appoint elders in every town, as I directed you" (Titus 1:5) after which he outlines the qualifications Titus should look for in such men. This pattern is not limited to the Pauline material. James urges those who are sick to "call the elders of the church

24 Clowney, *The Church,* 203.

to pray over him and anoint him with oil in the name of the Lord" (James 5:14). "One notices that in James it is not just any older person who is called, but officials, the elders of the church, which in this case is surely the *local congregation*."[25] This text assumes a relationship between the sick person and a particular group of elders who are the elders of the church, that is, his church.

Peter writes, "to the elders among you" (1 Peter 5:1). He admonishes them to shepherd God's flock "that is under your care." It must be admitted that there is both continuity and discontinuity between apostles and elders which are both referred to in this text. Peter reminds the elders of his apostolic qualification in describing himself as "a witness of the sufferings of Christ." However, he also describes himself as a "fellow elder" (*sumpresbuteros*) emphasizing his identification with them as elders called to "shepherd the flock." He is recognizing not merely a continuity of function but also the authority to fulfill that function.

> And, indeed, whoever will closely examine the words of Christ will easily perceive that they describe the stated and perpetual order, and not any temporary regulation of the Church.[26]

Any doubt that these leaders were to exercise authority melts away when the language of the recognition of that authority through submission is asserted. Members of the flock are called to defer and submit to the authority of the elders. The reason that human authority is to be respected is the very fact that, ultimately, that authority is from the Lord.

> It is the Holy Spirit who has made them overseers, and they are delegated by the head of the church. It is the obligation of the people and the elders to recognize that the rule exercised by the latter is by delegation from Christ and to him they are responsible.[27]

This theme is clear in the New Testament. The reason that citizens are to be submissive in paying taxes to the civil authorities is that "the authorities are God's servants, who give their full time to governing" (Romans 13:6).

---

25 Peter Davids, *Commentary on James* (Grands Rapids, MI: Wm. B. Eerdmans Publishing Co., 1982), 193, emphasis added.

26 John Calvin, *The Institutes of the Christian Religion*, vol. 2. (Philadelphia: Westminster Press, 1960), 488.

27 John Murray, *Collected Writings*, vol. 1 (Carlisle, PA: Banner of Truth Trust, 1976), 262.

One of the characteristics of the Good Shepherd's sheep is that they hear his voice and *follow* him. In turn, the sheep are to follow those elders called by him and given authority over various folds in the world. Paul encourages the Thessalonian believers to "respect those who work hard among you, who are over you in the Lord and who admonish you" (1 Thessalonians 5:12).

> Them that "are over you in the Lord" is not an official description of a technical order of ministry, but it is difficult to see who could be meant other than office-bearers in the church. The verb may be used of informal leadership, but it is also an official word, describing the function of those who are officers.[28]

Of great interest is the fact that the word translated "respect" in the New International Version is the verb *eidenia*, a form of the verb *oida*, which means "to know." Here, it means, "respect, appreciate the worth of."[29] Paul adds, "hold them in highest regard in love because of their work" (1 Thessalonians 5:13).

The author of Hebrews encouraged those to whom he wrote to "Obey your leaders and submit to their authority" (Hebrews 13:17). He goes on in that verse to state that this is necessary not only for the sake of the leader, but for their sake as well. "Obey them so that their work will be a joy, not a burden, for that would be of no advantage to you."

> Christian leadership is intended for the *advantage* of all, not just for the advantage of those who hold positions of authority, and good and successful leadership is to a considerable degree dependent on the willing response of obedience and submission on the part of those who are under authority.[30]

Therefore, not only are the shepherds to know the sheep and take responsibility for them, but the sheep are to know, that is, to respect, appreciate, and submit to those who are "over" them in the Lord. It is imperative for the health and growth

---

28 Leon Morris, *The First and Second Letter to the Thessalonians* (Grand Rapids, MI: Wm. B. Eerdmans Publishing Co., 1959), 166.

29 James Everett Frame, *A Critical and Exegetical Commentary on the Epistle of St. Paul to the Thessalonians* (Edinburgh: T and T Clark, 1912), 192.

30 Philip E. Hughes, *Commentary on the Epistle to the Hebrews* (Grand Rapids, MI: Wm. B. Eerdmans Publishing Co., 1977), 585, emphasis in original..

of the church that authoritative biblical leadership structures be in place. If the affirmation that there are some who are called to lead as pastors and elders is "hierarchical," so be it.

Ironically, Gibbs discusses not only the need for leaders but for "two-level" leadership.

> The first, or primary, level of leadership involves the ability "to keep the main thing the main thing." First-level leadership is concerned with challenges or insights that influence and at times threaten to subvert the overall operation.[31]

Then there is the second-level leader:

> At the second, *lower level,* leaders use their individual expertise in order to address a particular challenge. With some, this expertise is technical in nature. Others are systems people, who are skilled at connecting and sequencing.[32]

For all the talk about doing away with hierarchy, an *informal* hierarchy emerges nonetheless because, whatever you call it, leadership is required in the church. Even efforts to avoid the terminology of "office" come up short. Emerging theologian Ray Anderson demonstrates the dilemma.

> In this early [church] charismatic community the Spirit does not create offices but rather ministries. The need for ministries results in the creation of the office.[33]

The implication is that the "office" of elder in the church is not a divine directive but an expeditious creation of a needy community. Anderson summarizes that "leadership is more a function of community than an externally applied authority."[34]

It is quite interesting that one of the conclusions that Gibbs comes to is that "churches may be more effective if they move beyond the concept of a single leader to

---

31 Gibbs, *Leadership Next*, 64.

32 Ibid., emphasis added.

33 Ray S. Anderson, *An Emergent Theology for Emerging Churches* (Downers Grove, IL: InterVarsity Press, 2006), 171.

34 Ibid.

one in which leadership is exercised by a team with one individual serving as *primus inter pares* - first among equals.[35] This is already modeled, first of all, in the biblical concept of the plurality of elders. The New Testament testimony is clear that there were several elders in every church.[36] Gibbs acknowledges that Paul "established teams of elders to lead these fledgling churches."[37] The biblical picture of leadership is "team" leadership as it describes a plurality of elders leading the local church. It is likely that the *primus inter pares* was the pastor-teacher of Ephesians 4:11 who was also the one among the elders "whose work is preaching and teaching" (1 Timothy 5:17). The biblical picture answers Gibbs' concern.

Another issue that emerging leaders express is clearly met in the biblical view of how that authority is exercised. As shown earlier, emerging leaders are concerned with the exercise of power that "stifles people and creativity" and with the avoiding "all types of control."[38] However, the Scriptures are clear that those who exercise authoritative leadership are to do it under God for the wellbeing of those under that authority. Certainly, in the Lord's flock, leadership among God's people is always servant leadership. Peter writes that those who shepherd God's flock must do so, "... not because you must, but because you are willing, as God wants you to be; not greedy for money, *but eager to serve*" (1 Peter 5:2, emphasis added).

The Son of Man, the Chief Shepherd, came "not to be served but to serve, and to give his life as a ransom for many" (Matthew 20:28). The authority of the elder must also be exercised for the well-being of the flock "which he bought with his own blood" (Acts 20:28). Though there have been many shortcomings in expressing it throughout the history of the church, the biblical picture of leadership is *servant* leadership. "Control" is not harmful if it is used for the benefit of its recipients. A parent who exercises his control to pull a child out of the path of an oncoming car is demonstrating love in the exercise of that control. In the church, control is good when seeking to move a group in a godly direction (leadership) or to recover the lost sheep (discipline). The rod and staff were implements of care and control to the ancient shepherd, and the sheep were comforted by the sight (Psalm 23:4).

To keep this in proper perspective, the Scriptures are clear that the exercise of this authority is not in a vacuum, but rather it is exercised with accountability to the God who delegated it. All who hold derived authority are ultimately accountable to the One who gave that authority. Inasmuch as the elder's authority or "right to act"

35 Gibbs, *Leadership* Next, 64-65.
36 Acts 14:23; 20:17; Titus 1:5; James 5:14; 1 Peter 5:1.
37 Gibbs, *Leadership* Next, 117.
38 Supra, 2.

comes from the Lord, it follows that they are answerable to him for the manner in which they act. It is an accountability to the Lord for their care for his flock. The writer to the Hebrews reminds his readers of the following imperative. "Obey your leaders and submit to their authority. They keep watch over you *as men who must give account*" (Hebrews 13:17, emphasis added).

In commenting on this verse, Philip Edgecomb Hughes writes,

> They [leaders] are men who will have to give account to God, and this solemn consideration should affect not only the quality of their leadership but also the quality of the obedience with which the Christian community responds to that leadership.[39]

This concept is not new inasmuch as the "shepherds" of Israel were held accountable for their failure to care for God's flock.

> This is what the Sovereign LORD says: I am against the shepherds and will hold them accountable for my flock. I will remove them from tending the flock so that the shepherds can no longer feed themselves. I will rescue my flock from their mouths, and it will no longer be food for them (Ezekiel 34:10).

Rather than caring for the flock, these shepherds were taking care of themselves at the expense of the covenant people. Emerging church leaders are correct to take these matters to heart but not to dispense with biblical leadership structures so as to avoid its examples of abuse.

THE EMERGING CHURCH ON LEADERSHIP: THE ASCENT OF THE SITUATIONAL PERSPECTIVE?

In this brief analysis of the concept of leadership in the emerging church it becomes clear that its tendency is to give normative power to the context. Remember that the situational perspective is that which takes into consideration the culture and context. These concerns must be taken into consideration but there is great danger when concerns for cultural engagement overshadow biblical principles. In discuss-

---

39 Hughes, *Commentary on Hebrews*, 586.

ing the nuances of the emerging church movement, Scot McKnight identifies three approaches, or degrees of engagement. In identifying the postmodern mission field, some minister *to* postmoderns, others *with* postmoderns and others *as* postmoderns.[40] The first is direct engagement with the flawed foundations of relativism and the practices that flow from it. Ministering *with* postmoderns takes the approach that their work is *in* but not *of* postmodern values. "Such Christians view postmodernity as a present condition into which we are called to proclaim and live out the gospel."[41] Then there are those who choose to minister *as* postmoderns. The trouble comes when the "foundations" found in the norm of the Scriptures gives way to the "postfoundationalism" of those who minister *as* postmoderns, those who embrace the values of postmodernism.

Contextualization is the term that has been coined to express the legitimate integration of the situational perspective into ministry concerns. What difference should the context (place, people, culture, etc.) make in ministry, in how we understand leadership? It can sometimes be a delicate balance to find. If the context is not taken into account at all, *calcification* occurs, a hardening that does not consider the concerns of various cultures. However, when the distinctive principles of the normative perspective of the Scriptures are lost in the effort to contextualize, then *culturalization* occurs. Both of these extremes must be avoided if effective ministry is to be achieved. The contention of this essay is that the emerging church view of leadership has inched too closely to the culturalization end of the continuum. The connection between postmodern suspicion of authority and any hierarchy and the flattening of church structure can be seen again in Gibbs' argument.

> As society fragments and people exercise their freedom of choice, hierarchical structures crumble. The turfism of hierarchical organizations can especially frustrate younger people. They recognize that *lateral* and flexible structures are required to maintain unfettered access to the knowledge, wisdom, and resources necessary in today's fast-paced environment.[42]

This effort to identify with postmodernism has moved it away from key biblical principles of the legitimate existence and exercise of authority in the church and toward the extreme of culturalization. D.A. Carson has noted the same imbalance.

---

40 McKnight, "Five Streams," 37.

41 Ibid.

42 Gibbs, *Leadership Next*, 96, emphasis added.

> Is there at least some danger that what is being advocated is not so much a new kind of Christian in a new emerging church, but a church that is so submerging itself in the culture that it risks hopeless compromise?[43]

Ironically, in its efforts to contextualize, the emerging church has failed to give due attention to the fact that places in the world (the global south, for example) where the church is growing most dramatically[44] are not postmodern at all, but are modern or premodern for that matter. This highlights one of the dangers of elevating the situational perspective: reading the entire world through *your* cultural situatedness. For example, one of the marks of globalization is the fluidity of immigration patterns. This is not news to Christians in the United States, but perhaps its extent is.

> As we gain greater distance from the event, the passage of the Immigration Reform Act of 1965 increasingly looks like the most significant event of that much-Ballyhooeded decade. By 2000, the United States was home to 30 million immigrants, about 11% of the population. Over 13 million migrants arrived in the 1990's alone. Almost 5% of Americans have been in the country for a decade or less.[45]

Many of these immigrants are coming from modern or even premodern cultures. Has the emerging church movement taken this into consideration?

What about the aging population in the United States? The emerging church movement is concerned to reach postmoderns, specifically younger people. But what is the primary wave in American demographics? It is the progression of the baby boomers into retirement years. There is no better indicator of the significance of the advance of this wave than the preponderance of television advertisements by pharmaceutical companies addressing every possible malady an aging person could anticipate! However, to many in the emerging church movement this generation is suspect at best or disdained as the perpetrators of modernism at worst. The absence of generational diversity can impoverish a community, especially the leadership of a

---

43 Donald A. Carson, *Becoming Conversant With the Emerging Church* (Grand Rapids, MI: Zondervan, 2005), 44.

44 See Philip Jenkins, *The Next Christendom: The Coming of Global Christianity* and *The New Faces of Christianity* (London: Oxford University Press, 2002) and *The New Faces of Christianity: Believing the Bible in the Global South* (London: Oxford University Press, 2006).

45 Jenkins, *The Next* Christendom, 100.

community. Eddie Gibbs has observed in his interaction with younger leaders that "many have expressed their longing for mentoring by older leaders."[46] He goes on to mention the importance of this generational diversity to reach younger people.

> Those churches having the most influence among the under-thirty-five-year-old generation are those with 15-20 percent of the members in the over-sixty-year-old category. These seniors provide much-needed mentoring, accountability, encouragement and wise counsel.[47]

The antidote is to restore the balance provided by the normative perspective. After all, when it comes to the emerging movement view of leadership, it has been forced to recognize by mere pragmatic means principles that are already clearly articulated in the normative perspective of the Scriptures. Such principles include, among others, 1) the need for servant leadership; 2) the need for a parity (team) among leaders and; 3) the preferability of *primus inter pares* - first among equals. The fact that these principles have not been perfectly practiced through the history of the church does not change the fact that they are clearly taught in the scriptures. Rather than acknowledge the clear guidance about leadership found in the Scriptures, has the emerging church movement elevated "culture" to become the norm to which everything else must submit?

IMPLICATIONS FOR THEOLOGICAL EDUCATION

Here again the perspectival approach should be appreciated in terms of its value in training leaders. The normative perspective addresses the biblical standards for leaders including the description of the nature and functions of leadership within the church. This would also include subordinate standards such as confessional statements and ecclesiastical guidelines to which an individual might submit, given his ecclesial setting. They are called "subordinate" standards inasmuch as they are viewed as subordinate to the Scriptures and are legitimate only as far as they accurately reflect biblical principles.

The existential perspective would refer to the individual's assessment of his gifts and calling, in light of the standards and principles of the normative perspective. Does the individual exhibit the biblical character qualifications necessary to lead in

---

46 Gibbs, *Leadership* Next, 36.
47 Ibid.

the church? Does he posseess the requisite gifts for ministry? Has he experienced a "call" from the Lord? Has the Lord given him a burden for using his gifts among a particular people or a particular place? Is he willing to submit to the subordinate standards in his chosen ecclesial setting. These are matters for self-examination as well as for assessment by the appropriate ecclesial authorities.

The situational perspective takes into consideration the context in which that ministry leadership would be exercised. How are the biblical priorities of leadership to be applied by this leader in the particular cultural situation at hand? How is the "fit" of the leadership profile of an individual leader to the ministry in view? What leadership "style" might a particular ministry setting require? What are the specific challenges of the respective culture to advancing the mission of the Gospel?

Maximum effectiveness in leadership can be found only when all three of these perspectives are kept in consideration. However, as indicated previously, the existential and situational perspectives must bow before the normative, biblical perspective. With respect to the existential perspective, the nature of the understanding of the concept of "calling" must be biblical. The character qualifications of leaders are not to be derived from a common communal consensus but from the pages of the Bible. The nature and use of the gifts of the Spirit must reflect biblical principles. It is also the Bible that identifies what leaders are to do. With respect to the situational perspective, great care must be taken not to lose the truth of the normative perspective for the sake of the particular culture or ministry setting. Contextualization, properly understood, takes the concerns of the culture into consideration without compromising the truth of the Scriptures.

What does this have to do with theological education in a global setting? There has been significant criticism of traditional seminary-based theological education because it has often failed to give adequate attention to the situational and existential perspectives. This is certainly the concern of the emerging church movement. Here is Brian McLaren's assessment:

> My primary complaint about the current seminary system, however, is that it too often is a system of certification, not education. Not always, but too often seminaries recruit students who already know what they think and are not interested in having their thinking stretched or chal-

lenged, thank you very much. They'd rather learn stronger defenses and justifications and proofs for their current beliefs.[48]

Eddie Gibbs notes that "the present leadership training system is so elitist, slow, and expensive, that it constitutes a bottleneck rather than a fountain source of leaders."[49] Tony Campolo adds that seminaries "tend to require the wrong subjects. They seldom structure their academic programs and course requirements according to a rapidly changing world."[50]

Traditional seminary training is understood to be another outdated vestige of modernity.

There is no doubt that the very notion of curriculum, structure, and grades for that matter are *modern*. These critiques are not completely without value, not because seminaries (and it is risky to put all seminaries in the same pile) fail in their tendency to focus on "defenses and justifications and proofs for the current beliefs," but because they sometimes do not give considerable attention to, in perspectival terminology, the existential perspective (character, calling, and competence of the candidate) and the situational (how does all of this work in the world?) perspective. Here is how McLaren identifies the distinction:

> As we move beyond modernity, we lose our infatuation with analysis, knowledge, information, facts, belief systems—and with those who traffic in them. Instead we are attracted to leaders who possess the elusive quality of wisdom (think James 3:13-18), who practice spiritual disciplines, whose lives are characterized by depth of spiritual practice (not by just the tightness of belief system).[51]

But doesn't this "elusive quality of wisdom" find its ground in knowledge, facts, and a belief system (think James 1:21-25)? Isn't wisdom in the Scriptures always grounded in the knowledge of the truth revealed in the Bible?[52] Isn't wisdom merely the godly application of this knowledge to life? The emerging church's failure to sound clearly many biblical principles of leadership, including the need for authoritative

---

48 Brian D. McLaren and Tony Campolo, *Adventures in Missing the Point* (Grand Rapids, MI: Zondervan, 2003), 180.

49 Gibbs, *Leadership* Next, 205.

50 McLaren and Campolo, *Adventures in Missing the Point*, 176.

51 Ibid, 160.

52 Proverbs 18:15.

leadership structures and its appropriate exercise, may leave its leadership candidates devoid of wisdom in ministry. For example, with this approach to leadership, it is not surprising that many "younger leaders, as well as those who serve as their mentors, have observed reluctance on the part of younger leaders to accept leadership responsibility."[53] This is perfectly consistent given the emphasis in the movement on egalitarianism. The leader might ask, "Who am I to take responsibility to lead these people?" The answer is found in the normative perspective of the word of God which makes it clear that the authority of the leader comes together with the calling and gifting of the Lord of the church.

Who then emerges as a model of postmodern leadership? McLaren suggests Dorothy from *The Wizard of Oz.*

> Rather than being a person with all the answers, who is constantly informed of what's up and what's what and where to go, she is herself lost, a seeker, often vulnerable, often bewildered. These characteristics would disqualify her from modern leadership, but they serve as her best credentials for leadership in the emerging culture.[54]

McLaren goes on to contrast her collaborative, nurturing style with the "modern" fraud who is the wizard. He is probably overreaching in his analysis when he states,

> By exposing the Wizard as a fraud, the film was probing an unexpressed cultural doubt, giving voice to a rising misgiving, displaying an early pang of discontent with its dominant model of larger-than-life leadership.[55]

Do you remember how the story ends? It ends with the "wizard" not only meeting the needs of the scarecrow, lion, and tin man, but also offering to take Dorothy back home to Kansas in his balloon! However, after a futile attempt to board the balloon, it is actually the knowledge conveyed by Glinda, who instructs her to click her heals together and say, "There's no place like home." Dorothy quickly complies and the desired destination (Kansas) is realized. Apart from that knowledge, communicated and accepted, Dorothy would still be with the munchkins in Oz! This

---

53 Ibid.,108.
54 McLaren and Campolo, *Adventures in Missing the Point*, 158.
55 Ibid, 157-158.

isn't exactly the ringing example of postmodern leadership behavior that McLaren would have us believe.[56]

There is no doubt that adjustments need to be made continually to the traditional seminary approach.[57] Adjustments need to be made to *every* approach to ministry training all the time, but it is crucial never to become detached or even distant from the anchor of the objective propositional truth of God's Word. To some in the emerging movement, the previous statement is far too modern, but failure to embrace it will leave the emerging church adrift without an anchor, prone to the variable winds of the times and cultures in which we live.

CONCLUSION

As the waves of various movements wash over the church from generation to generation, there are always valuable things to be retained. The emerging church movement's concern for servant leadership and team leadership are valuable and reflect the concerns of Scripture. However, emerging movement efforts to flatten and remove structure with hopes of eliminating modern vestiges of hierarchy and authority compromise the biblical principles of authoritative leadership and office. Without this clear biblical commitment, eventually everyone will be left to do what is right in his own eyes.

The temptation will always be to elevate context and culture to the level of the normative, even in training for ministry leadership. Harvie Conn was on the cutting edge of working through the complicated matters of contextualization, and he clearly asserted the preeminence of the Scriptures as the norm.

> Scripture stands, its veracity untainted by either the cultures in which it comes to us or the cultures in which it goes. God's revelation can make use of our cultures but always stands in judgment over them.[58]

---

56 Don't forget that Dorothy left her friends behind, too! Not very postmodern.

57 See John Frame, "Proposals for a New North American Model" in Harvie M. Conn and Samuel Rowen, eds., *Missions and Theological Education in World Perspective* (Farmington: Associates of Urbanus, 1984); Roger S. Greenway, "Getting David out of Saul's Armor" in Manuel Ortiz and Susan S. Baker, eds., *The Urban Face of Mission* (Phillipsburg, NJ: Presbyterian & Reformed Publishers, 2002), 225-39; Robert Banks *Reenvisioning Theological Education* (Grand Rapids, MI: Wm. B. Eerdmans Publishing Co., 1999); and Timothy Z. Witmer, "Seminary: A Place to Prepare Pastors?," *Westminster Theological Journal* 69(2007): 229-46.

58 Harvie M. Conn, ed., *Inerrancy and Hermeneutic* (Grand Rapids, MI: Baker, 1988), 209.

What is to be valued and embraced from the waves that wash over the church? Those elements that call upon the church to revisit and recommit herself to fundamental biblical principles.

.15.

Theological Education in a Global Setting: The African Context

JONATHAN T. IORKIGHIR

What should occupy the minds of the church and every theological seminary or Bible school today is the relevance to the society of the theology that they teach. Our global community is experiencing such changes in thought, forms of expression and interaction that theological education today just cannot overlook these by clinging to old models of teaching. Theological education should support and serve the ministry of the church by giving direction and content to what the church does. It therefore follows that theology that is given and received at seminaries should be directly applicable to the context in which the church's ministry happens. Since the church exists in a geographical and cultural context, the theology of the church should also target the context of the church's ministry and appropriately hone its conclusions toward relevant application to the context in which the church does ministry. This is the major issue explored in this essay. How can we do theological education in today's global context, especially in Africa, in such a way that it has global relevance? The contention here is that the only way to have global relevance is for theological education to respond to the global context to which it is immediately applied.

Theological education in Africa has neglected the African context due to missionary influence and the resistance of African church leadership to come to terms with the African reality in theological education. In years gone by, Western and European missionaries went all over the world, especially in Asia and in Africa, preaching the gospel.[1] They also set up seminaries or Bible schools and equipped these schools with theological curricula and books that were directly taken from Western seminaries and used them to train local pastors in Asia and Africa. But in some cases, the missionaries worked hard to adapt those curricula to the needs of the natives to whom they ministered the gospel. However, the missionaries themselves, as students of these cultures, could not adequately adapt theological education to the needs of the local people. Their genuine attempts to provide relevant theological education in other contexts must be applauded but often ended up looking more or less like what one obtains in Western or European seminaries. When natives took over leadership of the church's education, they were resistant to changing the curricula for fear that they might be changing some cherished imported doctrines. Change became taboo. There is, therefore, the need to look at theological education today as it happens in Africa, especially with the rise of post-modernity and globalization, in such a way that it addresses the African situation of poverty, injustice, traditional religion, cultism, spirit encounter, HIV/AIDS, etc. To this end, we shall first clarify what we mean here by theological education and global setting, and then we shall observe how this challenges theological education both in the West and in Africa. We will follow up with a case study of a seminary in Nigeria. Finally we shall consider the type of theological education that is both globally relevant and contextually responsive to the unique African situation.

CLARIFYING THEOLOGICAL EDUCATION AND GLOBAL SETTING

What do we mean here by theological education, and what is a global setting? Essential to this essay is the claim that theological education has to be authentic and realistic. This means it must be education that is unreservedly theocentric and it must be theology that is rooted in God in his fullest revelation to us through his Son Jesus Christ. The fullest testimony of this revelation comes to us through God's Holy Scriptures, the Bible. It must be theology that focuses on the knowledge of God, the people of God and the purpose of God. I would, therefore, paraphrase Dieumeme Noelliste's definition of theological education as the equipping of the people of God

---

1 Adrian Hastings, in *African Christianity* (New York: Seabury Press, 1977), 2, wants us to acknowledge that freed African slaves were also very instrumental evangelizing African natives alongside with foreign missionaries, "The men who really carried the Christian faith along the West Coast in the mid-nineteenth century were nearly all Africans, many of them men and women rescued from the slave ships on the Atlantic and landed by the British navy at Freetown, in Sierra Leone."

with the knowledge and wisdom of God as deposited in the Bible for the purpose of personal renewal and meaningful participation in the fulfillment of God's purpose in the church and in the world.[2] In teaching theology in our age of globalization, it is mandatory to accent the uniqueness of divine revelation as it comes to us through the Word of God. Otherwise there are many competing theologies and all sorts of ideas and concepts of God such that you do not know what or which God (or god) in which an individual says he believes these days. Theological education today should emphasize the God of the Bible as he is revealed to us through his Son, Jesus Christ. God, Jesus Christ and the Bible must be uniquely upheld in any theological curriculum for it to attain relevance in today's world of relativity.

The next issue that needs clarification is the expression *global setting*. This rightly assumes that theological education should not happen in a vacuum, but in a setting, a context, and for us today that setting is global. A lot can be said about this, but we need only to state that this expression assumes a number of contexts that are represented on the face of the earth. On the continental level, we have the Asian, African, European, South American, North American, etc. contexts, and within these continents there is a wide number and variety of contexts defined by race, tribe or geography. All these contexts present their unique questions and needs to the theological educator. But the word 'global' does not just refer to the many contexts in the world; it also refers to what we call *globalization*. With the rise of globalization in the twenty-first century, whereby the whole world is becoming a small village, it may be asked whether we may still talk about various or multiple contexts. In our postmodern context, it might be a little simplistic to just look at globalization as referring to a multiplicity of disparate contexts that have nothing to do with each other. In attempting to respond to this question, it is important that we put in proper perspective what we mean here by globalization or a global setting. Globalization in itself is not about theology but it provides for us a new context for theological education.[3] But just what is globalization? Like many other concepts, globalization does not submit to a quick and easy definition.[4] However, we can set out by saying that globalization is propelled by the force of commerce and economics

2 Dieumeme Noelliste, *Toward A Theology of Theological Education: 3,500 Theological Institutions in the World* (Seoul: World Evangelical Fellowship Theological Commission, 1993), 7.

3 David A. Roozen, Alice Frazier Evans and Robert Evans, eds. *Changing the Way Seminaries Teach: Globalization and Theological Education* (Simsbury: Plowshares Institute, 1996), 8.

4 E. G. Singgih reviewing the book, *Changing the Way Seminaries Teach: Globalization and Theological Education* observes the difficulty of defining globalization that was encountered by authors of the book as well. He submits that the definition of the term is at best, ambiguous, in Noelliste, *Toward A Theology of Theological Education*, 8.

on the wings of modern technology and communication. It asserts that the whole world has become or is becoming one small village. Another point of view pushes this short definition further indicating that globalization means "overcoming the old obstacles of nationality, demography and geography and dealing universally without limiting boundaries."[5] In simpler terms, Roozen says:

> Globalization points to the increasing reality that the world is 'a single place' as peoples, cultures, societies, and civilizations previously more or less isolated from one another are now in regular and almost unavoidable contact.[6]

The implication of this is easy to recognize. If the whole world becomes a village and if geographical boundaries are overcome by this monster called globalization, where then do we still have local contexts? We only have one big context, the global context in which to do theology. If this is the case the topic here under discussion becomes highly unnecessary or even absurd. What this means is that we look more carefully at the concept of global theological education in such a way that neither are we too narrow-minded in our understanding of it nor do we refer to a concept that has a meaning different from what we intend to say and work with.

Maybe an illustration might help clarify this better. I sat in an internet café in my very little town of Gboko in Benue State, Nigeria, where the major language spoken is Tiv, the sixth largest tribe in Nigeria. Nigeria has over 400 languages (not dialects but distinct languages). While there I bought a laptop computer from the U.S. I paid for the laptop computer from a dealer in Seattle, Washington. Four days later I was sitting at the Heathrow Airport in London waiting for my flight to Philadelphia to attend some classes. I again contacted my computer dealer on the internet asking him to ensure that I receive my laptop at Westminster Theological Seminary in Philadelphia upon my arrival there. I arrived in Philadelphia and picked up the laptop—no problem. Six days before I was in Nigeria, 6,000 miles away, doing business with a dealer in Seattle, and now I was in Philadelphia using my laptop. It would take missionaries six months to have a letter sent to them in Nigeria from the U.S. in the 1970s and 1980s. Just a matter of six years ago I would not have been able to complete this transaction from my little village in Nigeria. Modern technology has improved communication and brought the whole world closer to the doorsteps of everyone, and a transaction like this one becomes easily

---

5 Mansfred Stegar, *Globalization: A Very Short Introduction* (Oxford: Oxford University Press, 2003), 10.
6 Roozen, *Changing the Way Seminaries Teach*, 185.

possible. This is a commercial aspect of globalization whereby Philadelphia, Seattle, London, and Gboko in Nigeria operate as though they were all in one small village. The same phenomenon applies to almost all areas of life.

In a small way, this shows how globalization in some way is eroding some contexts and making them into a mega culture. Cultural patterns once unapproved in several African contexts are now looked upon as the order of the day. For instance, ladies wear jeans made from an American factory in Malaysia and walk the streets of any African city with a cell phone in hand talking to friends far out of town setting dates and parties, etc. The parents do not bother what their daughters wear saying that the good old days with their good old cultures are now gone. Thus globalization asserts that all contexts are in a wave of constant change and so theological education in today's world has to live up to this global reality of changing cultures. It is theology that must be prepared to face the reality of change in changing contexts.

Globalization as outlined above conveys the idea that no cultural, religious, economic, political or social context is uninformed about the existence of other contexts, especially the global contexts.[7] What this means for our doing theology today is that we do it in such a way that it is responsive to the immediate cultural context but is also aware of the monster context out there, namely, globalization.

Globalization does not mean in any way that unique local contexts are extinct. We make a gross error of assuming that because of globalization there are no other cultures. This would be the same mistake the colonial masters and early missionaries made when they first came to Africa thinking Africans had no culture, had no religion, were unteachable, etc., and therefore were forced to think, learn and do things the western/European way.

THE CHALLENGE FOR A NEW WAY OF THEOLOGICAL EDUCATION

Globalization has placed a challenge on theological institutions around the world forcing them to rethink the way they teach theology. In North America, twelve seminaries came together to begin a five year project called the Pilot Immersion

---

7 Peter Beyer, in *Religion and Globalization* (London: Sage Publications, 1994), 2, captures this well when he says that globalization moves toward a single culture because the cultures clash as they are experienced all at once. So he feels that "globalizing social-structural and cultural forces furnish a common context that attenuates the differences among these ways of life.... Juxtaposition of particular cultures or identities not only brings differences into sharper profile, it makes it much more visible that the diverse ways of living are largely human constructions. In the contest of comparison no single one of them is self-evidently correct."

Project for the Globalization of Theological Education in North America (PIP/ GTE). The result of this project was the book, *Changing the Way Seminaries Teach: Globalization and Theological Education.* In this book, the seminaries come to the conclusion that globalization presents the church with challenges and opportunities to which the church must respond by the way it provides theological education to its leadership.[8]

Related to this, Roger Greenway rightly observes that certain seminaries are unable to meet the global challenge in training leaders for urban ministry in the U.S. when he says:

> Schools that are conservative and evangelical in theology are not able or willing to make the necessary changes to prepare an adequate number of people to serve effectively in urban contexts and minister in churches representing a wide range of spectrum of races, languages, cultures, and religious backgrounds.[9]

Elsewhere, two professors make the following critique: "We share the conviction that traditional theological education is not well suited for the equipping of urban Christian leaders.... Traditional forms produce nonfunctional or dysfunctional graduates."[10] By saying this, the two professors at Fuller Theological Seminary in Pasadena, California submit their agreement that seminaries are not able to meet the challenges of relevant theological education for urban pastoral leadership. Seeing this need for providing relevant theological education for today's world of globalization and urbanization, the Christian Reformed Church in North America (CRCNA) constituted a committee to look into the possibility of providing alternative routes for getting into the CRC ministry without necessarily having to go through the denominational seminary which offers traditional evangelical training.[11]

---

8 Roozen, Frazer & Evans, *Changing the Way Seminaries Teach*, 8.

9 Roger Greenway, "Getting David Out of Saul's Armor" in Manuel Ortiz and Susan S. Baker, eds., *The Urban Face of Mission: Ministering the Gospel in a Diverse and Changing World* (Phillipsburg, NJ: Presbyterian & Reformed Publishers, 2002), 226.

10 Edgar J. Ellison and J. Timothy Kauffman, *Developing Leaders for Urban Ministries* (New York: Peter Lang Publishing Co., 1993), 1.

11 A full report of the findings of this committee can be found in "Report from the Committee to Examine Alternate Routes Being Used to Enter the Ordained Ministry in the CRC," in *Christian Reformed Church in North America: Agenda for Synod, 2000* (Grand Rapids, MI: Christian Reformed Church in North America, 2000), 271-350.

If globalization presents a challenge for theological education in the U.S., the challenge is even more acute in Africa. As far back as 1983, the association for Theological Education by Extension (TEE) triggered the writing of the book, *Theological Education in Context: 100 Extension Programmes in Contemporary Africa.* The book acknowledged the limitations of the traditional theological education that was being given to the leadership of the churches in Africa, acknowledging also that there has been a powerful force at work in Africa that challenges that type of theological education:

> Theological institutions are being forced to examine their credibility by another powerful force namely the call for a more widely available and more practically-oriented education than has been traditionally offered in such institutions.... Pressures from both within and outside the church are calling it to an examination of its relevance to the life context in which it finds itself, and within this overall framework and context to examine more particularly its educational system.[12]

The challenge of globalization on theological education in Africa is more acute because as noted here, Africa needs a more practically oriented theology that directly addresses her contextual needs than what was and has been provided in the past in conventional seminaries. We noted earlier that African seminaries were set up and taught by European or American missionaries. What seminary students received was an academic-oriented theology that was abstract and not immediately applicable to the African situation. Today the situation has changed greatly as most African seminaries have Africans in the majority on their faculties. Nevertheless, most if not all the African faculty have been trained in overseas seminaries for a number of years, and when they return, one discovers that they have all been de-contextualized. They speak with a Western or European accent, dress like Americans and drink coffee in the seminary classrooms. The content of their theology is more or less cognitive and abstract bent on deciphering which scholar most accurately captures the trend of thought in John Calvin's Institutes or who best understands Van Til's apologetics. This information is good for Americans and, of course, anywhere, but for the most part it does not address the real issues of the context in which it is being taught. One wonders about the learning experience of the African who is

---

12 Jonathan Hogarth, Kiranga Gatimu and David Barrett, *Theological Education in Context: 100 Extension Programmes in Contemporary Africa* (Nairobi: Uzima Press, 1983), 4, 6.

pondering on why he is poor in the midst of much affluence in the world, what it all means that there is a God who cares and fights on the side of the oppressed and the poor, and why he cannot get out of his poverty while his fellow political leaders live in luxurious abundance.

To be more specific, it is important to trace briefly the history and development of the Reformed Theological Seminary, Mkar in Nigeria to illustrate what theological education in Africa has been. The historic beginnings of this seminary and its development until today depicts what has been outlined above.

THE CASE OF REFORMED THEOLOGICAL SEMINARY, MKAR IN NIGERIA

The Reformed Theological Seminary, Mkar in Nigeria (henceforth, RTS) is the official seminary of the Church of Christ in the Sudan among the Tiv (henceforth NKST).[13] The seminary was started in 1970 for two main reasons: To provide positive Reformed teaching to the leadership of the church and to supply enough pastors for the very fast growing church in Tiv land.

Through a somewhat contentious beginning fraught with denominational politics, RTS was started by indigenous African leaders but was soon taken over by the CRC in North America in terms of personnel and finance for infrastructure. When Timothy Monsma arrived at the seminary in 1974, he brought with him copies of the *Institutes*, copies of Young's *Old Testament Introduction* and copies of Berkhof's *Systematic Theology*. He also brought several other books written on theology by Western theologians. He designed the seminary curriculum to look like the one at Calvin Theological Seminary in Grand Rapids. So everything at RTS looked Western and was Western except the students.

Besides courses at RTS having a Western flair, most of the faculty who came to teach at the seminary were from the West.[14] While the missionaries taught at the seminary, there were also a few African faculty who taught alongside them, but issues of curriculum planning were completely handled by the missionaries.

---

13 The Church of Christ in the Sudan among the Tiv is popularly known in Nigeria by its Tiv acronym, NKST for its tribal language translation. The church has a large membership of over 100,000 with 500 ministers. By doctrinal persuasion, the church is Reformed being the product of the missionary activities of the Christian Reformed Church in North America and the Dutch Reformed Church Mission of South Africa.

14 Some of the names of the Western faculty from 1974-1992 are Timothy Monsma, Wilhelm Berrends, Sidney Anderson, Tina Vanstaalduinen, Rev. Brouwer, Dr. J. M. Zinkand, Rev. Hogeterp, Ryle Bierma. Apart from the long-term Western faculty there were a host of others who came on short-term basis.

So they designed the theological education at RTS to look like what they knew and what they had gone through themselves in their Western seminaries. In fact no one had even thought that theology could be taught differently from what one obtained in America.

While the RTS teaching curriculum looked very Reformed, just like the NKST church had desired, it never took into consideration some of the unique contextual issues present in the culture in which the students were going to minister after their graduation. The curriculum, while strong on content and sound theology, was seriously weak on practical theological issues. I went through the seminary and never heard anything about urban ministry. My class missed any course on pastoral theology and church administration, if these courses were offered.

Today much of the curriculum has not changed. It still has a strong emphasis on systematic theology and biblical studies. As to the content of the teaching, emphasis was placed on theoretical articulation of Christian doctrines, but now it is taught in simpler language that the students can understand. The strong weakness which remains in the curriculum is its uncontextualized nature. Ironically, even with the stress on systematic theology, nothing was taught on the doctrine of the Holy Spirit which should be and is a very real issue in African religiosity. The academic bent of the curriculum at the expense of a contextual theological education secures for the seminary the label of theological irrelevance despite the good things it teaches. Masamba ma Mpolo puts this well when he writes about irrelevant theological education in Africa:

> In most cases theological education has been too theoretical, academic, a carbon copy of Western culture, not geared toward the proclama-tion of the Kingdom of God but toward the maintenance of the church structures and the perpetuation of theological jargon. Most students who graduate from theological colleges and start their work in parishes find themselves distant from the laity.[15]

Well before Mpolo, the Consultation on Theology of the Indonesian Council of Churches had denounced this system of theological education as:

---

15 Masamba ma Mpolo, "Theological Education in the 1980's: Some Reflections on Curriculum Renewal in Africa," in *Ministerial Formation* (April 1980) 6-8.

a form and system of education inherited from the west which lays too heavy emphasis on historical-theological analyses of a highly academic character whose aim is to transmit the logical knowledge and tradition as a complete whole which is not sufficiently open to new developments. This system does not take account of the rapid social change experienced by the people. The system is not sufficiently directed toward or rooted in the reality of the local world view and is not sufficiently concerned with the concrete problems of the people.[16]

Written in 1971, this report echoes the issues globalization presents today and which theological education has to seek to address. Harvie Conn, writing on theological education in the *Westminster Theological Journal*, notes the way western style theological education further abstracts the students of other cultures from their contexts: "the impact of this structural methodology on third world churches is to leave them further abstracted from their own contexts and its problems."[17] And it cannot be better expressed than this.

All the current faculty at RTS are Africans from the same denomination, but all of them have been trained abroad either in America or South Korea or both. It was not until recently that two faculty members received graduate degrees at the Stellenbosch University in South Africa. However, one had attended and graduated from Westminster Theological Seminary in Escondido, California, before going to South Africa. Education is a such a powerful agent of change. It changes people from the inside out and the outlook on theological education of those African faculty at RTS, even though they are Africans, has greatly been colored by a western world view. As an example, I could not do this essay back in Nigeria (I did it in Philadelphia) because I thought I did not have access to the required written sources. I had some ideas about the essay but felt I needed to refer to an authority of some sort to support the points that I wanted to make. In this I was thinking like a Westerner, that a good essay must have a certain number of footnotes. Maybe I could have done a better essay had I gone out to ask real African church members what they felt about theological education today.

It is for the reasons illustrated above that it becomes evident that the challenge of globalization is more acute on African theological education than in the West.

---

16 Indonesian N.C.C. Consultation, "Our Hope for Theological Education in the Future," *South East Asia Journal of Theology*, 13, no. 1(1971): 25.

17 Harvie M. Conn, "Theological Education and the Search for Excellence," *The Westminster Theological Journal* 41, no. 1(Fall, 1978): 353.

It is time for African theologians to find ways of providing theological education that is both relevant to their immediate context and yet sensitive to the challenges of globalization. Otherwise Newbigin's challenge to the conventional theological education will always be appropriate:

> The pattern of ministry, and therefore of ministerial formation, introduced by the Western missions are now seen to have been the imposition of a style of leadership foreign to the cultures in which the church was being planted. The rapidly growing churches of today are those which rely on more indigenous patterns of leadership training. Leadership envisaged in our Western-style theological seminaries can only exist in a colonial situation where there are large foreign funds to support it.[18]

The following section will attempt to articulate how we should provide theological education in Africa that is both contextually relevant and open to the challenges of globalization. The proposal here hinges on the fact that theological education should be both textually faithful and contextually relevant as Shoki Coe aptly puts it as "text and context in theological education."[19]

PROVIDING A THEOLOGICAL EDUCATION FOR THE GLOBAL REALITIES OF AFRICA

Now we have come to the very practical aspect of this essay in which we must show what theological education in a global setting should look like. How do we African seminaries, most of which have a western educational history, provide theological education to the church that is biblically based, theologically valid, and contextualized to the realities in Africa, a continent marked by tribal diversity, cultural pluralism, severe social and economic turmoil, rapid change from rural to urban life and the fast infiltration of Western and European influence? This is not an easy task, but it is doable.

---

18 Leslie Newbigin, "Theological Education in World Perspective," *Growth Bulletin* 7(1974): 68.

19 Shoki Coe, writing under the name C. H. Huang in *Theological Education and Ministry. Reports from the North East Asia Theological Education Consultation. Seoul, Korea* (Taiwan: The Presbyterian Bookstore, 1967), 220-21, further explains what he means by text and context that "the excellence we seek in and ought to seek in theological education lies in that kind of living and dynamic interaction and correlation between our absolute faithfulness to the given Text, on the one hand, and the creative relevance to the context for which the Text is given, on the other."

African Traditional Reality

While we spend so much time trying to understand how to interpret the Bible and systematize our thoughts, the African theological student also needs to be a student of his culture, for it is only by understanding his cultural milieu that he can understand the message of the text. Unfortunately, many African seminaries do not even mention issues of cultural significance to theological students in the classroom. These include issues like witchcraft, polygamy, African traditional values, ancestral influence, spirit possession, etc. These are neglected mostly because the African professors themselves were taught to believe that some of these issues are just a figment of the mind and are not real. Top on the list of this deceit was witchcraft. But as African people went about their normal lives, they could not escape the fear of being bewitched or being tormented by witchcraft. While theological education in Africa has neglected this, globalization has come to bless it with the influx of other religions and worldviews close to the African doorstep. Theological education in Africa must engage these issues with seriousness.

World Religions

Globalization brings the religions of the world in touch with one another. Multinational corporations bring people from different countries with different religious affiliations in close contact with local people and their cultures. Theological training of the ministers of the future must be strengthened by the addition of a basic course on world religions as essential in the study of systematic theology. Just as Christians in the apostolic and post-apostolic age had to present their message and defend it within a hostile pagan atmosphere, we must be equally prepared to meet the challenge of our times. This does not mean a lesser emphasis on the traditional Reformed study in theology. The works of Charles Hodge, Louis Berkhof and Herman Bavinck still are needed. An analysis of Calvin's Institutes will never be outdated. These works are still very relevant to today's situation. However, something more is now required especially in Africa. We need to learn and understand the basic tenets and practices of the followers of other world religions, many of whom have suddenly become our neighbors.

Preachers today, especially in African cities, can testify to the presence of strange religious practices right behind their back yard. We are not only surrounded by Islam but also by a host of other faith persuasions. Sooner or later our pastors will encounter parishioners who ask questions not only about Islam but also about Hinduism, Buddhism, or the New Age. People are beginning to want some guidance not only on how to respond to their new Muslim neighbors or their friends whose children have married Muslims but also on why their son-in-law who works at the oil company is a vegetarian and wants his Christian wife to be the same for religious reasons. Thus African lay Christians, more than the clergy, rub shoulders in the business world with Hindus, Muslims, and Buddhists. The cultural atmosphere that surrounds the African Christian today keeps on telling him that all faiths are equal. The time has come to be better informed about the faiths and allegiances of our new neighbors from overseas. Many of them, in order to survive culturally, are asserting the uniqueness and relevance of their religious traditions. They advertise their faith through media, public meetings, and the internet. Theological education in African seminaries has to address the truth claims of these religions in order to better inform their students as they seek to do ministry in this new global setting.

Contextualization

Contextualization has received much attention from missions and other theological disciplines, and it will continue to be at the forefront of every discussion on theological education of any generation. This is because it has so much to offer to each generation as it seeks to do theology in its time and place. At this time of globalization we need the wisdom of contextualization to enable us to relate the gospel of Jesus Christ to our own unique situation, and the place to begin doing that is the seminary where theologians who assume church leadership are trained. Contextualization has received so many definitions from a variety of people, but in this essay we shall concern ourselves with Harvie Conn's views on the subject for the reason that he provides an understanding of contextualization that still upholds a scriptural check on how we practice it. Theology, says Conn,

> is the application of Scripture and Scripture alone, the inerrant Word of God addressed to the words and cultures of men. It calls all of God's people as prophets, priests and kings to the task of theology, to the task of applying Scripture as judge and savior to the whole texture and context of our culturally bound lives.[20]

Turning to contextualization of theology and ministry, Conn says,

> A contextual theology and a contextualized ministry call the body to address two questions to our cultures. How are the divine demands of

---

20 Conn, ""The Search for Excellence," 354.

> the gospel of the Kingdom communicated in cultural thought forms
> meaningful to the real issues and needs of the person and his society in
> that point of cultured time? How shall the man of God, as a member of
> the body of Christ and the fellowship of the Spirit, respond meaningfully
> and with integrity to the Scriptures so that he may live a full-orbed king-
> dom lifestyle in covenant obedience with the covenant community?[21]

Simply put, contextualization, as we can gather from Conn, is the communication of the gospel of the Kingdom of God in thought forms that are real and meaningful to a particular people at a particular time. With the issue at hand in this essay, we might then ask, how do we prepare theologians in such a way that they are able to minister in Africa in such a way that their gospel ministry realistically conveys to the Africans the gospel of the kingdom in ways and forms that are understandable to Africans during this time of globalization? The answer to this question lies in the reshaping of seminary curricula in Africa in such a way that they foster the teaching of issues that are of concern to Africans in their unique situation. We need to review three issues this reshaping will entail.

First, doing that requires the will power to withstand change that is meant for the good and health of the church in Africa. To remove some courses that were introduced by western missionaries in some seminary curricula in Africa is to invite disaster be-cause some of the churches are not prepared for it. One remembers when a colleague was dragged before the synod of his denomination for not using Louis Berkhof's *Systematic Theology* as the standard book for teaching the course at seminary. But to prolong that is to continue offering theological education that is further and further being abstracted from the people to whom we do ministry. Should we entertain fear of institutional churches? Greenway's counsel might give us courage:

> Trust God and insist on training that is appropriate to your religious and
> social context. Education should fit the needs and expectations of the
> people for whom it is designed.[22]

It also requires careful study of the African situation by theology professors in Africa and seeing how much globalization has changed that. One such situation that now requires careful attention and inclusion in our seminary curricula is the

---

21 Ibid.
22 Greenway, "Getting David Out of Saul's Armor," 226

influence of the occult or cultism on the African spiritual life. In recent years, cultism has become rampant in Nigerian universities, and the church is yet to find a way of combating this phenomenon. Christian A. Purefoy in *The Telegraph* writes about these cults under the caption, "War of the black magic cults brings death to Nigeria's universities." "In the last month alone, 13 of its students have been killed in clashes between cults calling themselves the 'Black Axe' and the 'Black Eye.'"[23] Nigerian movies depict this phenomenon in clear dimensions. The government has made legislations[24] against it and university authorities have combated it in various ways by expelling students involved in it or by suspending faculty. But the trend continues and appears to be on the increase every day. Since this is more of a spiritual matter, the church should have a better solution. Theological education curriculum in Africa should then include courses on cultism and a biblical response to it. This involves formulating a clear view of how the Spirit of God is the solution to this.

Second, how does the Bible address those issues? This is the bottom line question after all has been said and done. Actually, it is the first question as the Bible should determine where we go with our attempts at contextualization. Theological education should clearly point out how the Bible addresses the issues of poverty, spirit possession, cultism, salvation, protection from the evil spirit world, fecundity, ancestral worship, etc.

Third, since we are in the age of globalization, the curriculum should not just stop at attempting to present the gospel in African forms, it should also point out clearly how the West, Europe and Asia have struggled and are continuing to struggle with the issues of globalization in their own theological education setting. Sending students to the internet to seek out western solutions to these issues will be a good take on globalization and theology today.

---

23 Christian A. Purefoy, "War of the black magic cults brings death to Nigeria's universities," *The Telegraph*, April 20, 2005, http://www.telegraph.co.uk/news/worldnews/africaandindianocean/nigeria/, accessed 4/20/05. Several other Nigerian dailies carry horrifying news about the menace of cultism in Nigerian Universities. See Sina Babasola, "Death Toll Now 6 in Ibadan Varsity Cults Clash," *Vanguard*, June 23, 2004, www.vanguardngr.com, accessed 6/23/04 which carried the news that "Death toll in the bloody clash that occurred at the University of Ibadan at the weekend between rival cult groups has increased to six as tension continued to mount on the university campus." Also, see *The Guardian*, June 29, 2005; *Daily Champion*, Nigeria, May 4, 2005; *Daily Champion* (Lagos), September 2, 2004, via http://allafrica.com/.

24 The government even considered sending the Nigerian Army into Nigerian Universities to contain the menace of cultism. See "Soldiers may be deployed to varsities over cult activities," *The Daily Times*, November 10, 2003.

Social Justice

The church in Africa must stand up to issues of social justice in its prophetic voice against corruption and marginalization. It is only when theological education clearly identifies Christ as being the friend and liberator of the oppressed (Luke 4:28) that it can realistically claim to be addressing the African situation. The Bible has a great deal to say about poverty and the attitude of the "haves" toward the poor. Theological education in Africa should seek to clearly declare God's Word against poverty and corruption

Prayer and Spirit Encounter

Theological education has to address the issue of prayer and the work of the Holy Spirit in the life of the believer. The African comes from an animist background which places him under the constant fear of evil spirits. Theology should address this clearly pointing out how the Spirit of God is power over all other spirits, powers and principalities. Our battle is not just of flesh and blood but is against the spiritual realm even in heavenly places. Theological education in Africa should note that most Africans are coming out from this animistic background. Theology that engages the issue of spirit encounter will actually bring home the message right to the very need of those people

Worship

Theological education in Africa has to look carefully at the issue of worship. Africans prefer an expressive worship style which calls upon them to express their joy of salvation before God their Father. Indigenous music is important. Western guitars, pianos and drums can be used where necessary as the youth in the cities seem to connect best with such music. For this type of worship to happen, the pastor must lead the way. But if the pastor is not trained to handle and lead such worship, he cannot do it.

CONCLUSION

Not everything can be said here about the shape of theological education in Africa today, but this is enough to get us going on the path of realistic theological education in a global setting as it should happen in Africa. As we in Africa begin to consider these issues from a biblical perspective and reshape our theological curricula because the Bible says so, then we can be sure we are on the way to relevant theological education in a global setting.

.16.

Mentoring:
Developing Urban Leaders in Chicago

PEDRO AVILES

And the things you have heard me say in the presence of many witnesses entrust to reliable men who will also be qualified to teach others (2 Timothy 2:2).

INTRODUCTION

It was Jeremy's funeral. This young Latino, a member of the Chicago street gang called the Spanish Cobras, was killed by a bullet of a rival gang. At his wake there were more than thirty other Spanish Cobras (young men and women, mostly teenagers) all dressed in the green and black gang colors with cobras depicted on their clothing and tattoos of the same on their arms and necks.

As I quietly sat praying for the family and preparing to say a few words from the scriptures, the following questions kept crossing my mind, How is it that these inner city gangs can easily recruit so many teenagers and young adults, and then launch them into leadership roles in their corrupt clubs? Why is it that the church of Jesus in our city has much more difficulty retaining, recruiting, and developing into leaders the same teenagers and young adults? What needs do young adults find fulfilled in their association with gangs that they do not find fulfilled in our city churches?

The point of opening this essay with this story is to draw attention to the reality of my urban context. Inner city Chicago is the place where my church, Grace and Peace, has ministered for twenty-four years. From the beginning of my pastorate, my passion has been to raise indigenous leaders. I dream of many second and third generation young Latinos rising up to leadership roles in city churches and in our communities, urban leaders who are well equipped to impact their communities as they forcefully advance the gospel of God's kingdom.

My desire is to find young people like Jeremy, to lead them to embrace by faith Jesus Christ as their Master and Savior, and then to disciple them into leadership roles in the church. Through the years of ministry, it has been my privilege to see young men and women whom I have mentored decide to enter the ministry as church planters, educators, pastors, counselors, youth directors, community organizers, etc. All glory goes to God alone.

Much of what I learned in practice and in principles came through my own mentor, Manuel Ortiz. In addition, I have learned other mentorship practices from peer mentors, many conferences, seminars, training in graduate school, books, and from my own mentees. All of these have influenced my understanding of urban mentorship.

MENTORSHIP DEFINED

I often hear city pastors and youth pastors express the stress they feel of being over burdened with the load of ministry and the little support they receive from the few ill-equipped lay leaders that are available in their ministries. In addition, when I survey the present normal leadership development programs in their churches, I find that these programs are not meeting the demands in the ministry and the felt needs in our communities. There is an obvious lack of indigenous leaders laboring in our churches and in the city harvest fields.

In defining mentoring, I appreciate the insight Keith Anderson and Randy Reese provide when they explain the etymological root for the word mentor. They say that it derives from Greek mythology. Telemachus, Ulysses' son, was to be tutored by a person named "Mentor." He was to "provide an education of soul and spirit as well as mind, an education in wisdom and not merely in information."[1] From this root the word mentor has basically been understood as "a wise and trusted counselor or teacher."[2]

1 Keith R. Anderson and Randy D. Reese, *Spiritual Mentoring* (Downers Grove, IL: InterVarsity Press, 1999), 35.
2 *Webster's American Family Dictionary* (New York: Random House, Inc., 1998), 597.

Through their research Anderson and Reese define mentoring as "a triadic relationship between mentor, mentee, and the Holy Spirit, where the mentee can discover, through the already present action of God, intimacy with God, ultimate identity as a child of God and a unique voice for kingdom responsibility."[3] They rightly highlight the relational element which is at the "heart" of mentorship. At the calling of the twelve disciples, Jesus himself placed the relationship before the ministry to the other (Mark 3:14).

Robert Clinton has influenced leadership practices and development for twenty years. He refers to mentoring as "the process where a person with a serving, giving, encouraging attitude, the mentor, sees leadership potential in a still-to-be developed person, the protégé, and is able to promote or otherwise significantly influence the protégé along in the realization of potential."[4] Simply stated, "A mentoring process item refers to the process or results of a mentor helping a potential leader."[5] Here one can see the wisdom Clinton places in the process and the goal(s) in mentoring. Good leaders don't just arise from a passive model or practice. There must be intentionality in the process. Mentors must have goals and objectives; they must be proactive in their plans as they develop indigenous leaders.

In our postmodern urban world, a new wave of indigenous leaders is needed who can effectively address the plethora of problems impacting local churches and city neighborhoods. The other contributors to this volume have provided ample stats and evidences of the urban global condition. It is a sad reality that leadership development of indigenous men and women has not kept pace with our changing world. Local city churches, pastors, and community leaders must adopt leadership development principles and practices that surpass mediocrity. Urban churches are in desperate need of well equipped leaders to advance God's kingdom purposes throughout urban centers in this world.

What follows are some principles, values, guidelines, and practices which have greatly helped me as a Latino urban pastor in the mentoring and raising of indigenous leaders. In addition, I present some behavioral outcomes (the lifestyle) that must be demonstrated in an urban mentee.

This essay is divided into five topics. First, is the missional shift required in the mentor from the foundational discipleship mandate as found in the Great Commission to the higher expectation of urban leadership development. Next, is a refocus by the mentor to invest and transfer that missional mandate into the lives

---

3 Anderson and Reese, *Spiritual Mentoring*, 12.
4 Dr. J. Robert Clinton, *The Making of a Leader* (Colorado Springs: NavPress, 1988), 130.
5 Ibid.

of the next indigenous generation. The third theme is the urban mentee's need to embrace the God-sized assignment (calling) in the inner city. Then is the subject of the mentee "going beyond" Christianity 101 spiritual formation practices to more advanced leadership formation disciplines. Lastly, there is the audacious challenge for both the mentor and mentee in which the developed mentee (leader) is released to his/her ministry of advancing God's kingdom in new ministries throughout urban centers in this world.

I pray that this simple essay will launch many new mentorship ministries and many new indigenous urban leaders, leaders who are creatively and uniquely equipped for the diverse city/urban ministry in our global contexts.

THE GREAT MENTORSHIP MISSION

"Therefore go and make disciples of all nations" (Matt. 28:19-20).

"I left you in Crete to do what had been left undone and to appoint leaders for the churches in each town" (Titus 1:5 CEV).

Every person who calls himself/herself a follower of Christ is commanded by Jesus to be a witness, sharing with others the good news of the salvation found through faith in the resurrected Jesus. In addition, every Christian is responsible to take those who receive Christ as their God and Savior and to make them into disciples (obedient followers of Jesus) (Acts 1:8; Matt. 28:19-20). All are given this great commission.

Urban mentors on the other hand have a different or even a higher calling. Their mission is to go and make leaders of those new disciples. True, a mentor has the same great commission mandate. However, the mentor's mission is more than to make dedicated disciples. Their missional mandate goes beyond the great commission. An urban mentor is called to take these dedicated indigenous disciples and to fully equip them to become effective urban leaders who advance God's kingdom purposes in our inner cities. Mentors are called to a "trans-mission."

The reason I added the prefix "trans" to mission is to draw attention to the paradigm shift needed in urban leadership development ministry in our local churches and in para-church organizations. Webster's dictionary states that "trans" is borrowed from the Latin language meaning "across" and "through." In its verb form it denotes "movement" and in the form of an adjective it means "crossing" and "going beyond."[6] Therefore, mentors are driven to "go beyond," to move "across" the evangelistic mandate of the great commission to a high calling of a trans-mission. Urban mentors are to make urban leaders.

The Apostle Paul demonstrated this trans-mission mandate by his actions after he started a church. Among his first priorities for these new churches was the immediate establishment of indigenous leaders (elders, Acts 14:23). Later he commissioned Titus, his mentee, to do that same task of appointing leaders in the churches in other towns (Titus 1:5). He also gave Timothy, his other mentee, the same mandate and the instructions on the characteristic qualifications for these indigenous leaders (1 Tim. 3; 2 Tim. 2:2). Jesus' mission was to go into the world, to seek and save the lost. He carried out this mission by appointing the twelve apostles (sent ones). In following Jesus' and Paul's examples, mentors are to appoint and equip urban leaders who will carry out Jesus' mission.

In the urban setting, many ethnic minorities who are potential leaders are ostracized, oppressed, belittled, rejected, poorly educated, criticized for speaking improper English, and they experience racism, exploitation, and other degrading insults. Unfortunately, many of these minorities have little to no hope of advancement in their lives. They can relate to the Gentiles as Paul describes them in Eph. 2:12, "Remember that at that time you were separate from Christ, excluded from citizenship in Israel and foreigners to the covenants of the promise, without hope and without God in the world."

If urban mentors accept the challenge to dedicate themselves to the raising of indigenous leaders, they will most likely have to overcome the malaise in these mentees and in their ministries. "Without addressing this malaise among leaders and congregations, there will be little innovation in the missional life. The culture of belief and expectation in which these leaders and congregations are operating needs to be changed."[7] There is a hopelessness and an unhealthy self-perception or image that is found in many potential ethnic minority leaders in our cities in the U.S. Sometimes the mentor himself is the one with a negative perception of the indigenous people. They may believe that these ethnic minorities cannot possibly have the capacity to transform the city. Like the apostle Philip, who degraded Jesus' upbringing, "Nazareth! Can anything good come from there?" (John 1:46), some mentors believe that nothing good can come from inner city ethnic minorities.

---

6 *Webster's American Family Dictionary*, 989.

7 Alan J. Roxburgh and Fred Romanuk, *The Missional Leader* (San Francisco: Jossey-Bass, 2006), 16.

If mentors have little to no expectation of raising qualified urban leaders living under oppressive circumstances in the city, then they will reap to the level of their expectation. Low expectation is one reason there is a lack of ethnic minority leaders.

Thomas S. Rainer researched hundreds of churches that were reaching new members and were retaining those members. He said, "Effective assimilation churches have one primary characteristic that sets them apart from churches that do not keep their members in active involvement. Effective assimilation churches had high expectations of all their members."[8] This is true for church growth and for leadership development. Imparting hope, vision, and high expectations into the lives of the mentees is imperative in order to obtain positive results for growing leaders. A mentor with a high expectation in God's power and God's plan to grow indigenous leaders in urban centers will experience the joy of seeing leaders actually rise up to that hope. Günter Krallman identifies a major mentoring principle by the famous German poet J.W. Goethe who said, "Treat a man as if he already were what he potentially could be, and you make him what he should be."[9] A mentor must have the hope, the confidence, and the expectation that those he invests in are God's choice to be the most dynamic leaders a church and a city have ever seen. In a sense, urban mentors must have the same confidence God had for the Israelites living in an oppressive city of Babylon. God said, "'For I know the plans I have for you,' declares the Lord, 'plans to prosper you and not to harm you, plans to give you hope and a future'" (Jer. 29:11). Günter Krallman continued his thought by quoting B.E Goodwin II, "People have a tendency to try to live up to the genuine expectations of persons whom they admire and respect."[10] A mentor with a hope and vision for the mentee will not be disappointed for "hope does not disappoint us" (Rom. 5:5). Mentees will be challenged and captivated by the vision and high expectation of the mentor. Mentees will make genuine efforts to rise up to the hopes and expectations they hear and see. It is our role as mentors to impart that high transmission to the new leaders we develop.

---

8 Thomas S. Rainer, *High Expectations* (Nashville: Broadman & Holman Publishers, 1999), 23.

9 Günter Krallmann, *Mentoring for Mission* (Tyrone, GA: Authentic Publishing, 2002), 132.

10 Ibid. Endnotes quote from B.E Goodwin II, in his book, *The Effective Leader* (Dowers Grove, IL: InterVarsity Press, 1981), 41.

IMPRINTING THE MISSION ON
THE NEXT GENERATION

"… we will tell the next generation the praiseworthy deeds of the LORD, his power, and the wonders he has done… so the next generation would know them, even the children yet to be born, and they in turn would tell their children" (Ps 78:4, 6).

"We are losing about 85 % of our young adults."[11] Dr. Bob Oh, pastor of Oikos Community Church (a 1.5 and second generation Korean church), spoke these alarming words about Korean young adults at the October 2003 Intergenerational Ministry Conference in California. Other national leaders and I were invited to speak on the trends and challenges our particular ethnic groups are facing and to then present ethnic sensitive models of church growth.

Dr. Oh stated that in his research that although young Korean people are growing up in first generation Korean-speaking churches and have believing parents, they are not returning to their home churches or any other church after they complete their college education. The "generational transference" of the Christian faith, of worship traditions, and of confessions and creeds has found no permanent root in the lives of the next generation.[12]

Currently, mainline denominations and churches in the U.S. are becoming smaller and older. One cover story of the *Banner* magazine was called, "Where Did Our Young Adults Go?" In her article, Gayla R. Postma quotes David Kinnaman, a strategic leader of The Barna Group who said that "from high school graduation to age 25, there is a 42 percent drop in weekly church attendance, and by age 29, that drop increases to 58 percent." She continues, "Despite strong levels of spiritual activity during the teen years, most 20-somethings disengage from active participation in the Christian faith during their young adult years."[13]

The term "generational transference" is most often used to describe the enormous wealth that the U.S. senior generation will pass on as an inheritance to the next generation. The verb form of the word transfer means "to imprint, impress, or otherwise convey (a drawing, design, pattern, etc.) from one surface to another."[14]

---

11 Bob Oh, Intergenerational Ministry Conference, October 22-23, 2003, sponsored by Calvin Institute of Christian Worship, Calvin Theological Seminary, CRC Home Missions, and Korean Council of CRC.
12 Ibid.
13 Gayla R. Postma, "Where Did Our Young Adults Go?" *Banner,* August 2007: 18.
14 *Webster's American Family Dictionary*, 989.

Dr. Oh used this term in connection to the failure to imprint, and impress the Christian faith on the hearts of young Korean adults. He also used the word to describe the spiritual exodus of the young adults from their Korean churches, and to point out the lack of indigenous leaders. Although the Christian Korean community has a strong spiritual heritage, they are now facing the daunting reality that they have no one to whom they can transfer that heritage. In the U.S. there exists a major leadership vacuum. Spiritual generational transference has not occurred.

The scriptures provide us with examples of successful generational transference, as well as examples of failures in the development of the next generation of leaders. For examples of success, look at Moses. He mentored and spiritually transferred the teachings and practices of the Torah to the next leader, Joshua (Duet. 31). Elijah mentored the young Elisha who followed in his mentor's prophetic ministry (2 Kings 2). Barnabas is an excellent mentor who took both Paul then later John Mark under his oversight (Acts 9:27-28; 13:1-5; 15:37-38). Paul in turn recruited the young Timothy as his mentee (Acts 16:1-3; 1 Tim. 1:2; 4:20). These are just a few good examples.

Equally, we have ample examples of leaders who failed to transfer faith, doctrine and godliness to the next generation. The high priest Eli did not imprint the faith into his two sons (1 Samuel 2:12). Samuel, the prophet could not convey or impress godliness into his two sons (1 Samuel 8:1-3). Most of the kings of Israel after Solomon's reign failed in the spiritual generational transference to the next generation. In the scriptures we find that God is concerned about the spiritual transference of his deeds and his teaching. It is a command given to the Israelites. Paul commands it from Timothy. God's concern is not limited to the transference of faith to the next immediate generation. He is concerned that transference extends to the fourth generation (Ps. 78:4, 6; Joel 1:3; 2 Tim. 2:2).

Church leaders across the U.S. must adopt a different operational paradigm when it comes to their priorities in ministry. John Maxwell has taught in his leadership conferences and in his books what is known as the "Pareto Principle," or as some call it the "20/80 Principle." He wrote, "20 percent of your priorities will give you 80 percent of your production IF you spend your time, energy, money, and personnel on that top 20 percent of your priorities."[15] He also said, "20 percent of the people in an organization will be responsible for 80 percent of the company's success."[16]

---

15 John C. Maxwell, *Developing the Leader Within You* (Nashville: Thomas Nelson Publishers, 1993), 20.

16 Ibid., 21.

In the ministry context I have heard him say that 20 percent of the people in a congregation do 80 percent of the ministry.

The Bible states that "a man reaps what he sows" (Gal. 6:7). When one accepts this sowing and reaping truth plus the truth of the 20/80 Principle and sees the vacuum of urban leaders, one can safely conclude that city church leaders are not prioritizing nor sowing a significant amount of time, energy, and money into the 20 percent of potential indigenous lay leaders. What we have are pastors investing time and energy into developing good sermons and teachings, administrating their churches, and visiting and caring for the congregation. All of these things are important and good. However, in light of the lack of leaders it is evident that church leaders are not investing enough of their lives into the development of the next generation indigenous leaders. Effective generational transference is clearly absent.

What can be done to turn this trend around? A major shift in the thinking and value system of all present leaders must transpire. Therefore, I urge all urban pastors, youth pastors, directors of ministries, and mentors to rearrange their priorities so that their actions reflect an emphasis on spiritual generational transference. Leaders today must have a personal ongoing involvement in indigenous leadership development. The development of leaders cannot be abdicated and left solely in the hands of other people and institutions. Other people and educational institutions are not producing leaders for our inner cities or urban churches.

In the mentorship process my concern (goal) is not only that the mentee receive and own all that I have taught and modeled. In practice, I generally spend about 1 ½ hours per week for about two years mentoring a small group of potential urban leaders. In this process, I normally require that each urban mentee of mine is to also find another person whom they will mentor at another time of the week. My ultimate goal in mentoring an urban leader is to see him/her carry on the same practices with another person. I would not consider my mentoring ministry successful if the mentees alone became great leaders but did not embrace the spiritual generational transference principle. Unless I can see a third and, Lord willing, a fourth generation of new urban leaders following in the footsteps of their mentors, then I consider my mentoring ministry a failure. Paul's trans-mission was to make leaders who in turn would become makers of other leaders (2 Tim. 2:2). This priority and investment will increase the surety of "generational transference" and development of urban leaders unto a third and fourth generation. Therefore, urban leaders everywhere must reorganize their schedules and make mentoring a priority.

A GOD-SIZED APOSTOLIC CALLING

"The Lord has sought out a man after his own heart and appointed him leader of his people" (1 Sam. 13:14).

"I looked for a man among them who would build up the wall and stand before me in the gap on behalf of the land so I would not have to destroy it, but I found none" (Ezekiel 22:30).

How is it possible that no one heard the calling of God, and if they did, that no one responded to this calling? To think that the omniscient God found no one is amazing to me. Perhaps I should not be surprised. Sunday after Sunday city pastors are calling the members of their congregations to step up to the high calling of God and only a few respond. Few are hearing the King of Kings give the apostolic, conscripted call to service in the urban setting. However, blessed are the few who do hear and respond to God's appointment to minister in our cities.

The calling is no small matter. It is a God-sized calling, a God-sized assignment given to mentees in the city. The assignment has a greater focus than the growth of the local church, though it is primarily carried out in the local church. The focus of this assignment is the total transformation of the city. It is a calling to kingdom service going beyond shalom of the local ethnic church. Mentees are to seek the peace of the city (Jer. 29:7). Therefore, the calling is both to the local church and to the city. To reiterate, their assignment is larger than they can imagine, and it goes far beyond their known abilities.

The apostles received this missional mandate from Jesus when he said to them, "'Peace be with you! As the Father has sent me, I am sending you'" (John 20:21). They knew it was going to be great because Jesus also had said to them, "anyone who has faith in me will do what I have been doing. He will do even greater things than these, because I am going to the Father" (John 14:12). The mentees are called to greatness, to stand in the gap in the city.

We mentors, as instruments of God, are to call up and call out the mentees to this high conscripted calling. When the Spirit himself (John 22:22) is behind that calling, then those mentees who hear God's voice sense a compelling force to accept the mission. When Paul recruited young Timothy, he "did not hesitate to assign him tasks beyond his present powers."[17] When the teenager David heard the challenges

---

17 J. Oswald Sanders, *Spiritual Leadership* (Chicago: Moody Press, 1994), 149.

given by the gigantic soldier Goliath, the Holy Spirit compelled David into military service. God gave a God-sized assignment in response to a gigantic evil problem.

I live in a metropolitan global city with enormous challenges. I have no doubt that the high assignments of God are of a conscripted nature, meaning there is this compulsory demand that the mentee cannot resist. There is a charge to active service inspired by the Holy Spirit. As a result, it is my practice to challenge my mentees to take on ministry assignments that are just beyond their known abilities. I trust God is behind that challenge and I can trust him to compel all who are called. It is important that mentors never cheapen and compromise on the cost of urban ministry. The young adults of our community and our churches are looking for a mission worthy to live for and worthy to die for. I am blessed to have seen and to continue to see young ethnic minorities accept the challenge of the ministry.

Charles Van Engen uses the word "apostolic" as a key word to describe the missional dimension of the church. He said, "The gift that the church is apostolic would itself be a task for applying the apostolic gospel, living in the apostolic way, and being sent as apostles in the world."[18] The new believers understood this to be their task along with the first apostles. "The church's transferred apostolate was assumed by the disciples after Pentecost."[19] These new disciples "do not share with the apostles in the inspiration that first delivered Christ's gospel, but they share in the stewardship that ministers it."[20] The calling for mentees is to follow in the apostolic footsteps: forcefully advancing the full purpose of the kingdom of God in the city under the power of the Spirit, planting churches from urban center to urban center. These urban ambassadors will be motivated and compelled by the love of God, a love for the church and a love for the city (2 Cor. 5:14).

Denominational leaders and pastors alike ask me to inform them where they can find that next generation of urban leaders to mentor. Where do churches go to recruit indigenous leaders? For many, their first course of action is often to recruit leaders from colleges and seminaries. Some churches will also search out and recruit leaders from other churches.

As we read through the Gospels we learn that about six of the twelve disciples chosen by Jesus were from his neighborhood, by the Sea of Galilee. As stated earlier, Paul chose new indigenous leaders (elders) for the new churches from their own cities. I believe that our sovereign God has already selected the best leaders for our

---

18 Charles Van Engen, *God's Missionary People* (Grand Rapids, MI: Baker Book House, 1992), 65.
19 Ibid., 120.
20 Edmund P. Clowney, *Called to the Ministry* (Phillipsburg, NJ: Presbyterian & Reformed Publishers, 1964), 45.

churches. These leaders can be found right within our communities and within our churches. I believe that the best leaders most often overlooked are the young adults around us. Krallmann said in his book that the ones chosen by Jesus were most likely young people.[21] Initially, Christianity was a young people's movement. Peter who was married could have been the oldest among the twelve disciples. Jesus was probably the oldest in the group at the age of thirty. When I search for new urban mentees I look among the young adults in church and in our community. Often they are willing to count and pay the cost for ministry, they are motivated and are compelled and have a strength to overcome the evils of our communities (1 John 2:13,14).

We don't have to recruit people from outside our communities, transplanting from some other cultural context and then retrain them to minister within the city context. Conn and Ortiz said, "The kinds of leaders necessary for the task of urban mission already live in the targeted community. To exclude the community as a resource for selecting and developing leadership is to exhibit superior and paternalistic attitudes."[22] The indigenous mentees of our communities know the socioeconomic condition, the language, the values, and the cultural context of their neighborhoods. God has equipped them to serve our church and our neighborhoods. I have found them to be more faithful and committed in the long haul to the church and to the city.

What a joy it has been for me to raise spiritual sons and daughters who are now serving in leadership roles in churches and in the city. They catch the vision, they accept the calling. What are they called to? Core to the calling is what Clowney said, "Advancement in the kingdom is not by climbing but by kneeling. Since the Lord has become Servant of all, any special calling in his name must be a calling of humility, to service."[23] This humility connects us to the next topic of spiritual formation.

ADVANCE SPIRITUAL FORMATION

And we, who with unveiled faces all reflect the Lord's glory, are being transformed into his likeness with ever-increasing glory, which comes from the Lord, who is the Spirit (2 Cor. 3:18).

---

21 Krallmann, *Mentoring for Mission*, 52.

22 Havie M. Conn and Manuel Ortiz, *Urban Ministry* (Downers Grove, IL: InterVarsity Press, 2001), 412.

23 Clowney, *Called to the Ministry*, 43.

One thing I ask of the LORD, this is what I seek: that I may dwell in the house of the LORD all the days of my life, to gaze upon the beauty of the LORD and to seek him in his temple (Psalm 27:4).

When I consider the root causes for the moral failures in religious leaders today, it is clear to me that their failures are due to a disconnection (a character deficiency, loss of love) at the heart level for Christ. This may sound simplistic, however it is biblically true. In the final analysis, when God searches the heart to see what the true motivation is for the moral failures (Prov. 16:2; James 1:13-15), what is found is a rebellion or lack of love for God (John 14:15, 24). Jesus taught that when we commit adultery, it is first committed in the heart long before it is manifested in our actions. He would say that when we murder someone, it is first done in our hearts by our anger (Matt. 5:21-30).

Therefore, where do I begin in this topic of character-spiritual formation for our mentees? There are many skills (competencies) a leader must acquire, many principles and truths (content) they must learn, and many aspects of the fruit of the Spirit they must develop to be mature and effective leaders in the urban setting. Do we begin with the skills, with the content, or with character development? Dr. Robert J. Clinton said, "At the heart of any assessment of biblical qualifications for leadership lies the concept of integrity—that uncompromising adherence to a code of moral, artistic, or other values that reveals itself in sincerity, honesty, and candor and avoids deception or artificiality."[24] In order to qualify as a leader in the local church, the apostle Paul identified that a godly character is the first requirement (1 Tim. 3, Titus 1). Character-spiritual formation is the place to begin, but by the time a mentee is ready for leadership his character must be at a mature level.

On the shelves of local bookstores one can find leadership books by popular authors promoting situational leadership skills. They write about such topics as good management and administrative qualities for running the organization, the skills in creating and casting a great vision and mission, the importance of long-term strategy planning, the need for board and staff development, and practical techniques for planning good meetings just to name a few. Our educational Bible institutions on the other hand seem to primarily focus on providing a strong theological foundation in order to become an effective leader. A potential student-leader will be instructed in the historicity of the church, in biblical languages, in homiletics, in hermeneutics, in eschatology, in systematic theology, and in methods of ethnographic studies.

---

24 Clinton, *The Making of a Leader*, 58.

Upon completion of their three to four years of education, these men and women are then certified for full-time ministry.

For the record, I believe we need men and women well equipped with the managerial and administrative skills to lead in our churches, and I also believe we need these same leaders to gain a high level of theological training. As a pastor in the city of Chicago, a professor in a Christian college, and the director of my denominational lay leadership development program, I too promote and instruct in areas of skills and theology. However, I am aware that "we cannot mentor others from a theoretical position. Nor can we teach without practice. The mentor is a practitioner."[25] "This is important, because we tend to intellectualize and avoid the actual doing of ministry. We become intellectual missionaries and evangelists and teachers without ever getting real practice."[26] The unique way God has formed these men and women requires different ways to instruct with different concentrations in learning.

MENTEES PASSIONATELY PRESSING INTO THE PRESENCE OF CHRIST

Still, as I and many urban pastors assess leaders who are solely trained in skills and theology, we notice that something is missing. It is the single most important life-changing principle on which each new urban leader must focus his utmost attention. That is his real intimate relationship with Jesus Christ through his Spirit. To put this in another way, every mentee must press in to have written on the tablets of his heart a deeply rooted love for Christ that can weather any storm of life.

This vertical passion for an ongoing daily relationship with Jesus will transform them more than any other principle and practice they can learn in their lives. It is the first and greatest of all the commandments. Only as a mentee daily gazes into the face of Jesus will he/she experience the radiant sanctifying power of the glory of God. This gazing which is practiced through the spiritual disciplines is what transformed Moses on Mount Sinai (Ex. 34:29, 34-35), David as he worshipped God (Ps. 27:4), Isaiah as he saw the Lord (Is. 6:1-8), and John as he beheld Jesus on his throne (Rev. 1:1, 12-17). For all the scholarly training the apostle Paul acquired, he fully understood that nothing was as important in his life as the intimate experiential

---

25 Conn and Ortiz, *Urban Ministry*, 436.
26 Ibid.

knowledge of Jesus Christ. This was his utmost calling, to press heavenward with all his might (Phil. 3:7-14).

When Jesus was ready to appoint the apostles, as St. Mark wrote, "He appointed twelve—designating them apostles—that they might be with him and that he might send them out to preach" (Mark 3:14). Note that their first task was to "be with him." All transformation of the character of the mentee begins and continues in the intimate, abiding relationship with Jesus.

Urban churches need young urban leaders who are effectively mentored to have a contagious passionate love for Jesus Christ. The people of all ethnicities in our cities will be drawn to the glorious light of Christ radiating from the mentees' lives and then we will see the prophesy by Zechariah become a reality in our churches, "In those days ten men from all languages and nations will take a firm hold of one Jew by the hem of his robe and say, 'Let us go with you, because we have heard that God is with you'" (Zech. 8:23).

MENTORS PRACTICE WHAT THEY TEACH

How does a mentor transfer this high godly character, this intimate and passionate love for Jesus to the young urban leaders? You have heard it said, "More is caught than taught." In other words, this longing to press into a passionate love of Christ and to gaze into the face of Jesus must be clearly evident in the mentor's life. Yes, it starts with the mentor. I have witnessed that mentees are willing to show grace towards the weaknesses in skills that are evident in his leader if the mentee can see this single devotion to Jesus in the hearts of their mentors. A mentor must love the Lord his God with all his mind, soul, heart, and strength. He may fail in other areas, but above all a mentor must not fail in this one area. Let it be said by the mentee twenty years from now that he learned this most important life-lesson from his mentor: to love Jesus in all circumstances with all that is within him. When the leader Peter denied Jesus (failed in his walk), what was Jesus' central focus of restoration? "Peter, do you love me?" If Peter can have the love for Christ branded in his heart, then Peter can gain the fruit of the Spirit.

In my mentoring practices I train the mentees in the practices of the spiritual disciplines as we find them in the scriptures. When we study, for example, the kingdom lifestyle Jesus taught his disciples in the Sermon of the Mount (Matt. 5-7), we discover that disciples must practice the foundational spiritual disciplines of giving, prayer, fasting, simplicity and service in order to see the "blessed" godly characteristics manifested in their lives. In his book, *Celebration of Discipline*, Richard Foster identifies core spiritual disciplines as meditation, prayer, fasting, Bible study, simplicity, solitude, submission, service, confession, worship, guidance, and celebration.[27] Knowing that those I mentor will follow my example, I have determined to regularly practice all these disciplines for the purpose of igniting my own passionate love for Christ and to see the sanctifying work of his Spirit transform my inner being. Paul, the apostle and mentor, said, "Follow my example, as I follow the example of Christ" (1 Cor. 11:1). "Join with others in following my example, brothers, and take note of those who live according to the pattern we gave you" (Phil. 3:17).

PEER LEARNING PRACTICES

Having emphasized this point of intimacy with Christ, there are other skills and essential doctrines that I spend time imparting into the hearts and minds of my mentees. For example, in the area of doctrine, I require the mentees to read some of the very same books I had to read in seminary. This may not seem unusual except that the indigenous mentees I train usually have no more than a public high school diploma. We slowly walk through books by Louis Berkhof (*Systematic Theology*), by Eldin Villafañe (*Seek the Peace of the City*), by Haddon W. Robinson (*Biblical Preaching*) and/or by A .W. Tozer's (*The Pursuit of God*). We study these books with our Bibles in one hand and a dictionary in the other. The mentees are challenged by this level of instruction, yet each one has risen up to the challenge and is a better student of the Word because of it. Remember, you get what you expect.

My mentoring practices always center on a group experiencing together what they learn. Therefore, I normally have between three to six mentees meeting with me weekly for a period of two to three years. I mentor them in a small group. Jesus had his twelve and three of them were very close to him. In the process we actually end up teaching each other. I believe in peer learning. Günter Krallmann said,

> A team milieu provides a sense of belonging and security facilitates mutual encouragement, stimulation and challenge. It creates a favorable atmosphere for relational bonding and accountability. Within a circle of like-minded persons it is easier to keep vision alive, maintain motivation and commitment, smooth away character edges and compensate one

---

27 Richard Foster, *Celebration of Discipline* (San Francisco: HarperCollins, 1998).

another's weaknesses. Group backing enhances performance, producing better results through cooperation than would be achievable through solitary endeavor (Eccl. 4:9-12; Lev. 26:8).[28]

Whatever the topic, I am aiming for excellence. Whether I am training them in praying or preaching, evangelism or spiritual warfare, marriage or spiritual disciplines, hermeneutics or starting a small home group, I challenge each one to reach for more. The apostle Paul puts it this way, "Finally then, brethren, we request and exhort you in the Lord Jesus, that as you received from us instruction as to how you ought to walk and please God (just as you actually do walk), that you excel still more" (1 Thess. 4:1, NASB).

If all we do as urban mentors is prepare theologically sound mentees who can effectively administer their city ministries but we have not genuinely and deeply loved, then we have failed as mentors (1 Cor. 13:1-3). I have heard it said, "People won't care how much you know until they know how much you care." What Günter Krallmann wrote about nationals is true about the indigenous people in our cities, "Any cross-cultural missionary enterprise, including the development of leaders, should always be more personal than professional. What helps the nationals ought to be a higher concern than what serves our vision, plans or budget; from their viewpoint meeting people is more valuable than meeting deadlines."[29] The power of love has done more to remove the barriers and hindrances toward growth in Christ than any deep theological proposition I can teach. To succeed as a mentor I must passionately love Christ and faithfully love my mentees. The seeds planted in love will produce fruit in their spiritual formation.

RELEASING MENTEES INTO LEADERSHIP ROLES

"It was he who gave some to be apostles, some to be prophets, some to be evangelists, and some to be pastors and teachers, to prepare God's people for works of service, so that the body of Christ may be built up" (Eph. 4:11-12).

---

28 Krallmann, *Mentoring for Mission*, 58.
29 Ibid., 150.

In the mentoring process, it is crucial that mentees are given leadership roles in the ministry. It is not enough simply to teach them that they are part of a grand mission and have a God-sized assignment, or to ensure that they are faithfully practicing their spiritual disciplines. No, they must share in upper levels of leadership and decision making. If the young leaders are well equipped, then they will not be content unless they are actively fulfilling their leadership calling by having leadership responsibilities. What's my point? We urban pastors must release our mentees to function in significant leadership roles right by our sides in our churches and not always place them in roles below us. As mentors we are building a team of co-workers in the ministry. "Leaders build teams to multiply their influence.... Building teams is a core value for successful leadership in any organization or movement."[30] Paul viewed his mentees and others who ministered at his side as co-workers, "We sent Timothy, who is our brother and God's fellow worker in spreading the gospel of Christ, to strengthen and encourage you in your faith" (1 Thess. 3:2).

I am saddened when I see leaders (pastors) competing for power and prestige in and outside the church. I am equally sad to see the insecurities and resistance rise up in pastors when young men or women begin to demonstrate their spiritual giftedness and talents, and the congregation begins to acknowledge those gifts, thus following the lead of these young mentees. Too often I have witnessed the paternalistic attitudes of some pastors when they refuse to share leadership (power). But blessed is the pastor (urban leader) who can recognize the anointing upon their mentees, celebrate it, and release them to function in the fullness of their God-given abilities.

If the young leader is gifted as a worship leader why not let him lead and plan the services? If he is talented in teaching and/or preaching, then pastors should allow him to share the pulpit. If he excels in administration, then let the mentee chair the board meetings. The releasing of young leaders is not about position as much as it is about acknowledging the calling God has on their lives and ushering them into areas in ministry where they can function and use their gifts. "Mentoring can never be a step to higher ground—only to holy ground. Therefore, in mentoring the goal is not to equip for position but rather for function, that is, for service, so that the body of Christ may be built up (Eph. 4:12)."[31] "How else can a young person develop competence and confidence if not by stretching to try the impossible?"[32] This may appear to be risky for the urban pastor (what if the mentee ministers more

---

30 C. Gene Wilkes, *Jesus on Leadership* (Wheaton, IL: Tyndale House Publishers, Inc., 1998), 214.
31 Conn and Ortiz, *Urban Ministry*, 433.
32 Sanders, *Spiritual Leadership*, 149.

effectively than the pastor, what if the people start following the mentee instead of the pastor, what if, what if, etc.); however, the benefits to the advancement of God's kingdom in the local churches in the city will outweigh the fears. At times we pastors may lose some people and some influence; however, we will always gain more as we give away our mentees to fit in the body of Christ (that ministry) as God has determined.

In the spiritual formation process of the mentee, mentors can provide all the assessment tools (books and internet sites) that are available in order to help his mentee discover his spiritual gifts, his leadership style, and his personality type. Once a mentee understands how he is "SHAPED"[33] by God for ministry, and discovers the areas of his strengths, then it will be a wise mentor who releases this young protégé to function in the areas of his strength. Studies have indicated that "people who do have opportunity to focus on their strengths every day are six times as likely to be engaged in their jobs and more than three times as likely to report having an excellent quality of life in general."[34] This sharing of leadership is never without some tension. God's Word says, "As iron sharpens iron, so one man sharpens another" (Prov. 27:17). However, when pastors and their young leaders are operating from the areas of their strengths, the church (including the mentee and mentor) will be healthier and happier.

RELEASING MENTEES TO START NEW CITY MINISTRIES

"Then he said to his disciples, 'The harvest is plentiful but the workers are few. Ask the Lord of the harvest, therefore, to send out workers into his harvest field'" (Matt. 9:37-38).

There is an increased stirring of the Spirit of God in the hearts of pastors here in Chicago to fervently pray and ask for more leaders (workers) to work in the harvest. While these pastors pray, they also preach, teach, counsel, and spend years training their own people hoping someone will rise up and accept the leadership challenge.

Several times in my ministry life I experienced great disappointments when I invested much time, energy, and funds equipping a new emerging leader who was

---

33 Rick Warren, *Purpose Driven Life* (Grand Rapids, MI: Zondervan, 2002), 241-2.
34 Tom Rath, *Strengths Finder 2.0* (New York: Gallup Press, 2007), iii.

just about to be launched into a significant leadership role in my church only to hear him say to me, "Pastor, my wife and I have been praying and we believe God is calling us to another ministry (church)." It is frustrating to invest in someone and then see that another church reaps the benefit of my efforts.

In prayer I have complained to the Lord about how I expected these young leaders to work in "my" church and stay living within "my" community. Then he reminds me of his words in Matt. 9:38. In my heart I hear him say, "This young man was never your disciple, nor was the church yours, nor is the harvest field yours. All of these are mine." Now when I pray this prayer in Matthew 9, I recognize that God wants me to agree with him. He desires workers (mentees) to be "sent out" into "his" harvest field. How easy it is to forget this truth.

If we mentors faithfully follow our missional mandate to transfer to another indigenous generation the calling to urban ministry, then we must expect those we have equipped to imitate us by going into the mission field and reproducing other young leaders. On the other hand, if we mentor young men and women and they only become hard working Christians who do not reproduce other mission-minded disciples, then in effect we have produced Christian mules. Mules are very strong and hard working animals. However, unlike horses mules cannot reproduce. Developing Christian mules has been the limited goal of many pastors. In order to determine the success of our investment in our young leaders, we must see the evidence that they are advancing God's purposes in the city and are reproducing other disciples for the churches and the city. "The paramount goal in raising individuals up to maturity in Christ was not so much their personal spiritual welfare but their being equipped to spread the Gospel message, to multiply a Christlike testimony (cf. 1 Thess. 1:6-8)."[35] C. Gene Wilkes put it this way, "Mission continues when people are captured by it, equipped to do it, and 'teamed' to carry it on. When Jesus turned his motley crew of disciples into a team with a mission, he ensured that his work would continue long after he was gone." [36]

At times I ponder the difficulty it must have been for the church of Antioch to release two of their most gifted leaders; two men called to the mission of establishing new city churches in Asia Minor. "While they were worshiping the Lord and fasting, the Holy Spirit said, 'Set apart for me Barnabas and Saul for the work to which I have called them.' So after they had fasted and prayed, they placed their hands on them and sent them off" (Acts 13:2-3). Assuming our mentees are not leaving our

---

35 Krallmann, *Mentoring for Mission*, 190.

36 C. Gene Wilkes, *Jesus on Leadership* (Wheaton, IL: Tyndale House Publishers, Inc.. 1998), 213.

ministries for the wrong motives and assuming they are actually going off to do kingdom work, how do we release them? Most often, we don't want to release them. What if they stumble out there in the field? Wouldn't it be better for them to stay with us in our churches where it is safe and where they are effective in the ministry? "John R. Mott believed that leaders must multiply themselves by developing young leaders, giving them full play and adequate outlet for their abilities. Young people should feel the weight of heavy burdens, opportunity for initiative, and power for achievements. Foremost they must be trusted. Blunders are the inevitable price of training leaders."[37] As an inner city pastor who has released a number of young leaders, I continue to learn to trust the Great Shepherd. He has perfect wisdom over the care of the sheep, his people. He is the perfect head overseeing the right roles and functions for the parts of his body.

LOCAL CHURCH CELEBRATES A MENTEE'S CALLING TO THE CITY

How do I release these beloved young leaders? After processing this change of direction with the elders, and accepting that God is calling a young leader to plant a new church or start a new ministry in the city, during a Sunday service the church board will lay hands on our young leader, and we bless him and his family. We also give gifts and words of encouragement as we commission him to God's work in the city. On several occasions, we have permitted members of our congregation to follow him in the new ministry. We are both glad and sad during these events. We are sad to see the ones we love leaving us, but glad that they are pursuing the call of God to start new churches in the city.

When the releasing celebration is done with grace and with blessing, a wondering result follows. These very mentees will call you (their mentor, their pastor) again and again for guidance and wisdom in the ministry. In other words, the mentoring process continues but from a distance. This is a new and wonderful relationship of co-workers in God's harvest field. Meanwhile, we mentors are now starting the mentoring process all over again with another young indigenous person, and the cycle of mentoring continues.

---

37 Sanders, *Spiritual Leadership*, 145.

CONCLUSION

To summarize, in order to win our cities for Christ urban pastors, youth leaders and other leaders in parachurch organizations must fully adopt as their personal calling the missional mandate to raise young indigenous leaders for local churches and for the city. This will ensure that spiritual generational transference takes place. Included in the mandate, mentors embrace the value of "high expectations" of the mentees they equip. The expectations include that young leaders will sacrificially and obediently accept their God-sized calling that the Spirit assigns them through their mentor-pastor of becoming urban leaders winning their cities for God. The mentees are also expected to develop an intimate, passionate and radiant relationship with Christ by faithfully practicing their spiritual disciplines. These disciplines will eventually result in the transformation of their character so that they reflect Christ in all that they do and qualify as leaders. The final expectation is that these young urban leaders will plant other city churches and reproduce other indigenous leaders who have the ability to reproduce themselves in another generation (2 Tim. 2:2).

Jesus by his Spirit told the apostle Paul that he had many people in the city. As a result, Paul stayed in Corinth for a year and a half, teaching them the word of God (Acts 18:10-11). Jesus said that the fields are ready for the harvest but that the workers are few (Matt. 9:38). From all we have read in this volume it is clear that the harvest is in the urban centers of our world. In addition, the indigenous workers (mentees) are found in these cities. We urban mentors, like the apostle Paul, are running a race (1 Cor. 9:24-27). Let us run in such a way that we train and release an army of gifted urban leaders to advance God's kingdom in the cities of the world.

Author Profiles

John A. Algera received a B.A. from Calvin College, an M.Div. from Calvin Theological Seminary, and a D.Min. from Westminster Theological Seminary. Serving at Madison Avenue CRC since 1978, first as a youth pastor, then as co-pastor, and then as senior pastor, John is also the Church Multiplication Team Leader for Mid-Atlantic Ministries of the CRC in the Northeast assisting urban church planters and ministries.

Pedro Aviles received a B.A. from Trinity International University, an M.A. from North Park Seminary, and is presently a doctoral student at Trinity Evangelical Divinity school. He was pastor of Grace and Peace Community CRC in Chicago for 22 years and also served as interim principal of Humboldt Community Christian School, campus minister with InterVarsity Christian Fellowship, and now Assistant Professor of Church and Ministry Leadership at Trinity Christian College and is deeply involved in indigenous leadership development through Grace and Peace.

Susan S. Baker received a B.A. from Wheaton College and an M.A. and Ph.D. from Temple University. Ministering cross-culturally in Chicago's Puerto Rican barrio for 21 years, she has now been in Philadelphia serving with a multi-ethnic church for 21 years. Her ministry involvement includes being part of a ministry team involved in planting churches and developing Christian alternative education. Having taught at the Center for Urban Theological Studies for six years, she has been an adjunct professor in urban ministries at Westminster Theological Seminary for fifteen years and is now the Director of the seminary's Urban Mission program and is also co-director of the CRC Philadelphia Church Planting Initiative. She is the author of *Understanding Mainland Puerto Rican Poverty* and co-editor and contributor of *The Urban Face of Mission*.

Harvie M. Conn received a B.D. and Th.M. from Westminster Theological Seminary and was awarded a Litt.D. degree from Geneva College. Harvie was a world renowned missiologist and urbanologist before the Lord called him home in August, 1999. He served as a missionary to Korea for twelve years and then began teaching full time at Westminster Theological Seminary. Retiring in 1998, he was declared Professor of Missions, Emeritus until his death. He was a prolific author of articles and books including *Evangelism: Doing Justice and Preaching Grace, A Clarified Vision for Urban Mission, The American City and the Evangelical Church: A Historical Overview*, and *Eternal Word and Changing Worlds*, and he co-authored *Urban Ministry* with Manuel Ortiz.

Michael Eastman received a B.D. degree from the London School of Theology. He served as Chief Executive Officer of Frontier Youth Trust (FYT) in Great Britain from 1967 to 1998. In retirement he has continued as Executive Secretary of the Evangelical Coalition for Urban Mission, a partnership of seven parachurch agencies founded in 1980, of which FYT was a founder and member. He was an advisor to the Archbishops' Commission on Urban Priority Areas and was awarded an O.B.E. in the Queen's millennial year honours list for service to FYT and disadvantaged youth. His writings include editorship of *Ten Inner City Churches* and co-editor of *Urban Church: A Practitioner's Resource Book.*

Ignatius W. (Naas) Ferreira from South Africa received a B.A. at Potchefstroom University for Christian Higher Education, a Th.B. from the Seminary of Reformed Churches in Potchefstroom, a Th.M. at Potchefstroom University of Christian Higher Education, and is a D.Min. student at Westminster Theological Seminary. He has served at Reformed Church Wonderboompoort (Pretoria), Reformed Church Magol (Ellisaas), and Reformed Church Rietvallei (Pretoria) where he is currently senior pastor. He is also the Director of the newly formed Reformed Center for Urban Mission in Pretoria.

Ondrej Franka is Slovak living and ministering in Serbia. He received a diploma from Moody Bible Institute, a Degree in Foreign Trades at the High Commercial School in Serbia, an M.A. at Trinity Evangelical Divinity School, and a D.Min. at Westminster Theological Seminary. During the 1980s, while his country was under communist rule, he was an itinerant evangelist and teacher in the Slovak Baptist Association. The early post-communist years were dominated by ethnic cleansing and civil war, and Franka continued his ministry by founding and directing the KES Center in Serbia. In 2002 he was the founder and director of Antioch Church Planting Mission which has now planted ten churches in his country. In 2004 he became the first ordained pastor of Slovak Baptist Association in Serbia and has served with the New Baptist Church, Backi Petrovac, Serbia.

Mark R. Gornik received his M.Div. from Westminster Theological Seminary, a Th.M. from Princeton Theological Seminary, and his Ph.D. from the Centre for the Study of Christianity in the Non-Western World, University of Edinburgh.

Co-founder of New Song Ministries and Church in Baltimore, Maryland, he is currently the President and Director of City Seminary of New York. Author of *To Live in Peace: Biblical Faith and the Changing Inner City*, he has also penned a number of articles.

Jonathan Terzungwe Iorkighir hails from Benue State, Nigeria. He received a B.Th. from the Reformed Theological Seminary, Mkar, Nigeria, an M.Div. and Th.M. from Calvin Theological Seminary, a Th.M. from Westminster Theological Seminary, and is a D.Min. student at Westminster Theological Seminary. Ordained in 1989, he has been teaching at the Reformed Theological Seminary, Mkar, Nigeria, where he has recently been named the new Rector.

Jeffrey K. Jue received a B.A. from the University of California and an M.Div. from Westminster Theological Seminary, did graduate studies at the University of Geneva, Switzerland, and received a Ph.D. from the University of Aberdeen, Scotland. Currently Associate Professor and Coordinator of the Department of Church History at Westminster Theological Seminary, Jue has authored *Heaven Upon Earth: Joseph Meed* and *The Legacy of Millenarianism*. He has also contributed an essay in *Conversations: Asian American Evangelical Theologies in Formation* and an article in *Themelios*. A frequent guest speaker and lecturer, he is also on the board of China Horizon, an organization devoted to advancing theological education in the Chinese church.

Kyuboem Lee was born in Seoul, South Korea, moved to Nairobi, Kenya, at the age of ten with his missionary parents, and came to the U.S. for his education where he received a B.A. from Wheaton College and an M.Div. and D.Min. from Westminster Theological Seminary. He served as an assistant pastor at an African American church for seven years and then became the pastor of Germantown Hope Community Church, a multiethnic, community-oriented church plant in Philadelphia.

John S. Leonard received a B.A. from Belhaven College, an M.Div. from Reformed Theological Seminary, and a Ph.D. from Trinity Evangelical Divinity School. Ordained as a minister in the Presbyterian Church of America (PCA), he helped plant a church in Homestead, Florida, and served as a missionary in France for ten years with Arab World Ministries and PCA's Mission to the World working with North African Muslim immigrants. He is presently Associate Professor of Practical Theology at Westminster Theological Seminary and is planting a church in the Chestnut Hill/Mt. Airy section of Philadelphia.

Manuel Ortiz is a Puerto Rican born and raised in New York City. After being saved at the age of 30, he received a B.S. in Missions and Theology from Philadelphia College of Bible, an M.A. in Cross Cultural Communications from Wheaton Graduate School, and a D.Min. in Urban Mission from Westminster Theological Seminary. He ministered as part of a team in Chicago for fourteen years, planting five churches with indigenous Hispanic pastors, two elementary schools, and an extension school for theological education. Since moving to Philadelphia in 1987 to begin teaching full time at Westminster Theological Seminary, later serving as the Coordinator for the Practical Theology Department, and now retired as Professor of Ministry and Mission, Emeritus, he continues planting churches and beginning elementary schools, and is now co-director of the CRC Philadelphia Church Planting Initiative. His writings include *The Hispanic Challenge*, *One New People*, and *Urban Ministry* (co-authored with Harvie M. Conn). He also was co-editor and contributor to *The Urban Face of Mission* and has authored numerous articles.

William A. Shaw grew up in Belfast and studied theology at Queens University, Belfast. He entered the Presbyterian ministry where he was ordained and served in several posts before becoming the Director of Christian Community Development Project - The 174 Trust - in the Nationalist/Republican area of North Belfast. The 174 Trust is an organization dedicated to building peace and promoting reconciliation in Northern Ireland, a country with a long history of deep division between Protestants and Catholics.

Manuel Sosa hails originally from Guayaquil, Ecuador, has a Bachelor of Music degree from Texas A&I University and a M.Div. from Midwestern Theological Seminary, and has taken other graduate studies at Chicago St. University and Westminster Theological Seminary. After being a high school band director for seven years, he went into seminary studies and then was interim pastor at Primera Iglesia Bautista in Kansas City, MO, associate pastor at Nashua Baptist Church, also in Kansas City, and pastor of Memorial and Los Esteros Baptist churches in Guayaquil, Ecuador. For the last 23 years Sosa has been a missionary with the International Mission Board of the Southern Baptist Convention serving 18 years in Guayaquil as National Director of Theological Education by Extension, Dean of the Ecuador Theological Seminary, and Strategy Coordinator for the missionaries of Guayaquil, focusing on starting new works. For the last five years he has been in Santiago, Chile, serving as Administrator for the missionaries of the Chile Baptist Mission and in 2008 went to Buenos Aires, Argentina, to plant churches in the inner city.

Timothy Z. Witmer holds a B.A. from West Chester University, an M.Div. from Westminster Theological Seminary and a D.Min. from Reformed Theological Seminary. He has been engaged in pastoral ministry for more than 25 years and continues as the Minister of Preaching at Crossroads Community Church (Presbyterian Church in America) in Upper Darby, Pennsylvania. He is the founder and director of The Shepherd's Institute which trains church elders in the fine art of shepherding their flocks. He is currently Professor and Coordinator of the Department of Practical Theology at Westminster Theological Seminary where he also serves as Director of the Mentored Ministry program and the M.Div. program.

Bibliography

Ackroyd, Peter. *London: The Biography*. London: Vintage, 2001.

Ahlstrom, Sydney. *A Religious History of the American People*. New Haven, CT: Yale University Press, 1972.

Aikman, David. *Jesus in Beijing: How Christianity is Transforming China and Changing the Global Power Balance*. Washington, DC: Regnery Publishing, 2003.

Akins, Thomas Wade. *Pioneer Evangelism*. Rio de Janeiro, Brasil: Junta de Missões Nacionáis, Convençãs Brasileira, 1995.

Allen, John. *Rabble-Rouser for Peace: The Authorized Biography of Desmond Tutu*. New York: Free Press, 2006.

Anderson, Keith R. and Randy D. Reese. *Spiritual Mentoring*. Downers Grove, IL: InterVarsity Press, 1999.

Anderson, Ray S. *An Emergent Theology for Emerging Churches*. Downers Grove, IL: InterVarsity Press, 2006.

Armstrong, A.H., ed. *The Cambridge History of Later Greek and Early Medieval Philosophy*. New York: Cambridge University Press, 1967.

Banks, Robert. *Reenvisioning Theological Education*. Grand Rapids, MI: Wm. B. Eerdmans Publishing Co., 1999.

Banks, Robert and Julie Banks. *The Church Comes Home*. Peabody, MA: Hendrickson Publishers, Inc., Peabody, 1998.

Barker, Felix and Peter Jackson. *London: 2000 Years of a City and Its People*. Oondon: Cassell, 1974.

Barna, George. *Revolution*. Wheaton, IL: BarnaBooks, a division of Tyndale House Publishers, 2005.

Bavinck, J.H. *An Introduction to the Science of Missions*, trans. by David H. Freeman. Phillipsburg, NJ: Presbyterian & Reformed Publishers, 1960.

Bermant, Chaim. *London's East End: Point of Arrival*. New York: Macmillan Publishing Co., 1976.

Beyer, Peter. *Religion and Globalization*. London: Sage Publications, 1994.

Birkey, Del. *The House Church: A Model for Renewing the Church.* Scottdale, PA: Herald Press, 1998.

Brierly, Peter. *The Tide is Running Out: What the English Church Attendance Survey Reveals.* London: Christian Research, 2000.

_____. *Pulling Out of the Nose Dive: A Contemporary Picture of Churchgoing: What the 2005 English Church Census Reveals.* London: Christian Research, 2006.

Calvin, John. *The Institutes of the Christian Religion.* Philadelphia: Westminster Press, 1960.

Carnes, Tony and Fenggang Yang, eds. *Asian American Religious: The Making and Remaking of Borders and Boundaries.* New York: NYU Press, 2004.

Carson, Donald A. *Becoming Conversant with the Emerging Church.* Grand Rapids, MI: Zondervan, 2005.

Chadwick, Henry. *Early Christian Thought and the Classical Tradition.* New York: Oxford University Press, 1966.

Christian, Jayakumar. *God of the Empty-Handed: Poverty, Power and the Kingdom of God.* Monrovia, CA: MARC, 1999.

Clinton, Robert. *The Making of a Leader.* Colorado Springs: NavPress, 1988.

Clowney, Edmund P. *Called to the Ministry.* Phillipsburg, NJ: Presbyterian & Reformed Publishers, 1964.

_____. *The Church.* Downers Grove, IL: InterVarsity Press, 1995.

Conn, Harvie M. *Evangelism: Doing Justice and Preaching Grace.* Phillipsburg, NJ: Presbyterian & Reformed Publishers, 1982.

Conn, Harvie M., ed. *Inerrancy and Hermeneutic.* Grand Rapids, MI: Baker, 1988.

_____. *Planting and Growing Urban Churches: From Dream to Reality.* Grand Rapids, MI: Baker Books, 1997.

Conn, Harvie M. and Samuel Rowan, eds. *Missions and Theological Education in World Perspective.* Farmington: Associates of Urbanus, 1984.

Conn, Harvie M. and Manuel Ortiz. *Urban Ministry: The Kingdom, the City, and the People of God.* Downers Grove, IL: InterVarsity Press, 2001.

Costas, Orlando. *Christ Outside the Gate: Mission Beyond Christendom.* Maryknoll, NY: Orbis Books, 1984.

Dale, Tony and Felicity Dale. *Simply Church.* Austin, TX: Karis Publishing, 2002.

Davey, Andrew. *The Urban Challenge—The Eleventh Bishop Williams Memorial Lectuership*. Sherbrooke, Quebec: The Bishop Williams Memorial Fund Committee, 2005.

deGruchy, John W. *Reconciliation: Restoring Justice*. London: SCM Press, 2002.

Dennison, Jack. *City Reaching: On the Road to Community Transformation*. Pasadena, CA: William Carey Library, 1999.

Dunlop, John. *A Precarious Belonging: Presbyterians and the Conflict in Ireland*. Belfast: The Blackstaff Press, 1995.

Dyrness, William A. *Learning about Theology from the Third World*. Grand Rapids, MI: Zondervan, 1990.

Eastman, Michael and Stevie Lathan, eds. *Urban Church: A Practitioner's Resource Book*. London: SPCK, 2004.

Ellison, Edgar J. and J. Timothy Kauffman. *Developing Leaders for Urban Ministries*. New York: Peter Lang Publishing Co., 1993.

Escobar, Samuel. *The New Global Mission: The Gospel from Everywhere to Everyone*. Downers Grove, IL: InterVarsity Press, 2003.

Evangelical Coalition for Urban Mission. *Wineskins for the City: Report of Network of Urban Evangelicals (NUE) Annual Consultation*. London: Evangelical Coalition for Urban Mission, 2000.

Fitts, Robert. *The Church in the House: A Return to Simplicity*. Salem, OR: Preparing the Way Publishers, 2001.

Foster, Richard. *Celebration of Discipline*. San Francisco: HarperCollins, 1998.

Frame, John. *Van Til the Theologian*. Phillipsburg, NJ: Pilgrim, 1976.

_____. *The Doctrine of the Knowledge of God*. Philipsburg, NJ: Presbyterian & Reformed Publishers, 1987.

Gaede, S.D. *When Tolerance Is No Virtue: Political Correctness, Multiculturalism & the Future of Truth & Justice*. Downers Grove, IL: InterVarsity Press, 1993.

Garrison, David. *Church Planting Movements: How God is Redeeming a Lost World*. Midlothian, VA: WIGTake Resources, 2004.

Gibbs, Eddie. *Leadership Next*. Downers Grove, IL: InterVarsity Press, 2005.

Gibbs, Eddie and Ryan Bolger. *Emerging Churches: Creating Christian Community in Postmodern Cultures*. Grand Rapids, MI: Baker, 2005.

González, Justo L. *Mañana: Christian Theology from a Hispanic Perspective*. Nashville: Abingdon Press, 1990.

Goodwin, B.E., II. *The Effective Leader*. Downers Grove, IL: InterVarsity Press, 1981.

Gornik, Mark R. *To Live in Peace: Biblical Faith and the Changing Inner City*. Grand Rapids, MI: Wm. B. Eerdmans Publishing Co., 2002.

Goudzwaard, Bob. *Globalization and the Kingdom of God*. Grand Rapids, MI: Baker Books, 2001.

Green, Laurie. *The Impact of the Global: An Urban Theology*. Sheffield: New City Special, 2001.

Green, Michael. *Evangelism in the Early Church*. Grand Rapids, MI: Wm. B. Eerdmans Publishing Co., 1970.

Grogg, Viv. *Cry of the Urban Poor*. Monrovia, CA: MARC, 1992.

Guiness, Os. *Fit Bodies Fat Minds: Why Evangelicals Don't Think and What to Do About It*. Grand Rapids, MI: Baker Books, 1994.

Gundry, S. and A. Johnson, eds. *Tensions in Contemporary Theology*. Grand Rapids, MI: Baker, 1986.

Hart, D.G. *Deconstruction Evangelicalism: Conservative Protestantism and the Age of Billy Graham*. Grand Rapids, MI: Baker Books, 2004.

Hastings, Adrian. *African Christianity*. New York: Seabury Press, 1977.

Hauerwas, Stanley and Samuel Walls, eds. *The Blackwell Companion to Christian Ethics*. Malden: Blackwell, 2004.

Hesselgrave, David. *Communicating Christ Cross-Culturally*. Grand Rapids, MI: Zondervan, 1978.

Holifield, E. Brooks. *Theology in America: Christian Thought from the Age of the Puritans to the Civil War*. New Haven, CT: Yale University Press, 2003.

Hogarth, Jonathan, Kiranga Gatimu and David Barrett. *Theological Education in Context: 100 Extension Programmes in Contemporary Africa*. Nairobi: Uzima Press, 1983.

Howat, Irene and John Nicholls. *Streets Paved with Gold*. London: Christian Focus Publications, 2003.

Huang, C.H. *Theological Education and Ministry: Reports from the North East Asia Theological Education Consultation: Seoul, Korea*. Taiwan: The Presbyterian Bookstore, 1967.

Hudec, Ján. *Pútnici na Úzkej Ceste*. Ostrava: A-Alef, 1999.

Hurley, Michael, SJ. *Reconciliation in Religion and Society*. Antrim: Institute of Irish Studies, 1994.

Hyun, Jane. *Breaking the Bamboo Ceiling: Career Strategies for Asians: The Essential Guide to Getting In, Moving Up, and Reaching the Top*. New York: HarperBusiness Publishers, 2004.

International Mission Board. *Something New Under the Sun: New Directions at the International Mission Board*. Richmond, VA: International Mission Board, 1999.

Irving, Carter C. *A Strategy for Planting a Large Number of Churches in the Urban Los Angeles Area*. D.Min. diss., Fuller Theological Seminary, 1993.

Jaeger, Werner. *Early Christianity and Greek Paideia*. London: Oxford University Press, 1961.

Jenkins, Philip. *The Next Christendom: The Coming of Global Christianity*. New York: Oxford University Press, 2002.

_____. *The New Faces of Christianity: Believing the Bible in the Global South*. London: Oxford University Press, 2006.

Jeung, Russell. *Faithful Generations: Race and New Asian American Churches*. New Brunswick, NJ: Rutgers University Press, 2005.

Johnstone, Patrick and Jason Mandryk. *Operation World*. Waynesboro, GA: Paternoster, 2001.

Kelly, Gráinne and Brandon Hamber. *Reconciliation: Rhetoric or Relevant?* Belfast: Democratic Dialogue, 2005.

Kinkead, Maurice. *Mission and Community Development Resources for Responding to Social Need*. Belfast: Belfast Churches' Urban Development Committee, 1996.

Kirk, J. Andrew. *What is Mission? Theological Explorations*. Minneapolis: Fortress Press, 2000.

Kittel, Gerhard, ed. *Theological Dictionary of the New Testament*. Grand Rapids, MI: Wm. B. Eerdmans Publishing Co., 1964.

Krallmann, Günter. *Mentoring for Mission: A Handbook on Leadership Principles Exemplified by Jesus Christ*. Waynesboro, GA: Authentic Media, 2002.

Kreider, Larry and Floyd McClung. *Starting a House Church: A New Model for Living Out Your Faith*. Ventura, CA: Regal Books from Gospel Light, 2007.

Lane, Tim and Paul Tripp. *Relationships: A Mess Worth Making*. Greensboro: New Growth Press, 2006.

Lederach, John Paul. *The Journey Toward Reconciliation*. Scottdale, PA: Herald Press, 1999.

_____. *The Moral Imagination: The Art and Soul of Building Peace*. New York: Oxford University Press, 2005.

Liechty, Joseph and Cecelia Clegg. *Moving Beyond Sectarianism: Religion, Conflict and Reconciliation in Northern Ireland*. Dublin: The Columba Press, 2001.

Lundy, Derek. *Men that God Made Mad: A Journey Through Truth, Myth and Terror in Northern Ireland*. London: Jonathan Cape, 2006.

Marsden, George. *Understanding Fundamentalism and Evangelicalism*. Grand Rapids, MI: Wm. B. Eerdmans Publishers, 1994.

Matsuoka, F. and E.S. Fernandez, eds. *Realizing the America of Our Hearts: Theological Voice of Asian Americans*. St. Louis: Chalice Press, 2003.

Maxwell, John C. *Developing the Leader Within You*. Nashville: Thomas Nelson Publishers, 1993.

McLaren, Brian D. and Tony Campolo. *Adventures in Missing the Point*. Grand Rapids, MI: Zondervan, 2003.

McKnight, John. *The Careless Society: Community and Its Counterfeits*. New York: BasicBooks, 1995.

Meeks, Wayne A. *The First Urban Christians*. New Haven, CT: Yale University Press, 1983.

Meulemans, Bill. *Hope and Hate: Protestants and Catholics in the New Northern Ireland*. Belfast: Queens University of Belfast, 2008.

Min, P.G. and J.H. Kim, eds. *Religion in Asian America: Building Faith Communities*. Walnut Creek, CA: AltaMira Press, 2002.

Murray, John. *Collected Writings*. Carlisle, PA: Banner of Truth Trust, 1976.

Murray, Stuart. *Church After Christendom*. Waynesboro, GA: Paternoster Press, 2004.

Murray, Stuart and Anne Wilkinson-Hayes. *Hope from the Margins: New Ways of Being Church, Grove Evangelism Series*. Cambridge: Grove Books Limited, 2000.

Neighbour, Ralph W., Jr. *Where Do We Go From Here?" A Guidebook for the Cell Group Church*, rev. ed. Houston, TX: Touch Publications, 2000.

Newbigin, Lesslie. *The Gospel in a Pluralist Society*. Grand Rapids, MI: Wm. B. Eerdmans Publishing Co., 1989.

Noelliste, Dieumeme. *Toward a Theology of Theological Education: 3,500 Theological Institutions in the World*. Seoul: World Evangelical Fellowship Theological Commission, 1993.

Noll, Mark. *The Scandal of the Evangelical Mind*. Grand Rapids, MI: Wm. B. Eerdmans Publishing Co., 1994.

_____. *America's God: From Jonathan Edwards to Abraham Lincoln*. Oxford: Oxford University Press, 2002.

Novaković, Dragan. *Verske Zajednice na Razmedju Vekova.* Beograd: Institut za političke studije, 2003.

Ortiz, Manuel. *The Hispanic Challenge: Opportunities Confronting the Church.* Downers Grove, IL: InterVarsity Press, 1993.

_____. *One New People. Models for Developing a Multiethnic Church.* Downers Grove, IL: InterVarsity Press, 1996.

Ortiz, Manuel and Susan S. Baker, eds. *The Urban Face of Mission: Ministering the Gospel in a Diverse and Changing World.* Phillipsburg, NJ: Presbyterian & Reformed Publishers, 2002.

Ott, Craig and Harold A. Netland, eds., *Globalizing Theology: Belief and Practice in an Era of World Christianity.* Grand Rapids, MI: Baker Academic, 2006.

Packer, James I. *Knowing God.* Downers Grove, IL: InterVarsity Press, 1973.

Perkins, John M. *With Justice for All.* Ventura, CA: Regal Books, 1982.

Pocock, Michael, Gailyn Van Rheenen, and Douglas McConnell. *The Changing Face of World Missions: Engaging Contemporary Issues and Trends.* Grand Rapids, MI: Baker Academic, 2005.

Pocock, Michael and Joseph Henriques. *Cultural Change and Your Church: Helping Your Church Thrive in a Diverse Society.* Grand Rapids, MI: Baker Books, 2002.

Poirier, Alfred. *The Peacemaking Pastor.* Grand Rapids, MI: Baker, 2006.

Popple, Keith. *Analyzing Community Work: Its Theory and Practice.* Buckingham: Open University Press, 1995.

Poythress, Vern. *Symphonic Theology.* Grand Rapids, MI: Academie Books, 1987.

Priddy, Kenneth E. with J. Patrick. *Project 6:15: A Two-Year Commitment to Church Redevelopment.* Richmond, VA: United Front Ministries, 2003.

Rainer, Thomas S. *High Expectations.* Nashville: Broadman & Holman Publishers, 1999.

Ramachandra, Vinoth. *Faiths in Conflict? Christian Integrity in a Multicultural World.* Downers Grove, IL: InterVarsity Press, 1999.

Rankin, Jerry. *To the Ends of the Earth: Churches Fulfilling the Great Commission.* Ashville: Broadman & Holman Publishers, 2006.

Rath, Tom. *Strengths Finder 2.0.* New York: Gallup Press, 2007.

Reid, J.K.S. *Christian Apologetics.* Grand Rapids, MI: Wm. B. Eerdmans Publishing Co., 1969.

Ro, Bong-rin and Ruth Eshenaur, eds. *The Bible and Theology in Asian Contexts.* Taichung, Taiwan: Asia Theological Association, 1984.

Roembke, Lianne. *Building Credible Multicultural Teams*. Pasadena, CA: William Carey Library, 2000.

Roozen, David A., Alice Frazier Evans and Robert Evans, eds. *Changing the Way Seminaries Teach: Globalization and Theological Education*. Simsbury: Plowshares Institute, 1996.

Roxburgh, Alan J. and Fred Romanuk. *The Missional Leader*. San Francisco: Jossey-Bass, 2006.

Samuel, Vinay and Chris Sugden, eds. *Sharing Jesus in the Two-Thirds World*. Grand Rapids, MI: Wm. B. Eerdmans Publishing Co., 1983.

Sande, Ken. *The Peacemaker*. Grand Rapids, MI: Baker, 2004.

Sanders, J. Oswald. *Spiritual Leadership*. Chicago: Moody Press, 1994.

Sanneh, Lamin. *Whose Religion is Christianity?: The Gospel Beyond the West*. Grand Rapids, MI: Wm. B. Eerdmans Publishing Co., 2003.

Schlesinger, Arthur M., Jr. *The Disuniting of America: Reflections on a Multicultural Society*. New York: W.W. Norton & Co., 1992.

Schreiter, Robert J. *Constructing Local Theologies*. Maryknoll, NY: Orbis Books, 1985.

_____. *Reconciliation: Mission and Ministry in a Changing Social Order*. Maryknoll, NY: Orbis Books, 1992.

Schreiter, Robert J., ed. *Mission in the Third Millenium*. Maryknoll, NY: Orbis Books, 2001.

Sheppard, David. *Built as a City: God and the Urban World Today*. London: Hodder and Stoughton, 1974.

Shirlow, Peter and Brendan Murtagh, eds. *Belfast: Segregation, Violence and the City*. London: Pluto Press, 2006.

Sider, Ronald J., ed. *The Chicago Declaration*. Carol Stream, IL: Creation House, 1974.

Silber, Laura and Allan Little. *The Death of Yugoslavia*. London: Penguin Books, 1995.

Simpson, Wolfgang. *Houses that Change the World*. Emmelsball, Germany: C&P Publishing, 1999.

Snyder, Howard A., ed. *Global Good News: Mission in a New Context*. Nashville: Abingdon Press, 2001.

Spencer, Aída Besançon and William Spencer. *The Global God*. Grand Rapids, MI: Baker Book, 1998.

Steger, Manfred B. *Globalization: A Very Short Introduction*. New York: Oxford University Press, 2003.

Stetzer, Ed. *Planting Missional Churches: Planting a Church That's Biblically Sound and Reaching People in Culture*. Nashville: Broadman & Holman Publishers, 2006.

Strauch, Alexander. *Biblical Eldership*. Littleton, CO: Lewis and Roth, 1995.

Sturge, Mark. *Look What God Has Done: An Exploration of Black Christian Faith in Britain*. Bletchley: Scripture Union, 2005.

Sundkler, Bengt. *The Christian Ministry in Africa*. Uppsala: Swedish Institute of Missionary Research, 1960.

Takaki, Ronald. *Strangers from a Different Shore: A History of Asian Americans*. Boston: Penguin Books, 1989.

Takaki, Ronald, ed. *From Different Shores: Perspectives on Race and Ethnicity in America*. Oxford: Oxford University Press, 1994.

Taylor, John V. *The Primal Vision*. London: SCM Press, 1963.

Tiplady, Richard, ed. *One World or Many? The Impact of Globalisation on Mission*. Pasadena, CA: William Carey Library, 2003.

Tokunaga, Paul. *Invitation to Lead: Guidance for Emerging Asian American Leaders*. Downers Grove, IL: InterVarsity Press, 2003.

Tripp, Paul D. *Instruments in the Redeemer's Hands*. Phillipsburg, NJ: Presbyterian & Reformed Publishers, 2002.

Tseng, Timothy. *Asian American Religious Leadership Today: A Preliminary Inquiry*. Durham, NC: Duke University Press, 1998.

Tuan, Mia. *Forever Foreigners or Honorary Whites: The Asian Ethnic Experience Today*. New Brunswick, NJ: Rutgers University Press, 1998.

Tutu, Desmond. *No Future without Forgiveness*. New York: Doubleday, 1999.

Van Engen, Charles. *God's Missionary People*. Grand Rapids, MI: Baker Book House, 1992.

Van Til, Cornelius. *A Christian Theory of Knowledge*. Nutley, NJ: Presbyterian & Reformed Publishers, 1969.

Villa-Vincencio, Charles and Wilhelm Verwoerd, eds. *Looking Back, Reaching Forward: Reflections on the Truth and Reconciliation Commission*. Cape Town: University of Cape Town Press/ London: Zed Books, 2000.

Vincent, John, ed. *Faithfulness in the City*. Hawarden: Monad Press, 2003.

Viola, Frank and George Barna. *Pagan Christianity?: Exploring the Roots of Our Church Practices*. Wheaton, IL: Barna Books, a divsion of Tyndale House Publishers, 2008.

Volf, Miroslav. *Exclusion & Embrace: A Theological Exploration of Identity, Otherness, and Reconciliation*. Nashville: Abingdon Press, 1996.

von Harnack, Adolf. *History of Dogma*. New York: Dover, 1961.

Wagner, C. Peter. *Church Planting for a Greater Harvest: A Comprehensive Guide*. Ventura, CA: Regal Books, 1990.

Wallis, Jim. *The Soul of Politics: A Practical and Prophetic Vision for Change*. Maryknoll, NY: Orbis Books, 1994.

Warren, Rick. *Purpose Driven Life*. Grand Rapids, MI: Zondervan 2002.

Wells, David. *Above All Earthly Pow'rs: Christ in a Postmodern World*. Grand Rapids, MI: Wm. B. Eerdmans Publishing Co., 2005.

Wilkes, C. Gene. *Jesus on Leadership*. Wheaton, IL: Tyndale House Publishers, Inc., 1998.

Wolterstorff, Nicholas. *Until Justice and Peace Embrace*. Grand Rapids, MI: Wm. B. Eerdmans Publishing Co., 1983.

_____. *Justice: Rights and Wrongs*. Princeton: Princeton University Press, 2008.

Wu, Frank H. *Yellow: Race in America Beyond Black and White*. New York: BasicBooks, 2002.

Yang, Fengang. *Chinese Christians in America: Conversion, Assimilation, and Adhesive Identities*. University Park, PA: Penn State Press, 1999.

Yoder, John Howard. *Body Politics: Five Practices of the Christian Community Before the Watching World*. Scottdale, PA: Herald Press, 1992.

Yoo, D., ed. *New Spiritual Homes: Religion and Asian Americans*. Honolulu: University of Hawai'i Press, 1999.

Yu, Henry. *Thinking Orientals: Migration, Contact and Exoticism in Modern America*. New York: Oxford University Press, 2001.

Zdero, Rad. *The Global House Church Movement*. Pasadena, CA: William Carey Library, 2004.

Index

A

D

J

K

O

P

Q

R

S